W9-BLG-155
3 248 00341 7000

CELEBRATION OF

Angels

CELEBRATION OF
Angels

T i m o t h y   J o n e s

THOMAS NELSON PUBLISHERS
Nashville • Atlanta • London • Vancouver

Published in Nashville, Tennessee, by Thomas Nelson, Inc., Publishers, and distributed in Canada by Word Communications, Ltd., Richmond, British Columbia.

Unless otherwise noted, all Scripture quotations are from the NEW REVISED STANDARD VERSION of the Bible. Copyright © 1946, 1952, 1971, 1973, 1989 by the Division of Christian Education of the National Council of the Churches of Christ in the U.S.A. Used by permission.

Scripture quotations noted KJV are from The King James Version of the Holy Bible.

Scripture quotations noted NIV are from the HOLY BIBLE: NEW INTERNATIONAL VERSION®. Copyright © 1973, 1978, 1984 by International Bible Society. Used by permission of Zondervan Publishing House.

Scripture quotations noted RSV are from the Revised Standard Version of the Bible, copyrighted 1946, 1952, © 1971, 1973 by the Division of Christian Education of the National Council of the Churches of Christ in the U.S.A. and used by permission.

The Publisher would like to thank Dover Publications, Inc. for use of the *Dover Pictorial Archive Series*. Art has been reproduced from *The Complete Works of Albrecht Dürer*, Willi Kurth, ed. (New York: Dover, 1963); *The Doré Bible Illustrations* (Mineola, New York: Dover, 1974); and *The New Testament: A Pictorial Archive from Nineteenth-Century Sources*, Don Rice, ed. (Mineola, New York: Dover, 1986).

Jones, Timothy K., 1955–
Celebration of angels / Timothy Jones.
p.   cm.
Includes bibliographical references.
ISBN 0-7852-8241-6
1. Angels.   I. Title.
BT966.2.J65   1994
235'.3—dc20

Printed in the United States of America.
94   95   96   97   98 — 5   4   3   2   1

For Jill, Abram, Micah, and Bekah, whose patience and prayers
allowed this book to come into being.

Contents

Acknowledgments

My thanks to several people who offered invaluable feedback on early drafts of this book: Myrna Grant, Karen Mains, Kevin Miller, and last but by no means least, my wife, Jill Zook-Jones.

I am also grateful for the skillful work of my editors at Thomas Nelson: Laurie Clark, Amy Glass, and Janet Thoma.

Foreword

*F*or many years I taught overview courses in theology in which good angels were hardly mentioned. The invitation to write this foreword gives me a chance to make amends for my oversight. Angels ought not to be ignored, and I am sorry I did not pay more attention to them when I was younger.

The twentieth-century Western imagination has been haunted by the question, Are humans the sole rational inhabitants of this infinitely expanding universe? Our hearts feel, inarticulately perhaps but potently nonetheless, that surely it is not so. It is no wonder, therefore, that so many fictional fantasies of the *Star Trek* and *E.T.* type have been produced to massage our wishful thinking on this point; no wonder, either, that they have been so enormously popular. More recently there has appeared the rash of angel books that Timothy Jones surveys, many springing from New Age superstition and offering themselves as the religious counterpart of *Close Encounters of the Third Kind.* These ideas may and should be brushed aside as spectacularly wrong, but Jesus, the apostles, and the entire Bible join together to assure us that the feeling of our hearts is right. The world is alive, not just with the sound of music, as Julie Andrews sang, but with the movements of angels, darting to and fro on the King's business.

The nature of angels is as obscure to us as is the nature of the Triune God

himself, and what it feels like to be an angel is beyond our imagining. What we can understand, however, is the biblical witness to what angels do, as Timothy Jones ably demonstrates. First, they worship God, and as worshipers they are diligent observers of his work, in creation, in providence, and in redemption. As Francis Schaeffer wrote of the church before the watching world, so Paul the apostle writes of the church before the watching angels, explaining that part of the purpose of God in his plan of grace is that through observing all that he does for the perfection of the church, the "principalities and powers" (angelic hosts) might come to appreciate his fantastically resourceful wisdom (Eph. 3:10 KJV). Second, they convey messages to us from God (their name, in both Hebrew and Greek, means herald or messenger), and as messengers they fulfill a further role as our protectors, acting throughout as agents sent from God to do us service. Both as communicators and as guardians their work is ordinarily unnoticeable, and not until we get to heaven shall we know how much we owe to it.

When I teach theology nowadays, I try to celebrate the angels as I should. I hope that any who read these words will do the same. Certainly, what Timothy Jones has written here should help us all along this path.

J. I. Packer
Regent College
Vancouver, British Columbia

ries, tells how he once gave a lecture under the auspices of the Aspen Institute of Humanistic Studies. His topic? Angels and angelology. The response? "The announcement," he wrote, "drew an audience larger than any I have ever enjoyed in the last thirty years." The experience so moved him that he wrote a book on the philosophical significance of angels.[2]

Every time I walk into a bookstore, it seems, or browse through the stack of newspapers and magazines on my desk, I see more evidence of angel fascination. Angels or flying spirits appear in almost every civilization and religion, of course, but today they have become trendy, the focus of stories in supermarket tabloids and books for the New York literary set. People are curious about the celestial like never before. And they *believe*, according to a recent *Time*/CNN poll. A surprising 69 percent of Americans answered yes to the question, "Do you believe in the existence of angels?"[3] Belief in angels among teenagers, Gallup polls show, increased steadily from 64 percent in 1978 to 76 percent in 1992. Despite all we hear about the rising tide of skepticism and secularism, three out of four teens now believe in angels.

While I view much of culture's fascination with angels as wholesome, some is not. It occasionally, for instance, seems trivial or commercial. At a local bookstore I recently saw a counter display of AngelHeart™ pins. The card accompanying the gold pin said, "Whether you give or receive a special AngelHeart™, know that you have been touched by a magical essence that allows miracles to happen." With angel books proliferating, with angel seminars multiplying, and with angel paraphernalia becoming, as one news-

paper article coyly noted, a big business with "heavenly profits," I want to separate fad from fact.

Other expressions of angel interest sober me even more. A book with the innocuous-sounding title, *The Little Book of Angels,* argues that not only can we worship angels (something forbidden in Christian tradition), but also that "there is another sort of angelic rite: one in which they are specifically evoked and called down, either to give and receive messages, or to enter into the body of the ritualist. In its simplest manifestation this results in the phenomenon of possession."[4] Such occult dabbling under the name of angels makes me shudder, for reasons I'll give later. For now I'll simply say that all that goes under the name of the angelic is far from wholesome or holy. Satan can masquerade as an angel of light, noted Paul the apostle two millennia ago (2 Cor. 11:14). The subject of angels deserves wise discernment.

I'm also eager to write about angels because of a strange silence in the church. The Bible pays more attention to angels than many Christians. Sixteenth-century reformer John Calvin urged that we not "overlook such an illustrious and noble example" of God's creation,[5] but on this issue the church still is running to catch up with culture. Evangelist Billy Graham wrote that while he had heard or read of literally thousands of contemporary angel stories, he had never heard a sermon preached about them.[6]

Added to our neglect of angels, I detect in some church quarters a subtle disbelief. We may resemble those in sixteenth-century England, when

An angel announces Jesus' birth to shepherds nearby (Luke 2:10)

the great Puritan preacher Richard Baxter felt constrained to write a book called *The Certainty of the Worlds of Spirits*. He spoke of "many in the city of London" who professed unbelief in the life of the world to come and the reality of the supernatural, both demonic and angelic. "They take all such reports to be but the effects of error, deceit, and easy credulity," he wrote. "For the sake of such I have recited many credible instances in this book."[7] I will do something similar in mine.

I also suspect that angels make some of us uneasy. Contemplating them, we fear, may distract us from the everyday realities (and responsibilities) at hand. So we simply avoid discussing whether or not angels might show up at the bedside of a neighbor in the hospital or, even more daunting, appear to *us*. But if angels truly exist, if God made them to be part of his universe, we stand to benefit by considering and contemplating them.

I want to know more about angels for yet another reason: My questions have lately become personal. When I was growing up no grandmother told tales of angel guardians showing up to help in times of need. While angel art caught my eye every Christmas, nothing made me think much about what angels might have to do with me. Even graduate school religion classes never compelled me to ask how angels might matter for today. But now I'm eager to fill in the blanks. I want to know who and what angels are, how they move and intervene. Is there really an unseen world as real and trustworthy as the visible world? Have angels been "watching over me" as a popular song says? Do angelic visitors intervene without my knowing?

What should I make of the hosts of people on talk shows and in newspaper articles that suddenly are coming forward with stories of angel encounters?

It is possible to crawl out of bed, show up at the office, play with my children, and go to bed without thinking about any of this. But if an unseen world intersects my daily arena, I don't want to miss it. I want to be aware. While I do not want to overlook the Lord's everyday, quiet blessings by looking for angels, neither do I want to miss what he might want to do or show me through their ministry.

Some years ago I faced a difficult decision. The church my wife and I had been sent to Texas to launch was falling apart. I wanted to make a career change, but had no clear options. That my family and I wanted to relocate to the Midwest only compounded the difficulties, and my anxieties. As I sat by my phone one morning, thinking about the risks of moving and whether or not I should call a potential employer in Indiana, I had the oddest experience. For a split second I had a mental impression of a small figure standing by the phone, beckoning me to place the call. I say mental impression, but it was more an afterimage like those formed when you stare at a light and then look away.

I did call, and it set in motion events that would eventually lead to a job and a move that, for all the risks, were wonderfully timed. God used an image, a mental picture to assure me and urge me on. Was it an angel? I don't know. But the experience opened my mind to believe the gloriously odd may be more normal than we think. For the move we made that year, while

one of the riskiest, was one of the most significant I have ever made, paving the way for my entry into journalism and writing. Are there similar hints of divine intervention throughout your life?

G. K. Chesterton once wrote that the most wonderful thing about miracles is that they do sometimes happen.[8] Is the most wonderful thing about angels that they "happen," that in ways small and large they surround us with God's loving protection? I'd like to know more. And I want angel appearings to do for me what they did for so many figures in the Bible and the long story of God's people since: point me to God, in all his majesty and care. I may be thoroughly modern, but I believe that the reality of heaven itself sometimes touches my little world in ways I am just beginning to discover, ways we will explore throughout this book.

Chapter 2

Angels Watching Over Me?

Angels are unsatisfiable in their longing to do by all means all manner of good unto all the creatures, . . . especially the children of men.
Richard Hooker

$\mathcal{O}$ne day in the early 1960s, Olivia Sue Lambert was walking with a fellow graduate student, Alun, near their West Virginia University campus. The day was full of sunshine. But near a bend in the road leading to the locks on the Monongahela River, a figure suddenly appeared, dressed in a brilliant robe, carrying a warning.

"Go no farther," he said. "You are in grave danger. Turn around and go back the way you came. Go slowly." His appearance so overwhelmed Olivia's field of vision, she recalls, that he "blotted out the landscape" around her. Looking back, Olivia realizes that only something as dramatic as an angel appearance would have convinced her to stop walking. She and Alun immediately turned back.

Several years passed before Olivia made real sense of the encounter. One day, sitting in a doctor's waiting room, she saw a headline in a local paper: "The Morgantown Sniper Strikes Again." "I read with horror," she says, "about a person who had randomly killed over a period of years, striking in broad daylight, using a high-powered rifle atop a ridge overlooking the Monongahela—always at the bend of roads by the locks, the bend we had been approaching!"

In the doctor's waiting room, to the amused curiosity of others, Olivia blurted, "Thank you, Lord," because, she says, "I really understood then just how close Alun and I had come to danger, and how we had been saved that day by one of God's angels."

Southern Baptist church leader Ignatius Meimaris would not find

Olivia's story strange. Some years ago he was in graduate school, headed for a career in science. But he began to wonder if God was calling him to a career in the church. "One day," he recalls, "as I was going from the lab to the church where I worked with youth, I took the subway to downtown Boston. I waited for the train, and, when the doors opened, two older ladies came out. Behind them was a young man wearing a black turtleneck with a black zip-up jacket. As he and I passed, he just patted me on the shoulder very lightly and said, 'The Lord is with you, brother.'

"All of a sudden, I felt this tremendous, unexplainable comfort about the ministry and seminary. I naturally turned to see who that person was—maybe someone I had known. I looked up at the only stairs that were leading from the subway, and there were just the two ladies. He hadn't come out running, so I knew there was no way he would have had the time to run up the forty stairs. It had just been a second and a half. I looked to the left and right, but I didn't see one single soul. Later, when I read a book on angels, this scene came vividly back to mind."[1]

South Carolinian Gary Groetsch describes himself as a pragmatic, hard-edged businessman. But in 1979, when he was twenty-nine and cocky, Gary had an experience that blew apart his narrow world of sales reports and profit margins.

"My wife and I had just bought a new house in Rochester, New York, and we had gone out to buy wallpaper. I slowed for a turning car, but the

driver behind me didn't see me brake. He smacked into the back of our car."

No one was hurt, but when Gary saw what appeared to be a pool of gasoline on the pavement, he wasted no time getting out of the car. But he couldn't get his wife and one-year-old daughter out of the back seat. The locks on the back doors had jammed. Gary struggled to get his family out, when, he remembers, "Out of the blue a car came roaring down the road, going every bit of fifty-five miles an hour. I didn't see it until it was six inches from me."

Just then he heard a voice out of nowhere say, *"Jump!"* He insists it was not his wife's voice, or that of anyone at the scene.

Gary jumped, which kept him from getting crushed beneath the careening car, but he was hit anyway. The impact threw him eleven car lengths. (Three days later, a woman amazed Gary by bringing him his shoe, which had sailed some fifty yards into her house's second-story rain gutter.) Amazingly, just as he was falling, Gary remembers someone in a flowing white robe catching him, cushioning the impact. "Five minutes later I awoke on the asphalt, and I knew I had been saved by an angel. God sent someone because I wasn't supposed to die that day."

And his wife and child? "They didn't know I had been hit and, according to the people at the scene, their door suddenly opened. I thought, 'It's not just I who was protected. If she had been able to open the door earlier, she and the baby would have been hit, too.'"

Now, Gary, an active church youth leader and a devoted father of four, wonders why he was saved. "I should never have lived through the accident. And I certainly never should have walked again. But what happened made me realize that I'm here for a purpose. And I know now that God watches over us."

What do you make of stories like these? Were angels really involved? These accounts stretch my imagination, make me wonder. How do angels relate to lives filled with earthbound, everyday realities? What is the mission of angels among us? Questions like these form the heart of the first chapters of this book. I will tell a number of stories like those of Olivia, Ignatius, and Gary. They will be old and new, inauspicious and stunning, biblical and contemporary. And because Scripture, when it mentions angels usually describes them *doing* something, these early chapters will likewise focus on what angels *do*.

That harm may not befall us

Whether angel stories appear in the Bible or in conversation with a friend next door, one of the first and most elemental things we learn about the work of angels is that they *help* people. Caring for human beings ranks high on their list of duties.

Angels "keep vigil for our safety, take upon themselves our defense, direct our way, and take care that some harm may not befall us," Calvin wrote.[2] God employs angels to take care of us. That is not their only (or

even primary) assignment, but it is a significant one. God may use angels, as someone once suggested, not so much because God needs them, but because we need them; angels remind us tangibly that God exercises personal care over each of us. "Because I believe in angels," a friend of mine once said, "I can send my kids off to school on the bus every day, knowing they face dangers and pressures, but still not have an anxiety attack."

More can be said than that they serve as agents of providence. Angels evidence God's help in three significant ways.

ANGELS REMIND US THAT GOD NOTICES

Christian author Elisabeth Elliot tells that when her father was a small boy, he was climbing on an upper story of a house under construction. "He walked to the end of a board that was not nailed at the other end, and slowly it began to tip. He knew he was doomed, but inexplicably the board began to tip the other way, as though a hand had pushed it down again. He always wondered whether it was an angel's hand."[3] Was it?

If God cares so much that he draws near to us in the grit of daily choices and dark moments, why not? While the Bible affirms that God is the exalted God of the universe, it also emphasizes that even the very hairs of our head are numbered, as Jesus said (Matt. 10:30). Nothing, in other words, escapes God's notice.

Jesus once pointed to a child and said of children, "In heaven their angels continually see the face of my Father in heaven" (Matt. 18:10). How

surprising! Jewish tradition had said only the loftiest of angels had access to the supreme God, yet Jesus said that even angels who watch over the simplest and smallest stand close to God, intervening when God so directs.

My friend June told me how an angelic touch reminded her of God's provision for even the seemingly insignificant. June is a retired kindergarten teacher, a tall, stately, white-haired woman. I've known her for years—long enough to know she is not given to flights of fancy.

One night as she lay in bed, she says, "I felt a motion above my head, a slight moving of the air. I immediately knew it was the wings of an angel. I didn't see anything. There were no lights, no great drama. But I was so aware of a presence. I realized this is going on all the time; I just haven't known it. God's protective care surrounds me." I believe God gave June a wonderful gift. He reminded her that he noticed.

Of course, a powerful inner voice often whispers that we are nothing special, that our little lives cannot matter much to God. So we are dogged by a longing to be acknowledged. "What are human beings that you are mindful of them, mortals that you care for them?" asks David in Psalm 8. We yearn to know that the God who made us also holds our small lives in his hands. There is one sentence, writer Reynolds Price once wrote, that all humankind craves to hear: "The Maker of all things knows and wants me."[4] Every day as I wake, every night as I turn off my bedside light, and all the moments in between, I long to believe God sees me. It is what someone has called an "ache for cosmic specialness."[5]

A scene from the motion picture *Gandhi* captures this. As a young lawyer, Gandhi (an Indian) is walking a boardwalk with a white clergyman, contrary to South African law at the time. They are accosted by some rough-looking white men. Just then the mother of the ringleader calls from an upstairs window and commands the young man to go about his business. As Gandhi and the clergyman walk on, the clergyman talks about their good luck.

"*Luck?*" Gandhi asks. "But I thought you were a man of God."

"I am," replies the clergyman, "but I don't believe God plans his day around me!"[6]

The audience is supposed to laugh at the naïveté of thinking anything else. And the scene makes a point. God may not plan his day around me, but in his infinite mercy and constant care, his "eye is upon the sparrow," and all the more on us humans. We matter that much; after all, if God would give his Son's life for us, why could he not also send an angel? He will not always do so, of course. Indeed, most of us will never see a dramatic angelic appearance. But the fact that angels exist and occasionally come into view suggests great unseen activities on our behalf.

Two angel stories from biblical times drive home this point about the "noticing" of God. I believe it no accident that the first real angel story in the Bible involves the most common—and least important—of persons, an Egyptian slave girl named Hagar. Another surprise! I expect angels to ap-

pear to biblical celebrities like Jacob or Jesus. But to someone we would call a nobody?

Just as surprising are the circumstances surrounding the angel's appearance. It was no shining moment of virtue for the slave girl or her mistress, Sarai, wife of Abram. Despite God's promise that she and her husband would have many descendants, Sarai became depressed about her infertility. In accordance with a Middle Eastern provision for barrenness, she told Abram to sleep with her slave. "You see that the LORD has prevented me from bearing children . . . it may be that I shall obtain children by her" (Gen. 16:2).

"And Abram listened," the story tells us, describing a willingness in Abram that surely left mixed feelings in Sarai. When Hagar conceived by Abram, in her mingled insecurity and pride, Hagar "looked with contempt on her mistress" (Gen. 16:4). Sarai retaliated by dealing harshly with Hagar, and Hagar fled.

An angel found Hagar and told her to go back to her mistress. The angel adds an amazing promise: "I will so greatly multiply your offspring that they cannot be counted" (Gen. 16:10). Dumbstruck, simple Hagar confessed with quiet wonder, "Have I really seen God and remained alive after seeing him?" (Gen. 16:13). One writer concludes, "We are not told whether she actually saw the angel, but lonely and disgraced as she was, she knew that she had been found by him. . . . Armed with the knowledge that even she, a slave girl, was watched and protected, she was able to return to the

situation from which she had fled."[7] How I sometimes need such an assurance!

I am drawn to another story, likewise found early in the Old Testament narrative. Elijah was wrestling with his own littleness and seeming insignificance. He had just survived a showdown with the prophets of the pagan god Baal, a to-the-death competition which he won in the name of Israel's God. Israel's wicked king and queen, Ahab and Jezebel, furiously plotted revenge. Jezebel vowed to kill Elijah. Elijah did what anyone would do: He "got up and fled for his life" (1 Kings 19:3). He walked for a day into the wilderness and, finding a broom tree, he sat down and said, "It is enough; now, O LORD, take away my life, for I am no better than my ancestors" (1 Kings 19:4). He was a picture of discouragement.

But an angel awakened Elijah from sleep and offered him bread and water. He ate and fell asleep again. And again the angel awoke him: "'Get up and eat, otherwise the journey will be too much for you.' He got up, and ate and drank; then he went in the strength of that food forty days and forty nights" (1 Kings 19:7–8).

Artist Gustave Doré gives a wonderfully earthy quality to the story. He portrays the heavenly being descending to earth with a jug of water under one arm and a loaf of bread in the other. God does not let even the tangible, touchable aspects of our lives pass his notice.

Elijah nourished by an angel

ANGELS REMIND US THAT GOD SEES OUR DAILY DETAILS

It is good to know God notices, but there is more. He watches us with *interest*. And because God cares about us, he cares about even the details of our daily lives.

"We live lives of little things," I once heard someone say. So much of life happens in the daily arena of factory, shopping mall, school. Kissing my wife good-bye in the morning, standing at the sink washing dishes, waiting for a doctor's appointment, sitting at my office desk: Is God really paying attention? If he cares for us, if his love means anything, it must encompass in its view dirty diapers and divorces and job promotions.

God knows this is not always easy for us to remember. We tend to think that God will not bother with our daily anxieties or joys. We are apt to recall only the words of Ecclesiastes, "God is in heaven, and [we are] upon earth" (5:2b). But Martin Luther, the sixteenth-century church reformer, once said that angels are "our true and trusty servants, performing offices and works that one poor miserable mendicant would be ashamed to do for another."[8] God cares enough to occasionally send them to do good in the press of daily life.

Judith MacNutt, director of a counseling service, tells a vivid story that reminded her of this. She had just returned home from an evening with friends and was preparing for bed, thinking about the full load of clients she would see the next day. This is what happened:

"Tired and ready for sleep," she recalls, "I started to remove my jewelry: earrings, watch, necklace." Gasping, suddenly she noticed one of her ring fingers. A precious ring that, for her, held great sentimental value was gone.

"Rushing outside, I quickly checked my car to see if my ring had fallen to the floor. After vainly searching my car and my bedroom, I phoned the restaurant. Waiting while they looked for my ring, I prayed, 'Lord, please help them find it; please let it be there.' But after what seemed like an eternity, the manager phoned to report that no ring had been found.

"My memory went back to the brilliant summer day when my father had unexpectedly purchased the ring. We had flown together to the Bahamas to meet my older brother who had sailed there on his boat. Only rarely had we been together since I had left home in Kentucky following my mother's death seven years earlier.

"On that beautiful afternoon, I had invited my father to go shopping with me, since I wanted to buy a remembrance of our family vacation. After wandering through several shops my eyes spotted a tiny golden

ring—but as I started to buy it, my father surprised me by telling me he didn't like it."

Taking Judith's arm, her father took her to an elegant case where a woman of Judith's means would never dare look. "There," he said pointing, "there's a ring made for you!"

"Never before," recalls Judith, "had I seen a ring that danced with such light and beauty: a small diamond nestled between a circle of deep blue sapphires." She protested that it was too expensive, but her father insisted, "This ring is my gift of love to you. Whenever you wear it, remember that your father loves you."

"At that moment, tears of forgotten birthdays, bitter childhood memories, and disappointments were all forgotten. The little girl inside me felt loved and accepted by her daddy. The ring became a symbol of that marvelous healing."

But now, years later, it was lost. Judith struggled with Jesus' teaching that we should not be overly tied to earthly possessions, "but I felt he would surely understand my need for this one special attachment. I reached for my Bible and began to search for verses of promise." Finding comfort there, she was finally able

to release the ring. "Lord," she prayed, "I release that precious ring that symbolizes my daddy's love. Thank you for the joy it once gave me. Thank you for the healing it represented."

Once more at peace, Judith settled into the drowsy stillness that precedes sleep. "My last conscious thought was another prayer: 'Lord, you know I've released the ring. But if it's not a problem, would you mind sending an angel to bring it back to me?' "

It was a strange prayer, recalls Judith: "I had never in my life called on the Lord to send angels to do anything—much less return a ring."

The next day, getting started late, she rushed out the door to her car. As she turned the key to start the engine, something strange happened. "I heard an inner voice: 'Go back inside, your ring is there.' 'I must be dreaming,' I thought. The ring couldn't be inside." She backed out of the driveway.

"This time the voice became louder and more insistent: 'Go home!' Arguing with myself—and the voice—I found a place to turn around and headed back home. Feeling foolish, I unlocked the door and walked through my silent home, glancing here and there as I went from room to room. The bedroom was

the last place I entered. As I turned to leave, something sparkly caught my eye.

"I walked over to the rocker where I had sat the night before. On the flowered seat cushion lay my Bible just as I had left it. On top of my Bible, placed by unseen hands, was my beloved ring. Tears flooded my eyes, blurring my vision. This is impossible! I was astounded—the ring was real, not a dream, not a vision. I quickly placed it on my finger, laughing and crying at the same time. An indescribable mixture of joy, wonder, and relief filled my heart. I felt God tell me that he wanted me to know through this experience that my heavenly Father—not just my earthly father—loves me."[9]

Judith's was a lesson people have struggled to learn for centuries. While God will not magically dissolve every difficulty, while suffering is still very much with us, we at least know that he cares in ways big and small.

Once again the Bible fills out the picture and gives us a context for this item on an angel's job description. This time the story concerns Jacob. Isaac, Jacob's father, had just sent him on a several-days' journey to a relative's house to find a wife. One evening, as darkness approached, Jacob found a stone for a pillow and slept. He dreamed of a stairway stretching

Jacob's dream

between earth and heaven, upon which angels went up and down, up and down.

It may have dazzled him, but "Jacob's ladder" was no strange idea to people of the time. The neighboring Mesopotamians believed there was always one place where such a connection between heaven and earth was made. And at the top of such stairways, they taught, the gods dwelt in a lofty chamber. On certain occasions, the gods would come down to receive homage from the people.

But in Jacob's dream, God did not wait aloofly for worship, but gave a mind-boggling promise. He told Jacob, "I will give you and your descendants the land on which you are lying. . . . I am with you and will watch over you wherever you go, and I will bring you back to this land. I will not leave you until I have done what I have promised you" (Gen. 28:13–15 NIV). The God of the universe became "local"; he acted concretely.

But that did not settle it all for Jacob. As he was returning to Canaan after his long sojourn at the house of his uncle Laban, "the angels of God met him" (Gen. 32:1). That is all we know; we don't know what they did, how Jacob reacted, if he responded with awe or joy: only that he named the place *Mahanaim* (Two Camps), recognizing that on one side was his own ragtag band, and on the other, the company of God (Gen. 32:2).

But the angels were not through with Jacob. With his two wives, their children, servants, and flocks and herds, Jacob went to visit his brother Esau. Years before, of course, Jacob had cheated Esau out of his father's

blessing. Now Jacob must have wondered, "What will I find? Will Esau attack when I step foot on his turf?"

The night before the meeting, we read, Jacob met "a man" and "wrestled with him until daybreak" (Gen. 32:24). While the account never uses the word *angel,* the "man" was a heavenly being. Jewish and Christian tradition have long assumed that it was. Some commentators even argue it was God himself, appearing in tangible form (Jacob later names the spot *Peniel* [Face of God], for there he met God "face to face" [Gen. 32:30]). I am content to say that Jacob wrestled with an angel. Here, as in many biblical stories, the narrator spends little attention on distinguishing between the Sender and the sent, between God and the angelic messenger.

The angel did not best Jacob, and finally cried to be released. Sensing his wrestling partner's heavenly authority, Jacob countered, "I will not let you go, unless you bless me" (Gen. 32:26). Jacob received God's blessing—and a new name: Israel.

What does it mean? A powerful God sent an agent to fight a fearful man. He permitted this puny man to win, marked him with a limp as a sign, and gave him a new name that pointed to a grand future. It was God becoming what writer Reynolds Price called a "palpable God,"[10] a God who expresses his purposes for us in the daily and the concrete, the things we can see and taste and smell, a God who eventually honored our everyday world by one day becoming man to walk dusty roads and eat fish and bread.

As for Jacob and Esau's encounter the next day, once he saw his brother approaching, Esau ran to meet Jacob and "embraced him, and fell on his neck and kissed him, and they wept" (Gen. 33:4).

Jacob's numerous encounters with heavenly beings do not mean we should expect an angel at every turn. They do not appear (at least visibly) at every difficulty. On this Scripture is clear, especially when we hear Jesus' rigorous, ringing call to follow him whatever the cost. But it does mean that it is appropriate to ask God to send angels to watch over our days' pains and joys. The venerable *Book of Common Prayer*, used by Christians for centuries, includes this prayer:

> *E*verlasting God, you have ordained and constituted in a wonderful order the ministries of angels and mortals: mercifully grant that, as your holy angels always serve and worship you in heaven, so by your appointment they may help and defend us here on earth.[11]

ANGELS REMIND US THAT GOD PROTECTS

God does more than send angels, he grants them the insight and strength they need to protect us. Understanding angels' role in defending us, says one Bible scholar, "will increase our appreciation of a sovereign God whose creative ability, control of the universe, and interven-

tions on our behalf assure his glory and our good."[12] A character in Shakespeare's *Hamlet* puts it simpler: "Angels and ministers of grace defend us."[13]

Don and Caffy Whitney, a pastor and an artist, discovered this on their honeymoon. Here is their account of what happened:

> *We* were married in Fayetteville, Arkansas, on the night of January 8, 1977. The snow began to fall in the Ozarks just as we left the church, but we had no idea at the time that we were driving into the teeth of an eighteen-inch snowfall, the worst winter storm in Arkansas history.
>
> Road conditions rapidly deteriorated as we drove west across the Oklahoma border where the snow had been drifting longer. Not only did the blowing snow blind our vision, the blizzard obliterated the tracks of the few other travelers who had preceded us on the highway. For long stretches at a time, the only way to determine that we were actually on the road was for Don to stick his head out the window into the below-zero windchill and stay to the right of the dead weeds in the ditch whose tops could still barely be seen sticking out above the snow. We feared for our lives.

Our situation became so desperate that finally we agreed to stop at the next house we passed and ask if we could stay, even though it meant not only spending our first night together in a small country house with complete strangers, but probably most of our honeymoon as well. Heading toward a resort hotel on a secluded lake in northeastern Oklahoma, however, we were traveling on relatively minor two-lane roads and in a rural area. It seemed as though we'd never drive by a house. Finally we did, but no one was home! The same thing was true at the next house. We had no choice but to keep moving.

We went for miles without seeing another vehicle, and we were not at all sure we could find our way on these back roads. But about 1:30 A.M., headlights appeared out of the snow in our rearview mirror. To our surprise, the vehicle pulled out to pass in spite of the treacherous conditions. An old pickup moved around us and then settled comfortably in front of us at our same rate of speed. Comforted by his company, we decided to follow in the ruts made by his tires regardless of where he went.

For a half hour the truck turned this way and

that onto desolate country back roads, plowing a path for us through the fierce storm. Suddenly the old truck slowed to a stop in front of an arch across the road. From his headlights we could read on the arch the name of our resort. He had led us to the very spot we had been trying to reach! Then the pickup turned around, drove past us and out of sight into the blizzard and the night.

Why, of all places, did the driver of the truck head for such a remote location on such a horrible night? And why, after traveling for so long in the storm to get there, would he turn around at that point? Was it an angel that guided us safely out of danger and escorted us exactly where we needed to go? We could never prove to you that it was, but you could never convince us that it wasn't.[14]

God mercifully looked down on a young couple's plight. Was it an angel? I believe it was. The story is too odd, too full of the unexplained, too well attested by two sets of sane eyes for me to call it coincidence. But even if it was a human messenger who helped, I have no doubt that God was looking down with protective concern, providing an example of his caring intervention.

Then there's the story of Euphie Eallonardo, recounted in *Guideposts:*

It had been reckless of me, taking a before-dawn stroll through the tangle of streets behind the Los Angeles bus terminal. But I was a young woman arriving in the great city for the first time. My job interview was five hours away, and I couldn't wait to explore!

Now I'd lost my way in a skid row neighborhood. Hearing a car pass, I turned and, in the flash of light, saw three men lurking behind me, trying to keep out of sight in the shadows. Trembling with fright, I did what I always do when in need of help. I bowed my head and asked God to rescue me.

But when I looked up, a fourth man was striding toward me in the dark! *Dear God, I'm surrounded.* I was so scared, it took me a few seconds to realize that even in the blackness I could *see* this man. He was dressed in an immaculate workshirt and denim pants, and carried a lunchbox. He was about thirty, well over six feet. His face was stern but beautiful (the only word for it).

I ran up to him. "I'm lost and some men are following me," I said in desperation. "I took a walk from the bus depot—I'm so scared."

"Come," he said. "I'll take you to safety."

He was strong and made me feel safe.

"I . . . I don't know what would have happened if you hadn't come along."

"I do." His voice was resonant, deep.

"I prayed for help just before you came."

A smile touched his mouth and eyes. We were nearing the depot. "You are safe now."

"Thank you—so much," I said fervently.

He nodded. "Good-bye, Euphie."

Going into the lobby, it hit me. *Euphie!* Had he really used my first name? I whirled, burst out onto the sidewalk. But he had vanished.[15]

Do such stories of God's angelic protection have precedent in the Bible? One of the most-loved Bible stories suggests an answer. It involves the prophet Daniel's friends, Shadrach, Meshach, and Abednego.

It helps to know something about the setting for the story. Nebuchadnezzar, the king of Babylon in the sixth century B.C., had undertaken an impressive building campaign, with hanging gardens (one of the seven wonders of the ancient world) and a huge temple with a tower (ziggurat) dedicated to the pagan god Marduk. The ancient Greek historian Herodotus said the splendor of Babylon had no parallel.

It is no surprise, then, that such a powerful king could overtake and conquer the people of Israel. In a series of victories, Nebuchadnezzar took the people of Judah captive and deported them to Babylon. The youth

Daniel was taken captive in 605 B.C. Apparently showing great promise, Daniel was trained in the arts, letters, and wisdom in the Babylonian capital.

Because Daniel so impressed Nebuchadnezzar, the king appointed Daniel as a high governmental official. He made him "ruler over the whole province of Babylon and chief prefect over all the wise men of Babylon" (Dan. 2:48). It seems that one of Daniel's first requests was to ask the king to appoint Shadrach, Meshach, and Abednego as assistants.

Nebuchadnezzar also had built an idol, roughly one hundred feet high and ten feet wide, and set it in the plain of Dura. He told all his officials—princes, captains, and provincial rulers—to come to the dedication of the image. A herald announced that "whoever does not fall down and worship shall immediately be thrown into a furnace of blazing fire" (Dan. 3:6).

When Shadrach, Meshach, and Abednego refused to worship the idol, the king flew into a rage. "He ordered the furnace heated up seven times more than was customary, and ordered some of the strongest guards in his army to bind Shadrach, Meshach, and Abednego and to throw them into the furnace of blazing fire. Because the king's command was urgent and the furnace was so overheated, the raging flames killed the men who lifted Shadrach, Meshach, and Abednego" (Dan. 3:19b–20, 22).

The king, however, suddenly asked his counselors, "Was it not three men that we threw bound into the fire?" Yes, they answered. Astonished, he said, "But I see four men unbound, walking in the middle of the fire, and

they are not hurt; and the fourth has the appearance of a god" (Dan. 3:25b). When he discovered that the three men were not even singed by the fire, Nebuchadnezzar said, "Blessed be the God of Shadrach, Meshach, and Abednego, who has sent his angel and delivered his servants who trusted in him" (Dan. 3:28). God sent an angel on a mission of protection.

The New Testament has a counterpart story that finds its characters likewise rubbing their eyes with disbelief. During the time the early Christians were spreading their message in the ancient world, "King Herod laid violent hands upon some who belonged to the church. He had James, the brother of John, killed with the sword. After he saw that it pleased the Jews, he proceeded to arrest Peter also" (Acts 12:1–3).

Peter was imprisoned with "four squads of soldiers to guard him" (Acts 12:4b) and all the while "the church prayed fervently to God for him" (Acts 12:5b).

The night before Herod was to bring Peter before the people, "Peter, bound with two chains, was sleeping between two soldiers, while guards in front of the door were keeping watch over the prison. Suddenly an angel of the Lord appeared and a light shone in the cell" (Acts 12:6b–7a). The angel tapped Peter on the side and told him to get up quickly (even angels have to take seriously the circumstances of everyday life). The chains miraculously fell off Peter's wrists. The angel told him to dress and follow him. Then, verse 9: "Peter went out and followed him; he did not realize that what was happening with the angel's help was real." Soon, however, the an-

gel left, and Peter concludes, "Now I am sure that the Lord has sent his angel and rescued me from the hands of Herod and from all that the Jewish people were expecting" (Acts 12:11b).

Others were not so easily convinced. Peter went to the house of Mary, mother of John Mark, where many had gathered and were praying. A maid named Rhoda answered at the gate when Peter knocked, and heard Peter's voice. She was so overjoyed that she left Peter standing outside, and ran in to tell the others. Peter's praying friends told Rhoda she was crazy until Peter told them all how God rescued him through the angel. In the morning, "there was no small commotion among the soldiers over what had become of Peter" (Acts 12:18).

Where angels fit in

In the tough and sometimes miraculous business of living, what part do angels play? What does it mean to speak of God's watchful eye when in so many places in our world today "famine, sword, and fire crouch for employment" as Shakespeare wrote?[16] Because life contains times of both grace and pain, even agents of God's care do not save us from all harm.

Part of me, I find, wants to escape from life's hard realities. Who wouldn't like to forget that life contains moments of horror—concentration camps, abused children, starving masses? Or we wish to avoid the humdrum dailiness of life: deadlines at work, commutes through gridlocked traffic, another room to vacuum. We would like to spice it up, dream that

heavenly messengers live at our beck and call. We wouldn't mind celestial fireworks jolting us out of a dull day. But we must guard against the temptation to think of God's angels as celestial errand boys.

Still, other dangers are greater than expecting angel appearances at every turn: the danger that we will despair during the moments of pain that etch our lives, the danger that we will assume that the routine is all we can expect in life. We tend to forget that whatever happens in life, wherever we find ourselves, God is at work and taking care of us.

John Henry Newman, a nineteenth-century English church leader, wrote, "There have been ages of the world in which men have thought too much of angels, and paid them excessive honor; honored them so perversely as to forget the supreme worship due to Almighty God. This is the sin of a dark age. But the sin of what is called an educated age, such as our own, is just the reverse; to account slightly of them, or not at all; to ascribe all we see around us, not to their agency, but to certain assumed laws of nature."[17]

The work of his angels goes on still; we usually see only glimmerings of it. In your lifetime you may be aware of an angel helping you out of difficulty; you may not. The truly significant issue is something deeper. This understanding stole over Judith MacNutt in the wake of the angel-assisted recovery of her ring. After an early morning prayer service the following day, she lingered. "I remained on my knees at the back of the quiet church," she recounts. "As I thanked God for all he had done to bring

about this miracle, an overwhelming sense of the majesty of God filled the church."[18]

The sense of the Lord's majestic goodness can fill our lives as well, if we watch and listen. And whether angels appear to assist us, whether we see them vividly or only vaguely sense their unseen workings, God can employ them whenever he chooses. That should give us hope.

Chapter 3
Angels We Have Heard on Earth

*If heaven is willing to sing to us, it is little to ask
that we be ready to listen.*

Nancy Gibbs

*E*ven now, George Robbins cannot speak of his meeting with an angel without tears.

George is an eighty-something Midwesterner, a cherished uncle of a friend of mine, who five years ago was plunged into grief when his wife died. A devout Christian, George says that he and his wife "had a wonderful life serving the Lord and doing the things God wanted us to do." But cancer struck. "She had a mastectomy, and seemed fine. Seven years later, however, she developed another lump. The cancer moved into her lymph glands, then rapidly passed through her entire body.

"After her death," George recounts, "I experienced a black hole of despair unlike any I had ever experienced. I couldn't understand it; I knew my wife was in heaven, but darkness settled on me. For three nights I couldn't sleep. On the third night, at about two o'clock in the morning, I was praying. All of a sudden the whole room was illuminated. I didn't know what was happening. But then I saw an angel standing by my bed, in this very room. It was the most gorgeous thing I have ever seen, so beautiful I can't explain the radiance and the splendor." When pressed for more details, George will tell you that "the angel had flowing robes, long hair—seemed mostly feminine. This room was lit up with the presence." And, he stresses, "this was not a dream. I was awake.

"Then the being spoke to me: 'Peace be unto you.' That's all. But I knew then that everything would be all right. I felt a peace in my heart that was like when I was first converted to Christ. And all the darkness left. I've had

times of sorrow since; I still miss my wife. But I've never had that feeling of darkness again."

If the helping work of angels reminds us that God notices us, as we learned in the last chapter, the message-bearing work of angels reminds us that God also speaks to us. He is not a mute deity or a vaguely silent force. He is a God who communicates. And occasionally he uses angels as his means of communication.

I know many who suspect God never breaks through his silence. They believe that if God communicates, it is through fine principles: the Bible, or through a pastor, perhaps. He may even give us a general revelation, but a specific, personal word? No, they say. They would hear George's story and wonder, Was his angel interaction simply the effect of intense grief? Lack of sleep? A desperate need for assurance "projected" from the depths of his consciousness?

Our society is typically skeptical. "Why is it," asks comedian Lily Tomlin, "that when we speak to God we are said to be praying, but when God speaks to us we are said to be schizophrenic?"[1] If God is wondrously personal, as the entire Scriptures of Christian tradition repeatedly stress, why exclude the possibility of direct communication—from his side as well as ours? And why can't God use angels to bring us a message?

In the original languages of the Old and New Testaments, the words translated *angel* literally and simply mean *messenger.* And this is how we most often find angels at work in the Bible: carrying a message. When they

poke their celestial heads into stories of the Bible, more often than not it is to say something, guide a wandering nation, trumpet astonishing news, or set somebody straight.

Growing up in a churchgoing family, I always knew angels flew in and out of the nativity story, but I did not realize how persistently they bore messages throughout the rest of Scripture. Angels heralded many of the great acts of God. People are addressed by angels so commonly in Scripture that it's easy to list familiar names of those who were: Balaam, Elijah, Gideon, Isaiah, Daniel, Mary, John the Revelator. Even portions of books of the Bible—Daniel and Revelation—were mediated through angels.[2]

More remarkably, the New Testament says angels were the ones who "declared" or "ordained" the law of Moses—the Ten Commandments.[3] God used them to communicate one of the most vital parts of his instruction for his people. And angels show up with messages at crucial moments in Jesus' life: An angel announces to Mary that Jesus is to be born; an angel tells Jesus' shaken women followers that Jesus has been raised from the dead; and, in Acts, two angelic figures tell an awe-struck band of upward-gazing followers that Jesus had ascended into heaven.[4]

What does all this mean for today? Angels play a vital role as God's messengers to us even now. While their message-giving appearances are not exactly commonplace, angels are still God's celestial "secret agents." As the angel chorus articulates in John Milton's *Paradise Lost,*

> . . . God will deign
> to visit oft the dwellings of just Men
> Delighted, and with frequent intercourse
> Thither will send his winged Messengers
> On errands of supernal grace.[5]

This is not to say angels are God's primary way of communicating. They are not. God speaks supremely through Jesus' life, his death and resurrection, and his teachings. Jesus is the Word of God made flesh, John says in his gospel. And God reveals his will for us through the Bible, so that "everyone who belongs to God may be proficient," as Paul says in 2 Timothy 3:17. God also speaks through the "still small voice" of the Holy Spirit guiding us. Or he guides more subtly through spiritually wise friends or counselors. And when it comes to proclaiming Christ to the world, God has assigned that task primarily to the church, not angels.

Yet angels must not be forgotten. God has given them a role in conveying his will. They do this through their appearing in Scripture and in the lives of people today.

This message-bearing aspect of an angel's job description has a peculiar relevance to our current era, dubbed by some the Age of Communications. Ours is a day of exploding information technology; our bookcases, mailboxes, and computers threaten to bury us with facts and data; but they cannot guide our steps or make us wise. So when I ask, Is the God of the uni-

verse also the Shepherd of my personal life? when I wonder, Can he sometimes send a message to make his purposes clear? I look at angels and see more than a theoretical answer. I am reminded that messengers on "errands of supernal grace" have never stopped working.

Of course, angels do not act at cross purposes with God—revealing what he will not. The Bible's stories of angelic communication convey a sober sparseness of content. God does not send angels to satisfy our unhealthy curiosity. Nor do they dwell on the trivial. When speaking of angelic communication, then, we must exercise care.

But cautions noted, how should we understand the angels' roles as messengers? How did God use them in biblical times? What is the right place of these beings that God still sends for our surprise and benefit?

THEY BRING AN ENCOURAGING WORD

First, angels—the real angels spoken of in Scripture—sometimes communicate simple encouragement. Particularly when a servant of God faces anxiety or danger, God may send a messenger with a word of hope, a reminder of God's presence and care. The angel brings no mediation of new revelation, no secret unrevealed in Scripture. God simply sends a messenger to help keep his servant going. The angel makes real the truths we already know.

Take the story of Ivan Moiseyev, for instance. He was a young, vocal Christian drafted into the Soviet army in 1970. Openly expressing faith in

Christ was strictly forbidden in the Soviet Union then, and Vanya, as he was nicknamed, experienced a hell of interrogation and torture for his beliefs.

> *It* was a long walk to [the interrogator's] office, and as Ivan strode along the . . . streets of the base, he was giving praise to God for the time to pray. . . . It was a clear day. Something flashed and glittered in the sky overhead. . . . The trees in the small park in the central square of the base seemed dusted with a heavenly light. He lifted his eyes upward at the same instant that he heard a voice, "Vanya. Vanya."
>
> The voice was like a memory, unmistakable, clear, and strangely wordless. "Do not be afraid." Through the transparent form of the angel Ivan could see the large trees on the opposite side of the park. The form of the angel seemed to be moving. Staring, Ivan slowly resumed walking. The radiance of the angel lit the park far more brightly than the sun. But he was speaking again.
>
> "Do not be afraid. Go. I am with you."[6]

The words not only helped Vanya face that day's interrogation, but months of persecution. "Do not be afraid," said the angel; and Ivan, hear-

ing, could face long months of great hardship—and eventual martyrdom—and not lose his faith.

Then there's the story of a teenage girl, Heidi Thoma, and her mother, Janet. Here's how Janet recalls their angel encounter:

> *I* was on the West Coast, visiting a pastor who published with my firm. As I drove up to his church's parking lot, I couldn't figure out why cars were filling the parking lot on a weekday morning. Once in the building, I got my explanation. The crowd had come for the funeral service of a high-school senior killed in a car accident. Suddenly I thought of my own daughter, a high school senior, and prayed, "Lord, I'm here on your business. I'm trusting you to take care of things at home. Keep my daughter from anything like this."
>
> My prayer meant more than I knew. When I arrived at my suburban Chicago home that evening, a policeman rang the doorbell. My daughter, I learned, had crashed into a semitrailer truck when it illegally pulled out into a busy intersection. The policeman told me to contact the hospital immediately.
>
> At the hospital, Heidi told me that she had sat in

the car with blood streaming from a gash in her forehead. "But Mom," she said, "someone showed up on my side of the car. She held my hand and told me not to look into the rearview mirror." I realized later that her message-giving companion knew that Heidi would pass out at the sight. But Heidi couldn't resist looking, and seeing her reflection, she temporarily lost consciousness.

When Heidi recovered, she asked the police for the name of the kind helper at the scene of the collision. "I'd like to thank her," said Heidi.

"I'd tell you," the policeman answered, "but there was no woman at the scene of the accident. I was there from the beginning and would have seen her." Another witness agreed: no woman.

I wondered how to explain this. I went to the Scripture that says that children's angels "always see the face of my Father in heaven." There was no doubt in my mind that the Lord had answered my prayer at that memorial service. He sent an angel. On a day when I could not mother my injured daughter, God sent an agent to do his bidding and communicate words of encouragement to her.

In Scripture, we likewise see God's faithful heartened by the message of an angel, as happened in the Old Testament story of Gideon, an Israelite farmer and warrior.

In those days, Judges 6 tells us, the "Israelites did what was evil in the sight of the LORD, and the LORD gave them into the hand of Midian" (v. 1), their oppressive neighbors to the southeast. The people were despairing, but an angel "came and sat under the oak at Ophrah, which belonged to Joash the Abiezrite, as his son Gideon was beating out wheat in the wine press, to hide it from the Midianites" (Judg. 6:11). The angel then addressed Gideon specifically: "The LORD is with you, you mighty warrior" (Judg. 6:12).

"But sir," Gideon asked, "if the LORD is with us, why then has all this happened to us? And where are all his wonderful deeds that our ancestors recounted to us, saying, 'Did not the LORD bring us up from Egypt?' But now the LORD has cast us off, and given us into the hand of Midian" (Judg. 6:13).

Speaking through the angel, the Lord simply said, "Go in this might of yours and deliver Israel from the hand of Midian; I hereby commission you. . . . I will be with you, and you shall strike down the Midianites, every one of them" (Judg. 6:14, 16).

Gideon was not easily convinced, angel appearance or not. When faced with the combined encamped armies of not only the Midianites, but also the Amalekites and the people of the East, Gideon needed even more reas-

surance. He requested a sign: laying a fleece of wool on the threshing floor, he asked for it to be coated with dew in the morning, while everything all around would be dry. When he squeezed out enough dew the next morning to fill a bowl, he asked for the fleece that night to be dry, while everything around would be dewed (see Judg. 6).

In his patient mercy, the Lord complied, but he then put Gideon through a test of his own. He told Gideon to reduce the army of attackers to three hundred, all the more astounding given that the "Midianites and the Amalekites and all the people of the East lay along the valley as thick as locusts; and their camels were . . . countless as the sand on the seashore" (Judg. 7:12).

Gideon obeyed, his knees perhaps shaking, and got the Lord's go-ahead to advance. He led the people of Israel to victory, just as the angel had commissioned him to do (see Judg. 8). Surely Gideon would never have led this foolhardy campaign without the angel's appearance. God sent a messenger to make sure his purposes found fulfillment.

In the New Testament, God sent an angel to do something similar. In a dream, Paul the apostle saw an angel who carried a message of instruction and courage. Acts tells us Paul was headed to Rome and the prospect of prison. He needed to know that God's purposes for him would not be thwarted—especially when his ship was beset by a violent storm. The waves pounded the vessel, the winds wreaked havoc, and the crew had to toss the ship's cargo and tackle overboard. The storm would not go away. "Since

[they all] had been without food for a long time, Paul then stood up among them and said, '. . . Last night there stood by me an angel of the God to whom I belong and whom I worship, and he said, "Do not be afraid, Paul; you must stand before the emperor; and indeed, God has granted safety to all those who are sailing with you." So . . . I have faith in God that it will be exactly as I have been told' " (Acts 27:21–25). Paul still had a daunting journey, a trial, and imprisonment staring him down, but from that moment on Paul knew beyond doubting that God was watching, and orchestrating his purposes.

They Give Needed Guidance

Sometimes angels convey more than assurance; they also bring specific guidance. Angels may appear with knowledge that keeps someone from danger. They serve, in other words, as agents of God's guidance in people's lives. They remind us that God will not hesitate to communicate his will when we must know it, even if it takes rending the skies or stopping us in our daily rounds. I do not believe this is God's *preferred* means of communication; else why would he give us the Scriptures, send his prophets, and even become one of us in the person of Jesus?

But in his resourceful mercy, in his repertoire of ways to get our attention or keep us on the way of faithfulness, God may send an angel. We see this in a wonderfully odd story of pastor Sam Cathey of Graceway Baptist Church in Oklahoma City. Here he tells his story:

In 1967, my first year in [full-time evangelistic work], I had to rush back from [a series of revival services] to be with my family. My daughter had just been hospitalized with acute appendicitis, possible rupture, and possible peritonitis. They were trying to get her temperature down so they could operate in the morning.

I got on a plane in Los Angeles about two-thirty in the morning. I was heading to our home in Detroit. My heart was very heavy. [Because] it was my first year in evangelism, I was . . . unsure about what I was doing except I knew it was God's will. I didn't want to be away from the family, didn't want to be out on the road as I was. And here trouble had come the first few months of my new venture for Christ.

My seat was at the bulkhead, right behind the first class curtain. When we were airborne, a stewardess came by. She wore a red dress with blue trim. I asked her, "Do you mind if I go up into the first class cabin? There's nobody up there. I'm going home and I need to rest. May I go up there and make a bed?"

She said, "No, I'm sorry. I can't let you go up there. It's against the rules. We don't even have a stewardess up there."

She'd just walked away when another stewardess came through those curtains. This one was dressed in a blue uniform with red trim. She invited me to come up front and sit with her, and I gratefully agreed.

We sat facing each other, and she asked if I'd like some refreshments. I thanked her and she brought me some sandwich squares, olives, chips, and pop. I began to eat, and she began to talk.

She went on and on about the Lord, the Scripture, the sovereignty of God, grace, and God's love, care, and protection. I forgot I was hungry and sleepy and just listened. Now, mind you, not a word had been said about my daughter, Nola. Not one word. And I'd not identified myself in any way as a minister.

After a good while, we passed over Chicago. She stood and said, "See all those lights down there? Put your hands like so." She put my hands together and held them out there. "See, from way up here, it looks like you cover up the whole city of Chicago, doesn't it?" I agreed. "Now cup them so," and I cupped them. "From up here, it looks like you've got the whole city of Chicago in your hands, doesn't it?" Again, I agreed.

She then put her hand on my shoulder, looked at me full in the face, and said, "O thou man of God, Nola will be all right." With that statement, she wheeled around and went through those curtains into coach.

I was stunned. I'd not even mentioned Nola's name. A few seconds later, I got my composure and went after her. I couldn't find her. I ran into one of the other stewardesses and she asked where I'd been. I told her I'd been sitting in first class, and she said, "I told you, you can't go up there."

"Well, the head stewardess came and got me."

"I'm the head stewardess."

"No, I'm talking about the one dressed in blue with red trim."

"Oh, no, we don't have anybody like that on this plane. You've been dreaming."

"No, she took me up there and gave me some sandwiches and things."

"Now I know you've been dreaming. There's no food up there."

I said, "Let's go see." We went back up there, and there was a remnant. This stunned her.

I described the woman and the stewardess got the

other women together and they went from one end of that plane to the other, looking for the stewardess. We could not find her. So I told the stewardesses what she had said about Nola, my daughter, and they were just stunned, as was I. We looked everywhere. And of course, she was not to be found.

When I got off the plane that morning, my wife picked me up just grinning from ear to ear. She said the hospital had just called, the fever had broken, the blood test was clear. No indication of any kind of infection, no pain or anything, not even a need for surgery. They told us to come and get her and take her home.

Years later, when my daughter was twenty-six and the wife of a Baptist pastor, she went into a hospital for surgery. After the operation, the doctor came out and said, "Mrs. Cathey, we can't find a surgical scar indicating that Nola had her appendix taken out." My wife said, "No, she never did have it taken out." The doctor looked at her and said, "Well, we thought that while we were in there we would go ahead and clip that appendix. We found a surgical scar where the appendix was supposed to be, but there's no external surgical scar."

I know that's a wild, weird story, but it can be documented, especially the medical reports on my daughter. It is my earnest conviction that God sent that angel to me to encourage me, not only about my daughter, but to give me faith in my new venture as an evangelist, a faith that would keep me on the road for twenty-two more years.[7]

Angels likewise show up in the Bible to give specific guidance or direction, especially when it comes to people or events significant to God's purposes.

In one of the earliest angel stories in Scripture, the message brought by angels is crucial. Abraham was sitting at the shaded door of his tent on a hot day "by the oaks of Mamre" (Gen. 18:1). He looked up and saw three "men" standing nearby. Did he recognize them as divine visitors? We don't know. But with storied Middle Eastern hospitality, he rushed back in the tent ordering Sarah to bake bread.

He had a servant cook a choice, tender calf. He presented the meal of veal, bread, and cheese with pride to his guests. While they ate, the three visitors asked him where his wife Sarah was.

"There, in the tent."

Then, with no fanfare, no heavenly skywriting, one of the three said simply, "I will surely return to you in due season, and your wife Sarah shall

have a son" (Gen. 18:10). This "man" was an angel. In fact, in the middle of this chapter the text subtly shifts from "the men" to "the LORD" as the angel represents the Lord himself (see Gen. 18). (It even becomes a bit confusing to know exactly when the Lord himself is speaking and when [and how] he is using an angel.)

Sarah, we discover, was eavesdropping at the tent door behind Abraham. Sarah was old—"it had ceased to be with Sarah after the manner of women" (Gen. 18:11), the narrator delicately tells us.

So Sarah laughed. Not a hearty laugh, we can easily guess, but the sardonic laugh of someone whose hope has been eaten away by the decades. Was Abraham boiling with embarrassment before his honored guests?

All we know is that the guests were not put off by her scoffing. Instead, the focus shifts to the message of the Lord himself: "The LORD said to Abraham, 'Why did Sarah laugh . . . Is anything too wonderful for the LORD? At the set time I will return to you, in due season, and Sarah shall have a son'" (Gen. 18:13–14).

In this case, angels came to confirm for Abraham something God had already spoken: His descendants would be as the stars of heaven, he was told in Genesis 15:5.

What can we take away from such a story? The Lord had designs on Abraham. He had a clear role in mind for him among God's people, so he did not hesitate to dispatch messengers to make sure all would unfold as he intended.

In the New Testament book of Acts, we read about another angel coming with a specific word. Philip was preaching the gospel in the villages of Samaria, when an angel abruptly appeared with instructions. He told Philip, "Get up and go toward the south to the road that goes down from Jerusalem to Gaza" (Acts 8:26). Philip obeyed. In so doing he happened upon an important official from faraway Ethiopia. God guides further, this time speaking through the Spirit, telling Philip to go over to the Ethiopian's chariot. Philip heard the eunuch reading aloud the book of Isaiah, introduced himself, and began to explain how Jesus had fulfilled the passage that was perplexing the Ethiopian. The man believed, was baptized, and took his newfound faith with him as he went rejoicing on his way (see Acts 8:26–39). Had God not sent an angel, would Philip had found a man who needed to hear about Jesus Christ?

They Proclaim God's Ultimate Message

These stories already begin to suggest a final point about the angels' messenger assignment: God uses angels pre-eminently to convey news of his redemptive work. He delighted to use angels to tell people in New Testament times of the coming of Christ. And while the missionary task now belongs to the church, God may still use angels to point people to Christ. Perhaps this is the most important aspect of angels' message-carrying work.

Theologian Thomas Torrance wrote of this incident in the ministry of his father, a missionary in China:

One day he received a letter from a Chinese man who had never heard of the gospel, but who recounted that all his life he had been seeking for eternal life. The man had made long pilgrimages to various shrines and temples in pursuit of his quest.

"One night after many years he dreamed he was traveling along a mountain road. He came to a great stone arch with the words chiseled on it 'The Way to Eternal Life.' As he [prepared] to go through the arch, he was confronted by a man in white garments who asked what he wanted. When he told of his search for eternal life, he was told to enter, but in his excitement he woke up.

"As soon as morning arrived the Chinese man went to tell a friend about his dream, and on his way encountered a stranger in the village who thrust into his hand a piece of paper bearing the very words of his dream, 'The Way to Eternal Life.'

"It was a tract written by my father about Jesus as the Way, the Truth and the Life. . . . It had my father's name and address printed at the bottom. God had sent his angel to that Chinese pilgrim to show him the way to the Lord Jesus Christ."[8]

Here God used an angelic vision in a dream, and a stranger—presumably human—to communicate his truth and draw someone into the kingdom. While such contemporary stories help remind me that God is still communicating through angels, I find the most persuasive evidence for the gospel-bearing aspect of angels' work in the Bible itself. And the supreme examples of this appear in the events surrounding Jesus' birth.

It began with Zechariah, a priest of the Jewish temple in Palestine. Both he and his wife, Elizabeth, were "righteous before God" (Luke 1:6). Their great sadness was their inability to conceive a child. As he offered incense in the sanctuary "there appeared to him an angel of the Lord, standing at the right side of the altar of incense" (Luke 1:11). Zechariah was rattled. But the angel told him not to be afraid and promised, "Your wife Elizabeth will bear you a son, and you will name him John. You will have joy and gladness, and many will rejoice at his birth" (Luke 1:13–14).

Once he gathered his wits, Zechariah asked, "How will I know that this is so? For I am an old man, and my wife is getting on in years" (Luke 1:18). Eugene Peterson's rendering of this verse in *The Message* may be closer to what was actually going on in Zechariah: "Do you expect me to believe this? I'm an old man and my wife is an old woman."[9]

The angel replied with unflappable presence: "I am Gabriel. I stand in the presence of God, and I have been sent to speak to you and to bring you this good news" (Luke 1:19).

The angel Gabriel appearing to Zechariah

Despite Zechariah's initial skepticism, his wife indeed conceived the child who would eventually be known as John the Baptist.

Gabriel's work was not over. In the sixth month of her cousin Elizabeth's pregnancy, the virgin Mary also was greeted by the angel. "Do not be afraid, Mary," Gabriel says, "for you have found favor with God. And now, you will conceive in your womb and bear a son, and you will name him Jesus. He will be great, and will be called the Son of the Most High" (Luke 1:30–32).

Mary was astonished at the angel's message, but says, " 'Here am I, the servant of the Lord; let it be with me according to your word.' Then the angel departed from her" (Luke 1:38).

What did he look like? Who can know? But in a Roman fresco of the story dated from the end of the second or beginning of the third century A.D., preserved in the catacombs, the angel appears as a young man—unbearded, clothed in white.

The news of this birth is so world-shaking, so wildly important, so much the hinge upon which will swing all that God plans, that angels keep turning up in the Gospels' birth narratives. God makes sure that nothing at the periphery thwarts his purposes for this birth that forms, as Walter Wangerin observes, "the center of everything."[10]

God lets nothing stop this news from getting out. Joseph, for example, was met by an angel when he, concluding Mary was pregnant by another man, planned to "dismiss her quietly" (Matt. 1:19). He is told not to be

An angel appearing to Joseph in a dream

afraid to take Mary as his wife, that the child was conceived by the Holy Spirit. "You are to name him Jesus, for he will save his people from their sins" (Matt. 1:21).

In this drama, not only do angels communicate with the main characters, angels have much to do with shepherds. Christmas carols, bath-robed church pageants, stained-glass scenes have woven the appearance of the angelic host to the shepherds into the very fabric of our visualizations of Christmas.

In the region of the inn at Bethlehem where Mary delivered her child, Luke tells us, shepherds were watching their flocks by night. First one angel told them, "I am bringing you good news of great joy for all the people: to you is born this day in the city of David a Savior, who is the Messiah, the Lord" (Luke 2:10–11).

Then the angel was joined by a multitude of the heavenly host (literally, *army*), who praised and glorified God. While they are traditionally depicted as singing their praises, the text says only that they "said" them (see Luke 2:13–14). It is not hard, however, to imagine them finding spoken words too humdrum to chorus this news that would soon mean more than any of the shepherds imagined. Did it really happen as the story suggests? Because Luke tells us at the beginning of his Gospel that he wanted to write an orderly account after investigating everything carefully from the very first (see Luke 1:3), we can easily picture him trying to find the shepherds themselves, to hear with his own ears the wondrous

things they heard from God's celestial messengers that dark, awesome night.

ANGEL COMMUNIQUÉS TODAY

What should we expect by way of angel messages today?

I have a popular angel book in which the author tells of an angel named Enniss who revealed great "truths" to her. Such "revelations" led her to pen a twelve-hundred-word document on the heavenly order, replete with angels named Ascendar, Kennisha, and Tallithia. "I could see a fundamental difference," she writes, "in the way angels were at work in the world today in comparison with what I knew of their involvement in the past."[11]

I would argue that we should be wary of any who claim that angels are now revealing something new or different from what the Bible and Christian tradition tell us is true. Angels are not a supplement designed to strengthen an anemic biblical revelation. And while angels guide, they are not here to answer our every question about the mysteries of the heavenly realm. I find something unsettling about any author's claim to hundreds of pages of "revelations." We gain no clue in Scripture that angels work that way. "Here, as in all religious doctrine," said church reformer John Calvin four centuries ago, "we ought to hold to one rule of modesty and sobriety: not to speak, or guess, or even to seek to know, concerning obscure matters anything except what has been imparted to us by God's Word."[12]

Without that clarity, we may forget that angels do not show up to give us a new body of revelation, as Mormon founder Joseph Smith claimed for his angel Moroni. (Moroni, Smith declared, revealed to him the location of a hill where were to be found gold plates, which, when translated, became the Book of Mormon.) Here is a case where a claim for angel communication has led to serious error. Angels are not a competing means of divine communication. Angels do not call attention to themselves. Indeed, in Judges 13:17–18, Manoah asked an angel what his name was, only for the angel to refuse to tell him.

This is a point needing emphasis. Many New-Age-flavored angel books speak of angels as agents of divination (the practice of delving into the unknown through occult practices), despite Scripture's clear and repeated condemnation of divination as indicative of a lack of trust in God alone. Reading such unbiblical, demonically dangerous misguidance makes me anxious for all who are being led astray.

One book, *The Little Book of Angels*, goes even further. It speaks of evoking and "calling down" angels, not just to give messages, but to "enter into the body of the ritualist." In this experience of being possessed, the author explains, "the human soul is completely displaced by the spirit; after the trance, the person possessed can never remember what has happened or what the god has said." A Christian should instinctively know how grave the error here. But the author goes on not to identify such a "phenomenon" as a demonic practice to be avoided at all costs, but as a good: "Whether the

beings who indwell their human 'mounts' are called gods or spirits, we may certainly see them as Angels, since they come down from and return to heaven, and form the link between man's world and the realm of the high gods (or God), who never descend to earth." The "mounts," he continues, "obtain great benefits from their patron spirits. These benefits may be 'worldly'—such as good health, good crops—but they also include a numinous sense of well being which springs from the awareness of having been chosen by the Other World as a medium for its messages to mankind."[13] There is no awareness by the author that the "Other World" here described is really the demonic "underworld"!

Don Gilmore, a Congregationalist minister, wrote in 1981 a book called *Angels, Angels, Everywhere*, in which he advocated a kind of angel imaging, what he called "developing an angel consciousness." He offered suggestions on making contact with angelic reality through surrounding oneself with angel art, classical music, and slogans like "The host of God's angels watch over me." Problems arose, however. People started fabricating events, he now says. New Age enthusiasts took his suggestions too far, conjuring angel appearances where there were none. Now, he says, "Angels are angels. If the Lord chooses to reveal things to me through guardian angels, fine. But they're not seeking to have a conversation with us, nor should we with them."[14]

The angels of many trendy books are simply not the angels seen weaving in and out of the biblical story. Divination is categorically condemned in

the Bible and the historic teaching of the church. So is straining for glimpses into the cosmic realms without regard for God himself. Such practices open people to *dark* angels—fallen angels known as demons. Satan himself, says Paul the apostle, masquerades as an angel of light (2 Cor. 11:14).

This does not mean, that angels never come, never communicate. But God has given us all we need to know, all that is essential for our salvation, in Scripture and in Christ. We need not go as far as Martin Luther, who once wrote, "From the beginning of my Reformation I have asked God to send me neither dreams, nor visions, nor angels, but to give me the right understanding of His Word, the Holy Scriptures; for as long as I have God's Word, I know that I am walking in His way and that I shall not fall into any error or delusion."[15]

Luther did not want to be led astray by spiritual razzle-dazzle. He knew that the Word is sufficient, and something about that rings true for all of us. Christians should indeed not manufacture angel appearances or messages. This is confirmed by the fact that people in the Bible who met angels generally reacted with *surprise*. It is not our conjuring, but God's sovereign acting, that determines when angels appear.

But God's Word, which we and Luther trust, speaks of angels. So why exclude the possibility? Some Christians, noting that God secured our salvation at the Cross of Christ and gave us the Bible, say he sent a flourish of angels when Christ was born, perhaps, but has not since—and will not,

ever again. They claim that he has stopped sending messengers, stopped speaking dramatically.

But before long such a view leaves us asking if there is more. Just as human beings ache to know that they are noticed, they also yearn to know that the God who once spoke still speaks in the here and now. If it takes an angel to get through, will he go to those lengths? I say yes.

How are we to discern the messages we suspect are from angels? How can we stay open to God's leading?

First, guidance from God is to be sought only as part of a certain kind of life: one that University of Southern California philosopher Dallas Willard describes as "a life of loving fellowship with the King and his other subjects within the Kingdom of the Heavens."[16] Guidance for our decisions is not something we demand from God only when we grow anxious. God's guidance for us, Willard says, "is intended to develop into an intelligent, freely cooperative relationship between mature persons who love each other with the richness of genuine . . . love." We must therefore make our primary goal not just to have the guidance of God—from angels or anyone, but, as Willard says, to be mature persons in a right, loving relationship to him. "Only so will guidance itself come right."[17]

We also recognize that God guides us more generally in other ways, through the Bible, as we've previously noted. This is the part Luther got especially right. God also guides us daily as we live in an ongoing conversation with God, when God speaks quietly, with little rending of the skies. A

January 1992 cover story in *Newsweek* noted that not only do many Christians pray—talk to God—but for many, a major part of prayer is listening and "letting God guide me."[18]

We need to remember that God generally seems to prefer the quiet or unobtrusive. Indeed, I once heard someone say that God usually uses modest means to communicate his will, but if someone is especially deaf, God may have to resort to angels. Insistence on the spectacular indicates a *lack* of spiritual maturity.

Still, God may use a variety of means to address us: dramatic appearances, dreams and visions, an audible voice, the human voice of a trusted counselor, the still, small voice (our own feelings, impressions, and thoughts, which God influences), and, of course, angels. God can speak through any of these things.

While we should not try to manipulate God's messages to us, we should stay open to them. Speaking of Moses' experience of the Lord's presence in the burning bush of Genesis (described as an *angel* appearance in Acts 6), Dallas Willard says something important: "If we are not open to God addressing us whatever way *he* chooses, then we may walk right by the burning bush instead of, like Moses, saying, 'I will now turn aside, and see this great sight, why the bush is not burnt' (Ex. 3:3 KJV)."[19]

Chapter 4

A Battle for Good

Arouse yourself; . . . our Lord is speaking with you. Do not wander off. His elect angels surround you, do not be dismayed; the ranks of the demons stand facing you, so do not grow lax.

Fourth-century Evagrius

*I*t was perhaps my worst public speaking experience ever. When the owner of a local doll-making company saw an article I had written about angels, she asked me to speak at a luncheon and workshop organized around an angel theme.

When I arrived I found some seventy-five doll-making enthusiasts crowded into the restaurant meeting room. Frilly angel dolls adorned the display tables. At least one participant had followed the announcement's invitation to come dressed as her "favorite" angel. All were served a lunch of angel-hair pasta while a harpist played songs with angel themes. The em-cee led a parlor game with points going to those who brought angel dolls or, for even more points, had seen a *real* angel. My task was to talk for a half hour. Above the din of waiters serving lunches, the harpist playing, and many continuing their lunchtime conversations, I did my best. But I finished my talk with a growing sense that angels had been trivialized. They entered the program as a cute theme with a vaguely spiritual overlay, but little more.

When many in our culture hear *angel*, they think of children's dolls or chubby-cheeked cherubs painted with Renaissance flourish. The word evokes images of weakly feminine creatures adorned with feathered minions or haloed tinsel. It prompts for others nothing more than memories of miniature angels hung on Christmas trees or the angel lapel pins that were popular a few years ago. A character in Thomas Wolfe's novel *Look Home-ward, Angel* had a similarly anemic view. He describes a carved angel as

holding "a stone lily delicately, in one hand. The other hand was lifted in benediction . . . and its stupid face wore a smile of soft stone idiocy."[1]

While angels undoubtedly act with gentle care, angels sometimes show an altogether different side. Childlike sweetness and "soft stone idiocy" do little justice to the swift, formidable creatures that charge in and out of the stories of the Bible.

Indeed, one of the most common reactions to the wonder of angel appearances is fear. That they evoke alert and awestruck terror is attested by the frequency with which they greet those they visit with "Do not be afraid." The Bible portrays them as winds, flames of fire, and sentries at watch in God's awesome presence.

Even more striking, the Bible depicts angels as warriors, heavenly "bright squadrons" doing battle with demonic "foul fiends," as the sixteenth-century poet Edmund Spenser put it.[2]

For all my tendency to think of angels as pleasant, they are not goody-goodies who drown in sentiment and care nothing for God's justice. The Bible, as we will soon see, tells us that angels appear on the edges of our world with swords of righteous judgment. Author Madeline L'Engle writes, "All the angelic host as they are described in Scripture have a wild and radiant power that often takes us by surprise."[3]

That points us to three important truths about the sharp-edged side to the angels' mission.

Engaged in a battle

First, since the beginning of evil, good angels have been enlisted in a great cosmic battle against fallen angels: Satan and his minions, the demons. Milton built much of his epic poem *Paradise Lost* around

> The discord which befell, and War in Heav'n
> Among th'Angelic Powers, and the deep fall
> Of those too high aspiring, who rebell'd
> With Satan . . . .[4]

The Bible does not tell us a great deal (but surely as much as we need) about the Devil, the chief of fallen angels. He receives mention a number of times in the Old Testament, but we nowhere find an exhaustive account of what went wrong. The New Testament tells us the most. Satan was an angel, evidently perfect in his original angelic state (2 Peter 2:4 speaks of God not sparing the "angels when they sinned"). Pride seems to have caused Satan's downfall (1 Tim. 3:6). We also never get any hint that he is anything but an enemy of God's people, as his scriptural names suggest: Adversary, Accuser, Wicked One, Murderer.

This is an intriguing scenario. It has enough mystery that we might want to know more. No wonder Calvin once felt compelled to write of those who "grumble that Scripture does not in numerous passages set forth systematically and clearly the fall of the devils, its cause, manner,

Jesus rebukes Satan (Matt. 16:23)

time, and character." He concluded, however, that it is better to say little and touch upon the subject lightly. The Holy Spirit does not feed our curiosities with information that does not truly help us. "The Lord's purpose was to teach nothing in his sacred oracles except what we should learn to our edification. Therefore, lest we ourselves linger over superfluous matters, let us be content with this brief summary of the nature of devils: They were when first created angels of God, but by degeneration they ruined themselves, and became the instruments of ruin for others."[5]

The Bible also gives us a realistic assessment of Satan's power. Jesus in John 14:30 (KJV) calls him the "prince of this world," Paul in Ephesians 2:2, the "ruler of the power of the air." That he moves and works and is a force to contend with is nowhere disputed in Christian tradition. Good angels, the angels of light and grace that are the focus of this book, are not the only spiritual beings we have to deal with. Indeed, said Martin Luther, "It were not good for us to know how earnestly the holy angels strive for us against the devil, or how hard a combat it is. If we could see for how many angels one devil makes work, we should be in despair."[6]

Even if we do not see it all, we cannot avoid the effects of living in a battle zone. Human life—and the Christian's life in particular—entail elements of vigorous struggle.

The intense spiritual struggle Christians face was made especially profound for me by a story the great saint Corrie ten Boom told of the time she

and her sister Betsie were sent to a concentration camp for the crime of sheltering Jews in Nazi Germany. In the horror of all they met there, a prayer for angels' help saw a remarkable answer.

We were standing on the great open square in front of the administration building [of the concentration camp]. . . . We had thrown our arms around each other and drawn more closely about us the blanket we had carried with us. . . . It was very cold. We had already spent two days and nights outside. Now we were standing in a long line waiting in front of the bath-house. At the door of the somber, dark building was a pile of clothing, packages, suitcases, provisions and blankets, all thrown together in a colourful, chaotic heap. Gradually it became a mountain. All the possessions of the . . . new arrivals were being taken from them. . . .

The women coming out of the shower rooms had on a thin dress, an undershirt and a pair of wooden shoes—nothing more. A young woman beside me said, "This is worse than when [the Nazis] took everything out of my home." She told me about her pretty villa with its rose garden, her grand piano and so many other precious things. . . .

I felt Betsie shivering and pressed her closely to me. "O Lord, save us from this evil; Betsie is so frail," I pleaded. . . .

An officer appeared in the doorway and screamed at us hoarsely, "Do you have any objections to surrendering your clothes? We'll teach you Hollanders what Ravensbruck is like." The light shone on his cruel face. . . . For a few minutes we were quiet and spoke softly with the Savior. He was with us and knew what we were suffering, and he loved us.

"Lord, if thou dost ask this sacrifice of us, give us the strength to make it."

"Corrie, I am ready," whispered Betsie, softly.

"Then everything is all right," I answered.

I took her arm and together we entered the frightful building. At a table were women who took away all our possessions. . . . I asked a woman who was busy checking the possessions of the new arrivals if I might use the toilet. She pointed to a door, and I discovered that that convenience was nothing more than a hole in the shower room floor. Betsie stayed close beside me all the time. Suddenly I had an inspiration. "Quick, take off your woolen under-

wear," I whispered to her. I rolled it up with mine and laid the bundle in a corner. The spot was alive with cockroaches, but I didn't worry about that. I felt wonderfully relieved and happy. "The Lord is busy answering our prayers, Betsie," I whispered, "we shall not have to make the sacrifice of all our clothes."

We hurried back to the row of women waiting to be undressed. A little later, after we had had our showers and put on our shirts and shabby dresses, I hid the roll of underwear under my dress. It did bulge out obviously through my dress; but I prayed, "Lord, cause now thine angels to surround me; and let them not be transparent, for the guard must not see me." I felt perfectly at ease. Calmly I passed the guards. Everyone was checked, from the front, the sides, the back. Not a bulge escaped their eyes. The woman just in front of me had hidden a woolen vest under her dress; it was taken from her. They let me pass, for they did not see me. Betsie, right behind me, was searched.

But outside awaited another danger. On each side of the door were women who looked everyone over for the second time. They felt over the body of each

> one who passed. I knew that they would not see me,
> for the angels were still surrounding me. I was not
> even surprised when they passed me by; but within
> me rose the jubilant cry, "O Lord, if Thou dost so
> answer prayer, I can face even Ravensbruck un-
> afraid."[7]

Nothing less than the forces of a cosmic world participate with us in our daily rounds. We sometimes so fasten our eyes to scenes and struggles of daily life that we forget the real warfare that is going on about us and above us and within us. We play out our lives against a backdropped drama where heaven and hell contend.

To hear some believers talk about living faithfully, however, you might imagine it is a pleasant stroll. It means little more than occasional, pleasant visits to church services where the accent is always on the "positive." In this view, Christianity—religion—is anything that makes us feel warm inside or mist up.

Instead, Paul the apostle described the life of faith as a war. He used military imagery and spoke of standing against the assault of spiritual evil. "Put on the whole armor of God," he said in Ephesians 6:11. As we awaken in the morning, as we go through our routines in office, kitchen, or neighborhood, do we think about the battle that wages in the spheres of earth and heaven? Christians seem to have lost the recognition that a

war is on, that living faithfully often more resembles a battleground than a playground. Becoming a Christian is more than adopting certain beliefs; becoming a Christian means enlisting in a corps of troops under a commander doing battle against a foe whose "craft and power are great," as Martin Luther said in his great hymn "A Mighty Fortress Is Our God."

While Satan is not literally the hoofed, horned, and tailed figure of artists' fancy (such a depiction finds no warrant in the Bible), he is still very real, subtle, and much at work. And demons, while we do not finally know much about their essence, still influence, still speak lies into the hearts and minds of people, still move and work at the command of Satan.

When we think of biblical angels, then, we dare not confine them to nursery decorations or pretty stained glass. The first picture of angels given in the Bible, after all, includes a fiery sword and "cherubim," a kind of angel we will say more about later. As God "drove out" Adam and Eve from Paradise, "at the east of the garden of Eden he placed the cherubim, and a sword flaming and turning to guard the way to the tree of life" (Gen. 3:24). Frescoes by the Renaissance artist Raphael even depict the cherubim as fiery creatures, "their hair, wings, and limbs ending in glowing flames, while their faces are full of spirit and intelligence."[8]

We see this fiery, daunting side in many passages in the Bible. When the angels left Abraham by the oaks of Mamre in the story mentioned in

the last chapter, for instance, they headed straight for Sodom and Gomorrah (Gen. 18:16), towns renowned for their debauchery and wicked obstinacy against God. Abraham soon found out that the Lord was about to destroy Sodom and Gomorrah for their wickedness. Thinking of his kinsman Lot living there, Abraham convinced the Lord to at least reconsider.

But meanwhile, the angels "came to Sodom in the evening, and Lot was sitting in the gateway of Sodom" (Gen. 19:1) Here the pitch of the story rises. Lot offered his oddly celestial guests hospitality, but before they lay down, the men of Sodom, young and old, surrounded Lot's house. The townspeople wanted Lot to hand over his guests that they might know them—sexually. Lot refused. As the men began to attack, the angels moved into battle mode. They struck the men clamoring outside with blindness until the would-be intruders were "unable to find the door" (Gen. 19:11). Hardly a picture of dainty angels full of "soft stone idiocy"!

Come morning, the angels delivered Lot a clear, bracing message, as plainly as if they were all sitting around the breakfast table (which perhaps they were): "Get up, take your wife and your two daughters who are here, or else you will be consumed in the punishment of the city" (Gen. 19:15). But they did more than warn or give a message. When Lot and his family hesitated, the angels seized him, his wife, and their two daughters by the hand, "and they brought him out" (Gen. 19:15–16). The Lord rained fire on

Sodom and Gomorrah, but only after having sent angels on a battlefront mission of rescue and vindication.

A Bible story where angels are not specifically mentioned—but clearly meant—gives a similar picture. It begins with a striking portrait of the prophet Elisha. He was such a divinely anointed prophet that he advised the king of Israel of the plans of the enemy king of Aram in ways no one could humanly know. He had supernatural knowledge of the strategies of the Aramite king, alerting the king of Israel to avoid the places where the Aramite king was planning to attack. Finding himself inexplicably outfoxed by the Israelites in every military stratagem, the king concluded he had an inner-circle defector. No, his advisers told him, "it is Elisha, the prophet in Israel, who tells the king of Israel the words that you speak in your bedchamber" (2 Kings 6:12). At that, the king decided to pursue Elisha to Dothan. He sent horses and chariots and a great army which came by night and surrounded the city.

Elisha's attendant rose early the next morning and found that they were surrounded. He exclaimed to Elisha, "Alas, master! What shall we do?" (2 Kings 6:15).

Elisha, strangely calm, said simply, "Do not be afraid, for there are more with us than there are with them." Elisha then prayed, "O LORD, please open his eyes that he may see" (2 Kings 6:16–17).

What did the servant then see? The mountain was full of horses and chariots of fire all around Elisha. A heavenly army! Then, "when the Arameans came down against him, Elisha prayed to the LORD, and said,

'Strike this people, please, with blindness.' So he struck them with blindness as Elisha had asked" (2 Kings 6:18). Elisha then led the blind, unsuspecting men to a town ruled by the king of Israel. Elisha prayed that their sight would be restored, and then the king of Israel fed the men and sent them back to their master, vanquished by the unseen forces God sent to carry out his purposes.

Stories like these help us understand why one of the Bible's common references to God is Lord of *hosts,* a military word associated with those enlisted in war. *Hosts* sometimes refers to human armies, sometimes to the "starry host" of the skies, sun, moon, and stars, but especially to the heavenly army of God's angels. They appear with God and support his work, as seen in passages like this from 1 Kings 22:19: "Then Micaiah [the prophet] said, 'Therefore hear the word of the Lord: I saw the Lord sitting on his throne, with all the host of heaven standing beside him to the right and to the left of him.' "

And Isaiah said this:

> For thus the Lord said to me,
> As a lion or a young lion growls over its prey,
>   and—when a band of shepherds is called out against it—
> is not terrified by their shouting or daunted at their noise,
> so the Lord of hosts will come down
>   to fight upon Mount Zion and upon its hill.

> Like birds hovering overhead, so the LORD of hosts
>   will protect Jerusalem;
> he will protect and deliver it,
>   he will spare and rescue it (Isa. 31:4–5).

What is the nature of this spiritual battle? Many people's imaginations have been fed in recent years by Frank Peretti's angel-and-demon warfare novels, *This Present Darkness* and *Piercing the Darkness*. In the first book, which describes a diabolical plot by occultists to take over a small town, a demon called Lust and an angel named Triskal fight over the soul of a young woman:

> Triskal had glorified and was a shimmering white; his tattered wings filled the room and glimmered like a thousand rainbows. He held a gleaming sword in his hand, and the sword flashed and sang in blinding arcs as he engaged in a frenzied battle with Lust, a hideous demon with a black-scaled, slippery body like a lizard and a red tongue that lashed about his face like the tail of a snake. Lust was first defending himself, then lashing back with his glowing red sword, the crescent blade cutting crimson arcs through the air. The swords clashed with explosions of fire and light.

> "Let me be, I tell you!" Lust screamed, his
> wings propelling him like a trapped hornet about the
> room.[9]

Throughout the book, brawny, gladiator-like angels slug it out with leathery-skinned, black-winged demons, wielding punches and swords, gaining physical strength for the battle whenever the people of the town pray or pronounce the name of Jesus.

But when Paul speaks of *our* spiritual warfare, he urges us to don an armor that is anything but literal and physical. "Stand therefore," he wrote in Ephesians 6, "and fasten the belt of truth around your waist, and put on the breastplate of righteousness. As shoes for your feet put on whatever will make you ready to proclaim the gospel of peace. With all of these, take the shield of faith." Peretti's description of the nature of the battle is imaginative, but we should not conceive of that war as celestial supermen dueling with flying pests. The battle is at once more cosmic and more subtle than that. We face a war not against flesh and blood, as Paul says, but against *spiritual* forces of evil. Demons can harass, suggest, and even, to some extent, guide and influence the thoughts and choices of people. And while angels and demons can move and affect physical matter, to be sure, the battle has more to do with the triumph of spiritual truth than with swords, with God's unquenchable light than with sulphurous smells. The armor we are called to take up has a spiritual essence: truth, holi-

ness, faith, the Word of God, the Spirit of Christ. These are the true weapons.

Writer and monk Thomas Merton used an analogy for understanding how this influence works in us. Pictures and visions of supernatural things, he said, can be formed, or at least suggested, in our imaginations by agents outside ourselves, both good and bad: "The Devil . . . has the power to make you see things and think things as he wants you to see and think them. The natural mode of converse between spiritual beings is by the direct communication of ideas. The Devil, being a spirit, can so act upon the souls of men. It is quite evident that God can make use of other intelligences—his angels—to act in the same way upon the minds of men and make them see visions."[10]

The battles we face, the temptations we withstand or submit to, the good we accomplish, and the evil we leave unchallenged, are all ultimately part of a larger battlefield, one that, for now, stretches across creation into our daily lives and even our momentary thoughts. And God sends his appointed helpers to enter our own battlefields. That is why Martin Luther recommended praying at the end of each day "Let your holy angel have charge concerning us, that the wicked one have no power over us."[11]

Until recently, I found that I rarely thought of angels being at work in the battles of my life. But now I am more inclined to pray for myself or others that God's angels would fight their good fight. And I know that what-

ever the specifics of the battle that takes place between the angels and demons, it has to do ultimately with the powerful presence of the Lord of the Universe. That means it is never a futile fight.

Destined to win

If we share in the battle waged by armies of good and evil, a second truth needs forceful statement: God and his angels of light are more powerful than Satan and the forces of darkness. While we need to be alert, we need not fear. We tread paths "covered by shields of angels."[12]

No wonder Christian art in earlier centuries often depicted the archangel Michael clothed in knight's armor, with a sword or shield in hand. While our entertainment media excel in powerful images of evil—Darth Vaders and Freddie Kruegers—heroes of good tend to pale in comparison. Not so in heavenly truth. However angels may have been opposed in their work before the consummation of time, they have not been stopped from serving God now, forcefully and tangibly in the battle for the good.

My friend Pat Bailey, a pastor and mentor to what must by now be dozens of younger women, told me this story: When her son was eight years old, he was beset with bad dreams. "We would pray every night," she recalls, "that his angel would come and keep him safe. Once he asked if we should pray to see it. I said no." But just a few nights later her son said to her, "I know why I'm not supposed to ask. I prayed to see my angel, but then God told me the angel was too big. He said I'd be too afraid, that I just

had to believe the angel was there." That answer was so satisfying, Pat recalls, that from that time on her son stopped being fearful at night.

Glimpses of God's deployment of victorious angels seem even more common on the front lines of the mission field. Here is one story told by Billy Graham of John Paton, pioneer missionary in the New Hebrides Islands:

> Hostile natives surrounded his mission headquarters one night, intent on burning the Patons out and killing them. Paton and his wife prayed throughout the night that God would deliver. When daylight came, they were amazed to find that the attackers had left, unexplainably.
>
> A year later, the chief of the tribe became a Christian, and Paton asked him what had kept him and his men from burning down the house and killing them. The chief answered in surprise, "Who were all those men you had with you there?" The missionary answered, "There were no men there; just my wife and I." The chief argued that they had seen many men standing guard—hundreds of big men in shining garments with drawn swords. They seemed to circle the building so that the natives were afraid to attack. Paton realized it must have been angels.

Could it be that God had sent a legion of angels to protect His servants, whose lives were being endangered?[13]

The Christian draws his or her conviction about God's winning power from more than angel stories. In Christ's death on the cross and resurrection, Paul says, God "disarmed the rulers and authorities and made a public example of them, triumphing over them in it" (Col. 2:15). Even though Satan for a time wins skirmishes, even though evil is still real and powerful, the war has been won. Satan has been dealt his death blow.

Centuries ago Richard Baxter said no spirits, angelic or demonic, can ever frustrate God's love and mercy to his people, nor break any one of his promises to them. "Good spirits are servants, and evil ones slaves to Jesus Christ, our redeemer, and shall not frustrate his grace and undertaking."[14]

This backdrop of victory, the promise that "the angel of the LORD encamps around those who fear him, and delivers them" (Ps. 34:7), gives angels a significant part in the Lord's battle strategy. God "will command his angels concerning you," the psalm says, "to guard you in all your ways" (Ps. 91:11). We do not fight alone or with our own puny weapons and resources.

We may never see the final outcome or full extent of this victorious effort on our behalf, but the glimpses we gain from stories such as we read in

this book help it all seem more real. Several stories from the Bible illustrate that help even more vividly.

When Moses came down from Mount Sinai with the Ten Commandments, he gave the people a number of words the Lord spoke (Ex. 20:1). One was: "I am going to send an angel in front of you, to guard you on the way and to bring you to the place that I have prepared. Be attentive to him and listen to his voice; do not rebel against him. . . . But if you listen attentively to his voice and do all that I say, then I will be an enemy to your enemies and a foe to your foes. When my angel goes in front of you, and brings you to the Amorites, the Hittites, the Perizzites, the Canannites, the Hivites, and the Jebusites, and I blot them out, you shall not bow down to their gods" (Ex. 23:20–24).

As the people, still journeying toward the Promised Land, wondered about their future, they needed more than an angel of warm fuzzies and soft stone idiocy. They needed a sense of the angelic host, the armies of the Lord himself.

A later story from 2 Kings 18–19 illustrates this particularly well. "In the fourteenth year of King Hezekiah," we read, "King Sennacherib of Assyria came up against all the fortified cities of Judah and captured them" (2 Kings 18:13). When the prophet Isaiah got wind of Sennacherib's further threats, he told Hezekiah not to despair, that God would cause Sennacherib's downfall. But Sennacherib tried to intimidate Hezekiah through a letter: "Do not let your God on whom you rely deceive you by promising

that Jerusalem will not be given into the hand of the king of Assyria. See, you have heard what the kings of Assyria have done to all lands, destroying them utterly. Shall you be delivered?" (2 Kings 19:10–11).

After Hezekiah read the letter, he "went up to the house of the LORD and spread [the letter from Sennacherib] before the LORD. . . . And Hezekiah prayed before the LORD, and said: 'O LORD the God of Israel, who are enthroned above the cherubim, you are God, you alone, of all the kingdoms of the earth. . . . Incline your ear, O LORD, and hear; open your eyes, O LORD, and see; hear the words of Sennacherib, which he has sent to mock the living God" (2 Kings 19:14–16).

The story concludes, "The angel of the LORD set out and struck down one hundred eighty-five thousand in the camp of the Assyrians; when morning dawned, they were all dead bodies. Then King Sennacherib of Assyria left, went home, and lived at Nineveh. As he was worshiping in the house of his god Nisroch, his sons Adrammelech and Sharezer killed him with the sword" (2 Kings 19:35–37). Interestingly, the Greek historian Herodotus attributed the destruction of the Assyrian army to mice and bubonic plague. Whatever the specific agency, however God may have used an angel, rodents, and pestilence, God was victor.

Other stories from the Bible give us further glimpses of God's victorious power, such as the well-known and much-recited story of Daniel in the lions' den. Daniel, a sixth century B.C. Hebrew who served as a top administrator for King Darius of Babylonia, made the other officials jealous. They

conspired to have the king pass a decree that anyone who prayed to anyone other than the king would be thrown into a den of lions.

Daniel, who served the one true God, could not pray to the king, nor could he cease praying to God. Much to the king's regret, Daniel was thrown into the lion's den. But that is not the whole story:

> At break of day, the king got up and hurried to the den of lions. When he came near the den where Daniel was, he cried out anxiously to Daniel, "O Daniel, servant of the living God, has your God whom you faithfully serve been able to deliver you from the lions?" Daniel then said to the king, "O king, live forever! My God sent his angel and shut the lions' mouths so that they would not hurt me, because I was found blameless before him; and also before you, O king, I have done no wrong." Then the king was exceedingly glad (Dan. 6:19–23).

In the book that bears his name, an angel later points Daniel to a time when "Michael, the great prince, the protector of your people, shall arise. . . . At that time your people shall be delivered, everyone who is found written in the book" (Dan. 12:1). It is a picture of victory, of the ultimate power of good.

Jesus took such bold pictures and went further. In Mark 3:27 he likened the work he was beginning to someone entering a "strong man's house," to tie him up and "plunder his property." Luke 10:17–18 tells us that when the seventy disciples returned with joy, saying, "Lord, in your name even the demons submit to us!" Jesus replied, "I watched Satan fall from heaven like a flash of lightning."

Shift the tense to the future, and the scene to the last book of the Bible, and we see an even grander vision of victory:

> And war broke out in heaven; Michael and his angels fought against the dragon. The dragon and his angels fought back, but they were defeated, and there was no longer any place for them in heaven. The great dragon was thrown down, that ancient serpent, who is called the Devil and Satan, the deceiver of the whole world—he was thrown down to the earth, and his angels were thrown down with him. Then I heard a loud voice in heaven, proclaiming,
>
> > "Now have come the salvation and the power
> > > and the kingdom of our God
> > > and the authority of his Messiah,
> > for the accuser of our comrades

The crowned virgin and the fiery dragon (Rev. 12:1–4)

has been thrown down,
who accuses them day and night before our God.
But they have conquered him by the blood of the
    Lamb
    and by the word of their testimony,
for they did not cling to life even in the face of
    death.
Rejoice then, you heavens,
    and those who dwell in them!
But woe to the earth and the sea,
    for the devil has come down to you
with great wrath
    because he knows that his time is short!"[15]

For all the drama and vivid imagery we are given mostly tantalizing glimpses, not completed portraits, of what this victory is and will be. But the words of the Eastern Orthodox liturgy capture the feel:

Rank on rank the host of heaven spreads its vanguard on the way
    As the Light of light descendeth from the realms of endless day
    That the powers of hell may vanish as the darkness clears away.[16]

So does the Easter hymn "All Hail the Power of Jesus' Name" that declares, "Let angels prostrate fall / Bring forth the royal diadem and crown him Lord of all!"

Charged with executing judgment

A third aspect of the heavenly battle involving angels is not only victory, but vindication. God will not only ultimately win the great spiritual battle, he will also recompense.

God is a God of justice, and he uses angels to carry out his sovereign will. Evil will not always go unrewarded, and angels have a part in that ultimate restitution.

A friend I'll call Kendall understands this better than most. She is healing from a childhood that included satanic rituals and a youth that included the tough lessons of street life. While Kendall prefers to wear rugged jeans over anything, she has a quiet warmth and gentleness I appreciate. And God is doing something marvelous in her. Once, holy things had become so profane for her that simply being in a church created terror, evoking memories of black chants and unholy curses. That began to change when she became a Christian.

When her friend and spiritual mentor, Karen, decided to make it a habit to go to a church chapel to pray every Thursday morning for an hour and a half, Kendall thought just tagging along might help. Once there, Kendall would often get only as far as the back of the chapel, the pain was so great.

Sometimes the emotion and sense of Holy Presence was so strong that Kendall would shake. "Something very powerful is here," she once told Karen. "I'm sure of it."

Something happened there she will never forget. "One time when we went," Kendall told me, "I was feeling angry. I wanted to lash out at someone. I wanted to intimidate and even hit Karen. But then I saw the angel by the altar—not a painted one, a real one. The angel was muscular, bulky, eight feet tall. He stood there staring at me with arms crossed. After that, I knew I wasn't going to hurt any Christian, and I wasn't to touch Karen. He scared me to death. I thought, 'I'm not gonna mess with this guy. No, sir. Not gonna mess around at all.' " In Kendall's case, the angel brought warning; in Karen's, protective judgment. The angel stood between Kendall and her temptation to hurt one of God's people.

Oxford scholar and Christian apologist C. S. Lewis's fantasy series, *The Chronicles of Narnia*, captures something of this side of God and his agents. When two children in *The Lion, the Witch and the Wardrobe* first glimpse the awe-inspiring lion and Christ-figure Aslan, they do not know quite what to do or say. "People who have not been in Narnia," says the author, "sometimes think that a thing cannot be good and terrible at the same time. If the children had ever thought so, they were cured of it now."[17] That God can be both good and terrible means that he will not let evil go unrestrained, unvanquished.

But talk of God's vindicating power may seem tinny or insubstantial in

our day. Many Christians sing a hymn called "Onward Christian Soldiers"—full of victorious imagery and a musical style that cries for trumpet fanfare—but sometimes the church's "mighty army" seems more like an ineffective and forgotten subculture. We are just one voice in an increasingly pluralistic global village. The church seems pushed to the margins of importance and influence.

But the Scriptures ring with the assurance that all that we see is not all that is, that even if the wrongdoer prospers in some situations, God's battle against evil yet advances. Isaiah 24:21–24 is full of strong language:

> On that day the LORD will punish
> > the host of heaven in heaven,
> > and on earth the kings of the earth.
> They will be gathered together like prisoners in a pit;
> > they will be shut up in a prison,
> > and after many days they will be punished.
> Then the moon will be abashed, and the sun ashamed;
> for the LORD of hosts [which include the angels] will reign on
> > Mount Zion and in Jerusalem,
> and before his elders he will manifest his glory.

Acts, the chronicle of the earliest Christian church, contains in chapter 12 another example of angels carrying out God's judgment against wrongdoing. It was after Peter's angel-assisted jail break (which I recounted in

chapter two) and under the watch of Herod Antipas (ruler of Galilee and Perea). Acts tells us, "Now Herod was angry with the people of Tyre and Sidon. So they came to him in a body; and after winning over Blastus, the king's chamberlain, they asked for a reconciliation. . . . On an appointed day Herod put on his royal robes, took his seat on the platform, and delivered a public address to them. The people kept shouting, "The voice of a god, and not of a mortal!" And immediately, because he had not given the glory to God, an angel of the Lord struck him down, and he was eaten by worms and died. But the word of God continued to advance and gain adherents" (Acts 12:20–24).

The ancient Jewish historian Josephus gives an independent account, wherein he describes a "festival Herod was celebrating in honor of Claudius Caesar." Josephus tells us that Herod wore a silver robe, dazzling bright, and that when the people acclaimed him a god, he did not deny it. Josephus also noted that Herod was seized with violent pains and died five days later. The judgment he experienced from the "angel of the Lord" was divine retribution not only for his self-idolatry, but also for his persecution of the church.[18]

This judgment executed by God through angels may fall upon believers as well as unbelievers, as seen in 1 Chronicles 21:1–30. In this story, King David ordered a census to be taken of Israel. This census incurred God's wrath and judgment, ultimately carried out by an angel. Why the mere taking of a census was wrong is not made clear. In contrast, God commanded

one in Numbers 1:2–3. David's action must have grown out of pride in the size of his kingdom or a curiosity about the size of his military reserve (thereby revealing a lack of trust in God). First Chronicles 21:7 tells only that "God was displeased with this thing." The Lord then offered David a choice of punishments: "Either three years of famine; or three months of devastation by your foes, while the sword of your enemies overtakes you; or three days of the sword of the LORD, pestilence on the land, and the angel of the LORD destroying throughout all the territory of Israel" (1 Chron. 21:12). David answered that he would rather fall into the Lord's hands than human ones. So, we read, "the LORD sent a pestilence on Israel; and seventy thousand persons fell in Israel. And God sent an angel to Jerusalem to destroy it; but when he was about to destroy it, the LORD took note and relented concerning the calamity; he said to the destroying angel, 'Enough! Stay your hand' " (1 Chron. 21:14–15).

Does God send an angel of judgment against believers today when we sin? I see no indication in Scripture to support such a view. What happened with David was a judgment against a *people*, a nation which had a relationship to God unlike any before or since. But it does show that God has a passion for the right. He is not afraid to send his angel agents to combat evil.

In the New Testament view, angels' judging, sifting, vindicating work will happen most dramatically at the end of time, at the consummation of all history when Christ returns. It finds partial fulfillment now, in the small

ways that make up the little victories of daily life. But Jesus also spoke of a future day when he would return. Not only would he establish his kingdom, but "just as the weeds are collected and burned up with fire, so will it be at the end of the age. The Son of Man will send his angels, and they will collect out of his kingdom all causes of sin and all evildoers, and they will throw them into the furnace of fire, where there will be weeping and gnashing of teeth. Then the righteous will shine like the sun in the kingdom of their Father" (Matt. 13:40–43).

The devil's time, then, is indeed not long, as becomes even clearer when the apostle John outlines a series of mind-boggling, God-given visions in his Revelation, the last book of the Bible. While the devil's last spasm of harassment is yet to be (the "beast" in Revelation 13:7 was for a time "given authority over every tribe and people and language and nation"), God's ultimate victory is sure. And angels have a role: Revelation 14:6 tells of an angel "flying in midheaven, with an eternal gospel to proclaim to those who live on the earth—to every nation and tribe and language and people." Other angels are to come, including one who will swing his sickle "over the earth and [gather] the vintage of the earth," to be thrown into "the great wine press of the wrath of God" (Rev. 14:19). These are metaphors for a victory and reckoning. While there is harshness to these gritty pictures, they remind us that evil will not always be tolerated.

Then, in Revelation 20, an angel comes from heaven "holding in his hand the key to the bottomless pit and a great chain. He seized the dragon,

that ancient serpent, who is the Devil and Satan, and bound him for a thousand years, and threw him into the pit, and locked and sealed it over him, so that he would deceive the nations no more, until the thousand years were ended." Eventually he is thrown into the lake of fire and sulfur for final, eternal destruction.

This means that the harassing angels we know as Satan and the demons will one day trouble God's people no more. "The angels who did not keep their own position," Jude tells us, "but left their proper dwelling, he has kept in eternal chains in deepest darkness for the judgment of the great Day" (Jude 6). That day is coming as surely as anything.

These pictures are intended as more than dispassionate predictions. They are given pre-eminently to help us live—and live confidently, even as we face opposition in this interlude between Christ's victory on the cross and God's kingdom consummation. We remember that what is future is already in a real sense present. "Now is the judgment of this world," said Jesus in John; "now the ruler of this world will be driven out" (John 12:31). This means that for now Christians can believe God will continue to triumph.

At first glance, speaking of angels as ministers of battle and judgment seems intimidating, even frightening. But there is something very healthy about such "fear of the Lord." It makes us realize that the heavenly realm is more than a celestial candyland. We need a healthy corrective to offset much of the syrupy religion that has so captivated our culture. It should

be encouraging to us if we have sided with God's soon-to-be victorious hosts.

When it comes to angels, as Billy Graham reminds us, Christians "should never fail to sense the operation of angelic glory. It forever eclipses the world of demonic powers, as the sun does a candle's light."[19]

Chapter 5
Angels and the Drama of Heaven

In the house of God there is never-ending festival;
the angel choir makes eternal holiday;
the presence of God's face gives joy that never fails.
Augustine

$\mathcal{M}$y church often uses prayers during worship that were written in the early centuries of Christianity. Lately I have been struck by their mention of angels. Sunday after Sunday our pastor prays, "We praise you [Father Almighty], joining our voices with angels and archangels and with all the company of heaven. . . ." Then we sing an ancient hymn which begins, "Holy, holy, holy, Lord, God of power and might, heaven and earth are full of your glory. . . ." As I worship, I sometimes have a fleeting sense of heavenly throngs, surrounding with joy and adoration the throne of God.

That picture of worshipping angels captures yet another part of the angels' job description: Angels honor God with exuberant praise and adoring service. Angels not only worship, they direct *our* gaze to an awesome God. By their faithfulness to this fourth aspect in their job description, they help *us* live lives less focused on self and more centered on heaven. Angels point us heavenward in three important ways.

Angels lift my eyes above daily routine

Sometimes I find my concentration absorbed and captured by deadlines at work, by tasks crying for attention around the house, by the needs of my mother in failing health. I can become so engrossed in what someone calls "muchness and manyness" that I forget there is another world that frames my everyday one. Thinking about angels helps me not to become bogged down with my everyday grind.

"I throw myself down in my Chamber," poet John Donne wrote in 1621, "and I . . . invite God and his angels thither, and when they are there, I neglect God and his angels for the noise of a fly, for the rattling of a coach, for the whining of a door."[1] How poignantly true of my daily life! Sometimes faithfulness means hanging on to the stubborn conviction that the things that I see and taste and touch are not all there is. What someone called the tyranny of the urgent does not need to rule my every waking hour. The world of morning breath and gridlocked traffic and late-night office hours takes place against a backdrop that gives sense to it all.

One way angels remind us that the grit and limits of our normal lives do not confine God is by the sudden strangeness of their coming. Angels appear unpredictably, beyond our orchestrating. Poet Francis Thompson said,

> The angels keep their ancient places,
> Turn but a stone and start a wing,
> 'Tis ye, 'tis your estranged faces,
> That miss the many splendoured thing.[2]

But angels help us remember, when the urgencies screaming for attention make us forget, when we feel so estranged by stress or worldliness that we miss the many-splendoured things. They remind us to look beyond our everyday circumstance or stress.

"Sleight-of-hand magic," says novelist and theologian Frederick Buechner, "is based on the demonstrable fact that as a rule people see only what they expect to see. . . . Since we don't expect to see [angels], we don't. An angel spreads his glittering wings over us, and we say things like, 'It was one of those days that made you feel good just to be alive,' or 'I had a hunch everything was going to turn out all right,' or 'I don't know where I ever found the courage.' "[3]

I sometimes forget to credit the sheer force of God and his heavenly hosts at work all around me. Remembering that angels' efforts and not just my own are at work in my life helps me not lose sight when frantic busyness threatens to obliterate my awareness of the unseen.

This help may come subtly, almost imperceptibly. "Do not neglect to show hospitality to strangers," the writer to the Hebrews said in the New Testament, "for by doing that some have entertained angels without knowing it" (Heb. 13:2). God may catch us unawares. He may work through the seemingly simple or subtle circumstance.

V. Raymond Edman was a missionary to the Quichua Indians of Ecuador from 1923 to 1928. Later he was president of Wheaton College in Wheaton, Illinois, until his death in 1965. He tells this story of an angel encounter that pointed him to God:

After our marriage in the capital city of Quito, we were given our first assignment to a city whose envi-

rons had thousands of Quichua-speaking Indians. We lived on the outskirts of that city where we could reach both the Spanish-speaking citizens on the streets and in the marketplaces, and also the shy, suspicious Indians who passed our doorway on the way to market.

Our assignment was a difficult one. The people were quite unfriendly, and some were fanatical in their bitter opposition to our presence in their city. On occasion small crowds would gather to hurl insults, punctuated by stones both large and small. . . . As a result it was often difficult to get the bare necessities of life—fruits and vegetables, or charcoal for the kitchen stove. Added to these physical factors was an inward sense of human loneliness. . . .

Whenever we were not in the front part of the house we kept the gate locked with an iron chain and a great padlock. There was constant danger that some bare-footed stranger would tiptoe into an unoccupied room and depart with more than that with which he had entered. The gate had to be locked securely at night, of course, and the same was true when we had our meals.

One noon as we were eating we heard a rattling on the gate as though someone were asking for admission. I excused myself from the table and went to the porch. Then I saw an Indian woman standing outside the gate. She had reached one hand inside through the bars and was knocking on the chain with the padlock. Quickly I went down to inquire what she might want. She was no one I had ever seen before, and the small bundle she carried on her shoulder did not indicate that she had any vegetables to offer for sale.

As I approached the inside of the gate she began to speak softly in the mixture of Spanish and Quichua that was typical of the Indians who lived fairly close to the town. Pointing to a Gospel verse we had put on the porch she inquired, "Are you the people who have come to tell us about the living God?"

Her question startled me. No one had ever made that query before. Therefore with surprise I answered, "*Mamita* (little mother, the customary term for a woman of her years), yes, we are."

Then she raised the hand that was still inside the locked gate, and began to pray. I can still see that

hand and arm with its beads, in typical Indian style. She wore the large heavy hat of the mountain woman. She had a small bundle and the typical blue shawl over her shoulders. She wore the white home-spun waist with its primitive embroidery, and her dress was *balleta* (coarse woolen cloth) with a brightly colored homemade belt. . . .

She prayed for the blessing of God upon the inhabitants of this home. She asked that we have courage for the service committed to us, that we have joy in doing God's bidding, and prayed that many would hear and obey the words of the Gospel. Then she pronounced a blessing from God upon me.

The prayer concluded, she withdrew her hand. Then she smiled at me through the gate with a final, *Dios le bendiga* (God bless you). Her eyes fairly shone as she spoke those words, and then she bowed and turned to her left.

I was so astonished by all of this that for part of a minute I stood speechless and motionless. Quickly I remembered that it was the heat of the day, and that she should come in to eat with us. All the while I had held the key in my hand. In a matter

of seconds I had unlocked the gate and stepped out to call her back. She could not have gone five or ten yards.

But she was not there! Where could she have gone so quickly? It was at least fifty yards from our gate to the corner of the street and there was no gate along that stretch of wall, either on our side of the street or across the way.

I ran to the corner with the persuasion that if it had been possible for her to have reached that far then certainly she would be right there. Immediately I looked to the right, but she was not there. As I ran to the corner I could look down our street for nearly half a mile, and there were no openings in the wall in that direction. On both sides were large corrals. The same was true of the street to my left.

Where could she be? The closest gate was to my right and that nearly a block away. There I ran (and my days on the track team in school stood me in good stead at the age of twenty-four). I rushed inside the open gate and there my two closest neighbors were repairing the spokes in a large wooden wheel. Hastily I inquired, "Did an Indian woman just come in here?"

Both men looked up at once from their work and replied, "No sir."

"I mean just now," I insisted.

"No sir, we have been right here in the gate for an hour or more, and nobody has entered or left during that time."

I thanked them, and hastened back to the corner. There was not a soul in sight. At the noon hour there would be few on the road since it was time for lunch and the siesta.

She must be somewhere; but where could she have gone? I waited there nearly ten minutes looking in all directions, but no one appeared on the street. Slowly I retraced my steps to my own gate, and after locking it again went back to the table.

"Where have you been so long?" inquired [my] wife.

"There was an elderly Indian woman knocking on the gate. She prayed for us and invoked God's blessing upon us and then started on down the street. I unlocked the gate and stepped out to call her, but she was not along the wall as I had expected. So I ran to the corner and sought her, but in vain."

We spoke no more about the matter. However,

for days afterward my own heart remained strangely moved. It burned within me as I recalled that Indian woman's prayer, and it was strengthened by the blessing she had pronounced upon me. There seemed to be an aroma indescribably sweet and indefinable which certainly did not come from the flowers in the garden. Even now, as I write down these words . . . there comes anew the witness of God's Spirit to the ministry of that stranger.

After some days, I began to reflect upon that word in Hebrews 13:2 [about showing hospitality to strangers]. I began to understand that the Almighty had none of His earthly servants at hand to encourage two young missionaries, so He was pleased to send an angel from heaven. . . . Through all the [difficult moments that followed], and over the many years since then, there has remained the glow of God's blessings pronounced by someone who looked exactly like a little old Quichua Indian woman.[4]

My closest friend's mother told me a story of an angel who likewise helped her to sense God's nearness. She was one of several adults on a camping trip with a troop of teenage Explorer Scouts. She recalls,

It was a very cold New Year's weekend in Pennsylvania. We were approaching our camp on a back road because the front road was blocked with snow. But as we got close to the top of the ridge of the mountain, still a ways from the camp, our vehicles got stuck in the snow. We tried to push them, but our vehicles got stuck. Everything came to a screeching halt.

We began to worry. It was getting dark and colder. Everyone was "whistling by the graveyard," trying to act as if they weren't afraid. But if we couldn't get the vehicles going, we stood a chance of getting stuck out there and suffering from exposure.

I was standing by the side of the road when suddenly I saw a disturbance in the air. It was like angel wings fluttering, much as a butterfly would wave its wings, or on a hot day you'd see the currents of air.

I saw that and thought, "We're not alone." I went to the leader of the group and said, "I don't think we need to worry. I think we're going to be all right."

Then, with someone still pushing the cars, we got them going again. Eventually we pushed on through and got to camp in safety.

I didn't see glorious garments or a glowing countenance, but I knew we were not alone. For some reason I believed it was an angel and not the Lord. There was something fluttering there in the twilight, making a difference in the light. And that made all the difference for me, for us.

Angels acted even more dramatically in Scripture, pointing people past the circumstances of the immediate world. They showed up when Elijah, fleeing Ahab and Jezebel, was discouraged about his mission as a prophet. They showed up to touch the prophet Isaiah's life in the year King Uzziah died, a time of transition and uncertainty for the people of Israel.

In that year, Isaiah had a mind-rending vision of the Lord sitting on a throne where "the hem of his robe filled the temple" (Isa. 6:1). In the midst of this he saw angels:

> Seraphs were in attendance above [God]; each had six wings: with two they covered their faces, and with two they covered their feet, and with two they flew. And one called to another and said:
> "Holy, holy, holy is the LORD of hosts;
> the whole earth is full of his glory" (Isa. 6: 2–3).

The scene reminded Isaiah of the glorious holiness of God. When face-to-face with such overwhelming Presence, even the dazzling, sinless seraphim (a kind of angel we will describe in more detail later) were not fit to see (thus they covered their eyes), or be seen (they covered their feet). The horror and guilt of seeing his own sin threatened to drive Isaiah from the Lord, until a seraph came to touch Isaiah's mouth with a cleansing, burning coal. Then Isaiah heard the Lord calling. What could Isaiah say, but "Here am I; send me!"? (Isa. 6:8).

Here a vision of angels caught Isaiah up into something bigger than himself. He could only stand ready to be sent on a larger mission when faced with the force of heaven's Reality.

Have we become so bound to the duties and details of this life that we think little of the heavenly life? A spiritual life not anchored in the realities of heaven, as theologian J. I. Packer likes to say, cannot withstand the pressures of everyday realities. The secular view of reality, which says that only what we see, taste, smell, feel, and hear is real, will leave us empty.

Angels point my gaze to an unseen world

A second way angels help us is to encourage us to be free from the dailiness of life; they point our eyes to another world of spiritual realities.

"Our story here is part of a gigantic drama in which all heaven, earth, and hell strive," Thomas Howard writes. "A Christian is aware of living under titanic mysteries that arch and loom above his head."[5] Angels peri-

The four spirits leaving the presence of the Lord (Zech. 6)

odically "drop in" from this realm of mystery and wonder. Beyond the universe of rocks and tables and cars and hamburgers another carries on, a world we often miss, one of God and Satan, angels and demons, spirit and soul.

More than most of us have realized, the universe is mysterious, open-ended, rife with the unaccounted for and unfathomable. That is why angels are capturing the attention of our culture once again. That is why the secular world's attempt to oust the supernatural will backfire. That witchcraft, occultism, and New Age esoterica are flourishing only indicates that the human spirit cries out for something beyond our temporal world. Our hearts are restless, as Augustine once said, until they find their rest in God.[6] Sometimes angels help us see that.

That is how it happened for Diane Komp, pediatric oncologist and author of *A Window to Heaven*. She briefly tells of one of her patients, seven-year-old Anna.

> *T*oday many children with leukemia are cured, but this was not the case when Anna first became sick. Her therapy brought her periods of time when she was disease-free over the five years she received treatment, but she faced the end of her life at age seven. Before she died, she mustered the final energy to sit up in her hospital bed and say: "The angels—they're

so beautiful! Mommy, can you see them? Do you hear their singing? I've never heard such beautiful singing!" Then she laid back on her pillow and died.

Her parents reacted as if they had been given the most precious gift in the world. The hospital chaplain in attendance was more comfortable with the psychological than with the spiritual and he beat a hasty retreat to leave [me] alone with the grieving family. Together we contemplated a spiritual mystery that transcended our understanding and experience. For weeks to follow the thought that stuck in my head was: Have I found a reliable witness?[7]

That encounter, and others like it, eventually led Diane back to a life of faith.

Olive Fleming Liefeld, wife of Peter Fleming, one of five celebrated missionaries killed by Ecuador's Auca Indians more than three decades ago, gives a similarly intriguing account. On a return trip to Ecuador several years ago, Olive, after having been away for over thirty years, was finally able to piece together the concrete circumstances of her husband's death. To her and her traveling companions' amazement, they discovered that on the day the five men were killed, the tribespeople heard singing. Was it the

five men singing hymns as they awaited death at the hands of the fearful tribespeople? No, she found out from Dawa, a woman who had been an eyewitness to the killing on Palm Beach; the men's dead bodies were already lying on the beach. Fleming recounts, "Dawa in the woods and Kimo [one of the men who killed the missionaries] on the beach heard singing. . . . As they looked up over the tops of the trees they saw a large group of people. They were all singing, and it looked as if there were a hundred flashlights."

Flashlights?

"This is the only word for 'bright light' that they know," explained the interpreter. "But they said it was very bright and flashing. Then suddenly it disappeared."

Reflects Olive, "A host of people singing? Flashing lights? What had Kimo and Dawa seen? What did the people look like? Were they talking about angels?

". . . I wondered if they had invented the story to gain approval [since they knew our traveling party was made up of Christians]. No, that was impossible. It came out far too spontaneously between the two of them. Too much planning would have been required for them to correlate their facts. We all had watched their faces and their elaborate gesturing. There was no question that they had seen something.

". . . Soon the time came for us to leave the beach. My mind reeled with questions and images and memories as I watched Dawa holding her

little girl and Kimo making a new bamboo pole for the trip upriver. In a way, they personified the glimpse of eternity that I had sought thirty-three years earlier. . . . I had wanted God to give me a concrete sign—something I could see—to make it easier to trust him in this tragedy. But he didn't.

"As we climbed back into the canoe, I wondered if God had chosen instead to display the light of his glory—a glimpse of the unseen—to the fierce and primitive Aucas as they stood on this very beach. . . . Though [the missionaries who were killed] never had the chance to tell the Waorani [another name for Aucas] about their Lord, their death—and the miraculous aftermath—somehow prepared the first Aucas to embrace the gospel five years later."[8]

Especially at such crucial moments of God's work, it seems, such signs and glimpses of the unseen may be seen. This happened to Joshua millennia ago, and centuries before Isaiah's temple vision. Joshua was about to lead the people in an attack on the city of Jericho, which the Lord was directing the Israelites to occupy. This is what happened: "Once when Joshua was by Jericho, he looked up and saw a man standing before him with a drawn sword in his hand. Joshua went to him and said to him, 'Are you one of us, or one of our adversaries?' He replied, 'Neither; but as commander of the army of the LORD I have now come.' And Joshua fell on his face to the earth and worshipped, and he said to him, 'What do you command your servant, my lord?' The commander of the army of the LORD said to Joshua, 'Remove

The angel appearing to Joshua

the sandals from your feet, for the place where you stand is holy.' And Joshua did so (Josh. 5:13–15).

A note in my study Bible suggests that the end of this story seems to have been lost; some command is expected after verse 15, but none seems to come. Or was the command simply that Joshua recognize that he stood in the presence of genuine holiness? Then again, because the account of Israel's actual conquest of Jericho follows right on the heels of this encounter, perhaps the story tells us simply that when Joshua needed assurance of the presence of the heavenly realm, God supplied it.

Angels help me worship god

Angels live not for themselves but in loving service to God. They move in the heavenly reaches in a way we do not, so angels can worshipfully point us toward God. Their presence reminds us that when we come together to praise and honor God, we do more than simply sing or pray; we also join with the angels in the heavenly spheres.

This is significant in two ways. Many Christians are ego-centered, focused on "felt needs" and strategies for self-enhancement. It almost seems that faith is designed solely to make us happier, better adjusted people in this life—without also fitting us to live in the life to come. Worship sometimes seems to focus only on our needs, our feelings. Thinking about angels, however, reminds us that our worship is part of something much big-

ger. It echoes the heavenly worship that surrounds the throne of the Lamb. Thinking about the heavenly, angelic realm can enlarge our picture of God. If we consider that the "angel choir makes eternal holiday,"[9] as Augustine said, we may find our times in church not so distracted by the anxieties and concerns that capture our attention.

The church frequently misses this ongoing, supernatural dimension of worship. For years I have recited in church the line of the Lord's Prayer, "Your will be done, on earth *as it is in heaven*" (Matt. 6:9–13), without realizing that in so doing I was acknowledging the heavenly realms where angels surround the throne of God, doing his will through service and adoration. Thinking of angels can remind me of what I in turn am made to be and do. "The chief end of man is to glorify God and enjoy him forever," says the centuries-old statement of faith known as the Westminster Shorter Catechism.[10] Worshipping and glorifying God is central to our existence, and angels remind us of that.

Throughout Scripture, angels never draw attention to themselves. They always point to the Lord who sent them. Angels are always subservient to the Lord they serve. They direct us to glorify and worship God alone. Indeed, twice an angel made clear to John in Revelation, "You must not [worship me]! I am a fellow servant with you and your comrades who hold the testimony of Jesus. Worship God!" (Rev. 19:10; 22:9).

The church's early leaders knew something that we, so tempted to a

mechanistic view of the universe, have lost. Augustine wrote in the fourth century that the importance of praising God is made evident by the whole of creation, earthly *and* heavenly. Augustine noted that all creation praises God—fire, hail, mountains, fruitful trees, even reptiles, along with "kings of the earth and all peoples. . . . Moreover," he wrote, "let these from the heavens praise you: let all your angels praise you in the height . . . all your powers, sun, moon, all stars and light, the heaven of heavens. . . ."[11]

Believers from earlier times seemed more familiar with the heavenly dimension of our lives. Recently I stumbled across an oddly titled but intriguing-looking book in the library of a Catholic retreat house and monastery: *The Syriac Fathers on Prayer and the Spiritual Life*. It contained the largely forgotten works of early Middle Eastern Christians. Martyrius, for example, wrote in the seventh century of the "splendor of [God's glory]":

> *The* seraphs of fire stand there to honor him, the ranks of the many-eyed cherubim escort his majestic Being, the bands of spiritual powers dash around ministering to him, the throngs of angels fly hither and thither with their wings, and all orders of spiritual beings serve his Being in awe, crying, "Holy" in trembling and love, as they cover their faces with their wings at the splendour of his great and fearful

radiance, ceaselessly crying out to one another the threefold sanctification of his exalted glory, saying "Holy, holy, holy, Lord Almighty, with whose glories both heaven and earth are full."[12]

Words tumble over words, in a breathless attempt to capture something so beyond our senses and imaginations that it cannot be captured. Martyrius also wrote,

> $\mathcal{L}$et us also ponder this: how we, who are mortal, being continually bespattered with the mud of sins, have been held worthy to stand before the King of Kings and Lord of Lords who dwells in the resplendent light that none can approach, to whose honour thousands upon thousands and myriads and myriads of angels and archangels minister as they stand before Him in fear and trembling.[13]

I find Martyrius's glimpses, his sense of fear and trembling in the presence of Tremendous Mystery, wonderfully stretching for my vision.

Fast-forwarding through Christian history we find another witness to the glories of the celestial worship service in poet John Milton. Milton has Adam telling Eve,

> Millions of spiritual creatures walk the earth
> Unseen, both when we wake, and when we sleep:
> All these with ceaseless praise his works behold
> Both day and night.[14]

And sometimes, says Milton's Adam, "echoing hill or thicket" they hear "celestial voices . . . signing their great Creator: oft in bands." Their voices "divide the night," he says, "and lift our thoughts to heaven."[15]

Milton's poetic imagination filled in details of the heavenly picture not found in Scripture, of course, and they are suggestions of what might be, not authoritative pronouncements of what is. It is not revealed knowledge or truth as much as it is poetry. But he does not too far exceed the glimpses of Scripture. For while God does not tell us all we in our curiosity might like to know, the Bible is full of wonderfully suggestive sketches of heavenly worship.

The prophet Daniel, for example, had this to say of a mind-expanding vision:

> As I watched,
> thrones were set in place,
>   and an Ancient One took his throne,
> his clothing was white as snow,
>   and the hair of his head like pure wool;
> his throne was fiery flames,
>   and its wheels were burning fire.

> A stream of fire issued
>> and flowed out from his presence.
> A thousand thousands served him,
>> and ten thousand times ten thousand stood
>> attending him (Dan. 7:9–10).

Who are these "thousand thousands" and "ten thousand times ten thousand" but angels? The angels about whom the psalmist wrote when he urged,

> Praise the LORD!
> Praise the LORD from the heavens;
>> praise him in the heights!
> Praise him, all his angels;
>> praise him, all his host! (Ps. 148:1–2).

In Revelation we see even more. John wrote of six-winged "living creatures" who day and night without ceasing sing, "holy, holy, holy, the Lord God the Almighty, who was and is and is to come" (Rev. 4:8). We can only conclude that these living creatures are part of some angelic order. Then, later, John paints this wonderful scene of the heavenly company surrounding Jesus, the Lamb of God:

Then I saw between the throne and the four living creatures and among the elders a Lamb standing as if it had been slaughtered. . . . He went and took the scroll from the right hand of the one who was seated on the throne. When he had taken the scroll, the four living creatures and the twenty-four elders fell before the Lamb, each holding a harp and golden bowls full of incense, which are the prayers of the saints. They sing a new song:

> "You are worthy to take the scroll
> and to open its seals,
> for you were slaughtered and by your blood you
> ransomed for God
> saints from every tribe and language and
> people and nation;
> you have made them to be a kingdom and
> priests serving our God,
> and they will reign on earth."

Then I looked, and I heard the voice of many angels surrounding the throne and the living creatures and the elders; they numbered myriads of myriads and thousands of thousands, singing with full voice,

"Worthy is the Lamb that was slaughtered
to receive power and wealth and wisdom and might
and honor and glory and blessing!" (Rev. 5:6–12)

When Scripture pulls back the curtain on heaven, I want to live with a greater awareness of that glorious world. Too often I let the pressures and looming tasks of my life hide it from view. But I now find myself praying that God will help me to hear, with the ears of my soul, the worship services of the supernal hosts, the hallelujahs and praises that fill the heavens in the presence of Almighty God. I want my eyes opened, if only for occasional moments, to see the high company we are all in when we worship and praise God. The Puritan saint Richard Baxter wrote,

> Ye holy angels bright,
> Who wait at God's right hand,
> Or through the realms of light
> Fly at your Lord's command,
> Assist our song,
> Or else the theme
> Too high doth seem,
> For mortal tongue.[16]

Part 2:

Almost Everything You Wanted to Know About Angels

[Patriarch Tychon] was seized with a kind of ecstasy and overheard the singing of angels, the beauty of which he was afterwards unable to describe; neither could he at the moment grasp the words of that song, but was aware of it only as the harmony of many voices.

A Treasury of Russian Spirituality

Chapter 6
Angel Myths

[In Holy Scripture angels] *are not an absurdity or curiosity which we are at liberty to reinterpret, to deny, or to replace by curiosities of our own invention.*
Karl Barth

$\mathcal{L}$ately I've made a habit of looking for angel books whenever I visit a bookstore. It's rare that I don't find a new one on the shelves. Perhaps you've noticed angels appearing in other unexpected places. Angels are trendy. Mail-order houses specialize in angel statuettes, pictures, and a host of other celestial collectibles. Leading "angelologists" grace the sets of daytime TV talk shows. While this fascination partly reflects wholesome spiritual hunger, I'm troubled because I also detect an unhealthy angel confusion.

Some of what I see being said and written seems shallow, such as the book that counsels, "Simply be the angel you are. Think beautiful thoughts. . . . You can never fail when you are in line with the angel in you."[1]

I worry even more about other manifestations of angel-mania. Not every new "truth" about angels squares with the revelations of the Bible or the tested wisdom of the church. Not all that purports to be spiritual is authentic. I have come to believe that not everyone who speaks of angel encounters is discerning. The result is that many people have unanswered questions, unwitting misconceptions, and persistent myths. These need confronting before we can go far in saying what angels truly are.

Six unheavenly myths

MYTH ONE: ALL THAT CAN BE SAID ABOUT ANGELS
IS A MATTER OF PERSONAL OPINION OR EXPERIENCE

This myth holds that anything to do with the heavenly realm is ultimately a matter of your opinion or mine. Some subscribers to this myth even wonder whether or not angels exist. For example, "Some people think their guardian angel is their higher self," one author says. "Others think their guardian angel is a separate being." The typical bottom line: "Choose the explanation that fits you best."[2] One well-known writer describes her angel "handbook" not as a book to help us understand God's provisions through angels, but as "a book about all of us, just as we are inside right now, a road map to the higher realms within us."[3]

The angels of the most popular books do not necessarily bear any resemblance to the angels that weave in and out of the Bible. "There is no correct way to perceive angels," says one book. "They come to us very much on their own terms, appearing to us in ways that are highly personal to each individual."[4] "The only way to know an angel is by your feeling," says another prominent angel writer.[5]

But are angels just our "spiritual" thoughts? Do they populate a landscape, as one angel book asserts, "in which reality, myth, fantasy, legend, dreams and supernatural visions all appear hopelessly entangled"?[6]

Questions like these are centuries old. The Sadducees of Jesus' day, a religious sect often criticized in the New Testament, taught that angels were only impulses God inspired in people, or mere examples of his power, not real beings.

Others since have tried in various ways to "demythologize" angels—to say that however much the idea of angels might inspire us, they are not real. They are seen only by those who believe in them or think they encounter them. This stands against not only virtually every major worldwide religious tradition (for which the existence of an unseen world is fundamental to faith) but also against the clear testimony of Scripture. The words of Jesus in the New Testament alone deal a death blow to such views; he referred to angels clearly and unblushingly. He said the angels of children, to give just one example, "continually see the face of my Father in heaven" (Matt. 18:10).

The Bible tells us that angels are *real*. While the Bible does not enter some metaphysical stratosphere discussing their precise nature (more on that in the next chapter), it clearly teaches that angels exist apart from us. Angels are not merely a figment of someone's overheated imagination. They are a largely invisible, but unmistakable, part of creation.

The nature of angels had something to do with the purported medieval debate over how many angels can dance on the head of a pin. The debate never actually took place, but medieval theologians did indeed conjecture that angels must have no physical bodies, and must exist as pure spirit. But exist they did.

If wondering about angels' nature seems like arcane speculation, irrelevant to today, consider how it points to larger realities: It reminds us that something powerful exists beyond what we see, taste, or touch. As one writer concluded, God "has created a universe that is incredibly rich and has both material and spiritual components. Both aspects are real. There are pins, and we should try not to sit on them, and there are angels, real messengers of a real God who do his bidding. . . . God has created both a visible, material world and material beings, and a spiritual, immaterial world and its beings—and us, who have a share of both."[7]

MYTH TWO: ANGELS' ONLY MISSION IS TO PROTECT US FROM HARM

I recently saw a set of "Angelic Messenger Cards—A Divination System for Spiritual Self-Discovery" at my local bookstore. The copy on the package declared, "The angels are teaching us an entirely new and deeply meaningful way to hear their guidance. If you love flowers, you will benefit greatly by working with these Angelic Messenger Cards and real flowers to 'intuit your own personal guidance.' "[8]

Many angel books today have a strong self-help flavor. One talks of "freeing your inner angel child." Subtitles promise "An angel-guided journey into creativity" or "The angels' guide to personal growth."[9] Angels are seen as a means to an end: prosperity, peace of mind, increased personal confidence. That makes them friendly, tame little deities, but not the vigorous, God-enflamed angelic beings of the Bible.

Worse, some misguided voices claim we can manipulate angels to give us personal guidance. "The angels are opening to us as never before," exult the authors of *Ask Your Angels*.[10] They present the channeled wisdom of Abigrael, an angelic messenger they claim was sent to instruct them. They lead New Age–flavored workshops on getting in touch with "celestials" and aligning with angelic "energy fields." Troubled by a career decision? Unsure about a romance? Consult the "Angel Oracle" cards you can make yourself by following the instructions in the book.

The idea that God made angels like a heavenly room service to cater to our discomforts or whims has found a foothold even in some orthodox Christian circles. Some talk of "activating" God's heavenly hosts for our daily needs.

While Scripture "strongly insists," as Calvin reminds us, "that angels are dispensers and administrators of God's beneficence toward us,"[11] that far from says it all. They help us, but they live first for God and serve us in submission *to him.* They take their cues from God, not our ambitions or whims. They may serve us, but it is not simply to make us "feel better." It is to enable us to live more fully as God intends.

Indeed, as a friend pointed out to me recently, angels in the Bible often complicate the lives of those they meet. Think of Abraham, reminded by the three heavenly visitors that he and Sarah would bear a son and become the destined parents of a multitude. But such promises turned him into a wanderer; he ended up traveling, "not knowing where he was going" (Heb.

11:8). Or think of Mary, told by Gabriel that she would have a Son who would be Savior. Good news, to be sure. A shining moment of faith, yes. But where did it lead? Her son, the Son of God, died an agonizing death while young. He became "a man of suffering and acquainted with infirmity" (Isa. 53:3). We get no sense that she giddily sought the angel's appearance in the first place. The years would cure her of any temptation to see his appearance as an easy spiritual high. An angel visit becomes an occasion of *responsibility,* not sentimental or spiritual self-indulgence. Those visited by angels usually talk of a new seriousness and commitment in the wake of their encounter.

That is true of Gary Groetsch, the businessman whose account of being "caught" by a roadside angel I told in the second chapter. He will tell you that his angel encounter not only convinced him that "there is something beyond what we know today," it also made him realize that he is here for a purpose. He wants to repay some of what God in his goodness has done. He gives of himself to his family, church, daily friendships in a way he never did before his encounter. Nor is it an accident that Walt Shepard, with whose story I began this book, is now a full-time pastor.

Myth Three: Every Person Has a Guardian Angel

Many people who claim to have been helped by an angel will refer to "my guardian angel." And many have been comforted by belief in angel guardians, instilling confidence that God does not leave us alone in the bat-

tles of life. Catholics especially are taught from birth that each of us has one. Do we?

Belief in a guardian angel has long precedent. In pre-Christian Roman religions, adherents believed in protective spirits—every man had a Genius, every woman had a Juno. Some of the church's earliest theologians argued for the idea. Origen, for example, said that "every human soul is under the direction of an angel who is like a father."[12] Basil said that "an angel is put in charge of every believer, provided we do not drive him out by sin. He guards the soul like an army."[13] Other early Christian teachers said that persons simultaneously have an angel and a demon within. The angel, they thought, drew the soul toward good; the demon tugged the soul toward evil.

Perhaps medieval Christian teacher Thomas Aquinas had the most to say. Every person has a guardian angel, he said in his *Summa Theologica*.[14] This is true even for unbelievers destined for "perdition," he argued, if only to protect them from some of the harm they might do to themselves or others. This angel, he said, is assigned to each person at birth, as one of the gifts of providence, though the angel takes on a new role at baptism. Aquinas's teaching is seen as authoritative in churches in the Catholic tradition. What should be said in response?

The truth is, the Bible never teaches that each of us has a specific angel. True, the story in Acts of Peter being rescued from prison speaks of *his* angel (Acts 12:15). But that verse only reports what some people at the disci-

ples' meeting house said. It may reflect a common view of the time, but it is not thereby presented as revealed truth. And while Matthew 18:10 teaches that guardian angels watch over children, it does not say that each child has a particular angel. It is possible, of course. But we have no proof from Scripture.

Perhaps even more pertinent, doesn't the doctrine of one guardian angel actually *limit* God? John Calvin allowed for the possibility of a guardian angel; but what is even better, he says, is that "the care of each one of us is not the task of one angel only, but all with one consent watch over our salvation." Indeed, he said, referring to Jesus' parable of the lost sinner in Luke 15:7, "it is said of all the angels together that they rejoice more over the turning of one sinner to repentance than over ninety-nine righteous men who have stood fast in righteousness. . . . If the fact that all the heavenly host are keeping watch for his safety will not satisfy a man, I do not see what benefit he could derive from knowing that one angel has been given to him as his especial guardian."[15]

God assures us that his angels are always nearby, ready to help. That is what matters. Far better than the notion that we each have one angel is the conviction that God can employ legions of angels, as Jesus said in Matthew 26:53, should he choose. While the guardian angel myth seems to promise us assurance, it ends up not going far enough.

Myth Four: The Angels Are Organized in Three Elaborate Hierarchies

Scripture uses different names for angels. It suggests they have different functions, and perhaps even come in different kinds. So why is this traditional, pervasive teaching a myth?

It helps first to understand some background. In the early centuries of the church, Jerome and Ambrose constructed lists of angels that included nine named ranks: seraphim, cherubim, thrones, dominations (or dominions), virtues, powers, principalities, archangels, and angels. In this they were drawing on scattered Bible verses that mention these names, such as Ephesians 1:21; 3:10; and 6:12; and Colossians 1:16–20.

It was an unknown sixth-century Christian that set the teaching in plaster. Pseudo-Dionysius, as he is usually called (he was once thought to be the Dionysius converted by Paul's preaching and mentioned in Acts 17:34) elaborated on Jerome and Ambrose's views. He said that the community of angels is divided into three hierarchies; each of these in turn contains three choirs. The topmost hierarchy is comprised of seraphim, cherubim, and thrones; the second hierarchy, dominions, virtues, and powers; the third hierarchy, principalities, archangels, and angels.

This order, he explained in his *Celestial Hierarchies*, points to grades in angels' creaturely "perfection." The classes signify varying levels of closeness to God. The angels of the first hierarchy enjoy the closest communion with God; they enlighten the second hierarchy, which in turn enlightens the

third. Cherubim, then, are closest to God's presence, while angels (who relate most often to humankind) are the farthest.

This is an imaginative framework. Philosopher Mortimer Adler finds such speculation to be "highly entertaining."[16] Eugene Peterson, professor of spiritual theology at Regent College in Vancouver, once told me that he finds all this "an imaginative living into the reality of God." Peterson gives this analogy: If you walk in the woods with a friend who knows the names of scores of trees and flowers and shrubs, you say, "Wow, there's a lot more going on here than I ever thought." Pseudo-Dionysius's hierarchies evoke the same reaction. He uses angelology to prayerfully enter into the reality of God. To stretch our imagination, I have concluded, it may have value, but as theology, it has problems.

Dionysius's system attracted many medieval thinkers. But it was not Scripture, not divinely revealed truth. Dionysius simply had no way to determine if his nine-fold ordering was literally true. Nor do we. Even Paul the apostle, who claimed to have been caught up into the "third heaven" (2 Cor. 12:2), hinted that such things are not to be told: They have to do with things "no mortal is permitted to repeat" (2 Cor. 12:4).

Indeed, in Scripture, we gain only glimpses and fragments of how the angels might be organized. Here is what we can say with some confidence about those mentioned with greatest frequency or clarity:

Cherubim. These heavenly beings are often depicted in mysterious fashion, as though the writers were straining to explain something "surpass-

ingly supernatural."[17] Their appearance and character seem beyond our imagination's ability to conceive. And their portraits are diverse. Cherubim were stationed with flaming swords to guard the entrance to the Garden of Eden when Adam and Eve were expelled (Gen. 3:24). Two representations of cherubim were placed on top of the ark in the tabernacle (which contained the stone tablets of the Ten Commandments); and their likenesses were fashioned into the inner curtains and veil of the tabernacle (Ex. 26:1, 31). Ezekiel describes a vision of cherubim, each with four faces and four wings. They appear next to the storied wheels within wheels, and together they "darted to and fro, like a flash of lightning" (Ezek. 1:14).

What sense can we make of this? Cherubim seem to be proclaimers and protectors of God's glory and presence. They guard holy ground, his throne. I wish we could say more! But there is enough in these pictures to remind us that the heavenly realms contain glorious realities.

Seraphim. These are mentioned by name only in Isaiah 6:2. They seem to be distinct from the cherubim, though they both share a multi-winged, striking appearance. They lead heaven in the worship of God. If cherubim guard the holiness of God, seraphim seem to prepare people for the proper approach to God.

Archangels. The term itself appears only twice in Scripture (1 Thess. 4:16; Jude 9), but there are other references to the archangel Michael. He is said to have his own angels (Rev. 12:7) and to be the prince and protector of the nation of Israel (Dan. 10:13, 21; 12:1). In the apocryphal books of

Adam and Eve driven out of Eden

Enoch and Tobit (not accepted as Scripture by Protestants), names of other archangels are mentioned, including Gabriel and Raphael. Biblical writers seem to consider Gabriel an archangel, though nowhere is that explicitly said.

Other names. In addition to the nine names or classes of angels picked up in Pseudo-Dionysius's system, Scripture uses other terms, including *living creatures* in Revelation 4:6–9; 14:3 (seen by some as another name for cherubim, by others as a synonym for seraphim); *sons of God* (Job 1:6; 2:1; and 38:7 RSV), and *watchers* (Dan. 4:13, 17), a name that suggests vigilance. There are others, too.

Are there differences between principalities or powers, between dominions or thrones? These seem to point to simple differences in rank or dignity among the angels, but we cannot say more. We cannot know, and God has not seen fit to reveal to us in Scripture, precisely what the ordering of the angelic realm is like. He certainly could have. He seems to prefer instead that we hold it among those mysteries which wait until the Last Day for a full accounting. However tantalizing the recorded glimpses of angels in Scripture are, they are ultimately just that: glimpses. We can take great comfort, however, in knowing that populating the heavenly spheres are creatures so great they boggle and frustrate our every attempt to pin them down. That makes me all the more expectant for the life that awaits us after death. How many of my questions about angels will finally be answered!

"There was a holy watcher, coming down from heaven" (Dan. 4:13).

MYTH FIVE: WE CAN PRAY TO ANGELS

Occasionally people speak of "calling" on their angel. One New Age book, for example, claims, "We're all capable of walking down a street and having a conversation with our angels. . . . Talking with angels is the most natural thing in the world. . . . When you *Ask Your Angels*, you can be sure that you will be answered."[18]

Such misconceptions are not limited to New Age angelologists. One Christian writer claims the Lord told him that while most people think God tells the angels what to do, most of the time we are the ones who give them their assignments. You sometimes get the idea that angels are what make things happen, not God. Why is that a problem?

Because *God himself* is the one on whom we must call for help. Only in him must our focus and confidence lie. And God is eminently available. "Even before a word is on my tongue, O LORD," Psalm 139:4 says, "you know it completely." And Jesus was speaking of our heavenly Father, not angels, when he urged, "Ask, and it will be given you; search, and you will find; knock, and the door will be opened for you." He went on to use an apt analogy: "Is there anyone among you who, if your child asks for a fish, will give a snake instead of a fish? . . . If you then, who are evil, know how to give good gifts to your children, how much more will the heavenly Father give the Holy Spirit to those who ask him!" (Luke 11:9, 11, 13). Prayer need never be something we fear we must get just right for God to hear.

Jesus reminded us that our Father "knows what [we] need before [we] ask him" (Matt. 6:8).

Why turn to angels when we can turn to the Lord of the universe without hesitation? He can dispatch angels at his word of command, he can help us directly, or, he may, in his sovereign will, allow us to remain in our trial so that we develop greater character. Whatever the outcome, it is ultimately God who matters, and with whom we have to deal. This leads to the sixth and final myth.

MYTH SIX: ANGELS ARE NECESSARY INTERMEDIARIES BETWEEN US AND AN INACCESSIBLE GOD

"Man experiences a relationship with God through a relationship with the Angel," notes one angel book. "Virtually nothing can occur without the intervention of the Angels. . . . The Angelic World . . . constitutes the very relationship between the world and God."[19]

Such thinking assigns exaggerated authority to angels. There is no warrant for such authority in the Bible. The angel in Revelation twice tells John not to worship him (19:10; 22:9). Angels in Scripture repeatedly recognize their subservient role before God. We never get any sense that they are the main ones with whom we are to deal. *Angel,* as we have noted, literally means *messenger.* Angels are sent. The messenger is never more important than the Sender.

This means we do not need a gallery of saints or angels to address God. In the New Testament, Christ is the star at center stage in the great drama of redemption; angels are stage hands.

The temptation to make angels the center of the spiritual life harks back to New Testament times. Paul wrote the New Testament letter to the Colossians, many scholars believe, to correct those who taught, among other things, that angelic beings had control over human affairs, even all creation. People in Colossae were anxiously trying to acquire secret knowledge of the celestial beings. They had to learn the names of angels and master ways to catch their attention. They began to so honor angels that the reverence due God alone was transferred to them. So Paul urged in the letter to the Colossians, noted Calvin, that "not only is Christ to be preferred before all angels but that he is the author of all good things that they have."[20] "Do not let anyone who delights in false humility and the worship of angels disqualify you for the prize," Paul said. "Such a person goes into great detail about what he has seen. . . . He has lost connection with the Head [Jesus]" (Col. 2:18–19 NIV).

Paul knew that an inflated view of angels blocks our view of Christ's position as our one mediator; it diminishes Christ's glory. Instead, as Paul said, "[Christ] is before all things, and in him all things hold together. He is the head of the body, the church; he is the beginning, the firstborn from the dead, so that he might come to have first place in everything. For in him all the fullness of God was pleased to dwell" (Col. 1:17–19).

Author and theology professor J. I. Packer once stumbled upon an analogy for the Holy Spirit that also suggests a truth about angels:

> *I* remember walking to church one winter evening to preach on the words [of Jesus about the Holy Spirit], "He will glorify me" (John 16:14). [S]eeing the building floodlit as I turned a corner, [I realized] that this was exactly the illustration my message needed. When floodlighting is well done, the floodlights are placed so that you do not see them; in fact, you are not supposed to see where the light is coming from; what you are meant to see is just the building on which the floodlights are trained. The intended effect is to make it visible when otherwise it would not be seen for the darkness, and to maximize its dignity by throwing all its details into relief so that you can see it properly. This perfectly illustrates the Spirit's new covenant role. He is, so to speak, the hidden floodlight shining on the Savior.[21]

Because angels perform a similar function, they do not call attention to themselves. They are not to be the focus of our spiritual longings. They may help us but, like the Holy Spirit, they point beyond themselves to Christ, who is our hope and salvation.

Chapter 7
Most-Often Asked Questions About Angels

[An angel] *is a member of that family of wondrous beings who, ere the worlds were made, millions of ages back, have stood around the throne of God . . . and served him with a keen ecstactic love.*

John Henry Newman

$\mathcal{M}$y friend Marshall Shelley still has questions about little Mandy, his profoundly retarded and disabled daughter who lived only two years. At least a few of his questions concern angels.

One week, when Mandy was hospitalized with influenza, she lapsed into a coma. Sometime that week, an aide told a Christian nurse attending Mandy, "I've known I've needed to do something to get God into my life, but it never seemed to be the right time. I'd like you to help me do that now, and I'd like to do it here in Mandy's room, because every time I walk by her room, I see angels hovering over her crib."

"I was never able to get a fuller description of the 'angels,' " Marshall said, "but whatever it was this woman saw or sensed, something about it unlocked her spirit, opening her to God."

By morning Mandy had rallied, only strengthening Marshall's conviction that something far beyond the ordinary was at work that night—something that had to do with angels. But the specifics are still a mystery.

Like Marshall, many of us have questions about angels: What do they look like? Where do they come from? Now that we have examined angel myths—what angels are not—we can look carefully at what they are.

We do face limits in how much we can say, however. While the words *angel* or *angels* appear 340 times in the Bible, angels' existence is assumed, not explained. What we can gather are more like gleanings. We learn some of their characteristics, but only in ways incidental to the verses or stories

in which they appear. "Their entries are sudden and brief," writes English professor and author Thomas Howard, "and then they exit. [Archangel] Michael himself is mentioned in only three books of the Bible, and in every case the reference is very brief and mysterious, as though we were given a glimpse through a cranny out onto huge vistas where heavenly dramas were in progress."[1]

Even if we were given more raw data, would our understanding allow us to grasp it all? Fourth-century theologian Gregory of Nazianzus once said our minds go into a spin trying to speak of the elusive nature of angels.[2]

Because we are limited both by what we are told in Scripture and by what our minds can grasp, one modern theologian suggests we can discuss angels only "softly and incidentally."[3] Softly and incidentally, then, what can we say? While we cannot discover all that we might like to know, we can learn from the questions people have asked for centuries about angels.

The controversial questions

WHERE DO ANGELS COME FROM?

Angels come from heaven, which is God's dwelling place, his "holy habitation" (Deut. 26:15). Scripture's vivid imagery for heaven (city streets paved with gold) notwithstanding, it forms a wondrous realm we cannot begin to imagine. And what most makes it a place of blessed, eternal wonder is God himself. He is present in a special way. That is where angels dwell, and from whence they come.

People who have met angels do not find this hard to believe. Many of them describe beings who convey an aura of reverent mystery and holiness. They talk of messengers whose eyes shine with radiance, whose mere appearance communicates peace, whose luminous presence conveys power. Angels appear to have dropped in from a heavenly country.

In a still larger sense, angels have their origin in the God who created them, perhaps before time itself. The Nicene Creed, the great statement of faith affirmed every Sunday in many churches, suggests God's role in creating angels: "We believe in one God, the Father, the Almighty, *maker of heaven and earth, of all that is, seen and unseen.*" The creed echoes Psalm 148, which declares, "Praise him, all his angels; praise him, all his host! . . . for he commanded *and they were created*" (vv. 2, 5).

If they are created beings, when did it happen?

All angels appear to have been created at or near the same time. We hear no hint in Scripture of angels being continually created, and they certainly did not and do not evolve from human beings or other creatures. They were created as angels. Because angels do not procreate (Matt. 22:28–30), we can conclude that each angel is a direct creation of God. This is probably why angels are sometimes called the "sons of God" in Scripture (Job 1:6; 2:1 RSV); the word *son* seems to indicate a direct creation

of God, as in the case of Adam (Luke 3:38), or as in the recreation of believers in Christ (Gal. 3:26; Eph. 2:8–10).

We also know that "all the sons of God" shouted with joy at the creation of the earth (Job 38:7 RSV), and that Satan, a fallen angel, was already on the scene by Genesis 3 to tempt Adam and Eve. Both suggest that angels were created before us. Can we say more?

Not much more. Augustine, writing in the early fifth century, used elaborate reasoning to argue that angels were created on the first day of creation as recorded in Genesis. How did he arrive at that? He argued first that angels had to have been created in the first six days of the creation of the world, since we are told "all things were created and ordered and the work was completed in six days." Augustine next argued that angels had to have been created on the first day because that was when God created light, and angels are "participators of [God's] eternal light."[4]

More recent scholars find Augustine's circuitous reasoning unconvincing. John Calvin, one of the brilliant minds of the Protestant Reformation, once asked, "What point . . . is there in anxiously investigating on what day, apart from the stars and planets, the other more remote heavenly hosts began also to exist?"[5] I agree with Calvin that we cannot fully, finally know the when. The fact of angels' creation, however, is beyond doubt.

Do Angels Have Bodies?

Angels are more than mere thoughts or ideas. That much we know. But what is the physical (or nonphysical) nature of their existence?

Early church teachers Origen and Augustine suggested that angels could have "subtle" bodies, different from ours, and certainly less limited. The church council held at Nicea in A.D. 784 maintained that angels have bodies composed of ether or light. Poet/theologian John Milton went further. His angels in *Paradise Lost* eat and excrete and even enjoy a kind of attraction and love, what C. S. Lewis called "transexuality."[6] Milton's Raphael "with a smile that glowed / Celestial rosy red," blushingly explained to Adam and Eve,

> Whatever pure thou in the body enjoy'st
> (And pure thou wert created) we enjoy
> In eminence, and obstacle find none
> of membrane, joint or limb.[7]

Those who reason that angels have some kind of body argue two points: first, the idea of a bodiless being contradicts the very nature of creatureliness; and second, angels seem to be subject to spatial limitations and move from place to place, which implies that they have some physical aspect.

Throughout church history, however, the view that angels have physical bodies has attracted only a minority. The church's Council of Lateran (A.D.

1215) decided that angels had no bodies. Thomas Aquinas, the Medieval theologian named "Angelic Doctor" for all he wrote about angels, went further. He taught that angels are pure intellect or spirit without bodies. "There must be some incorporeal creatures," he argued. Indeed, "the perfection of the universe," created by God by his intellect and will, "requires the existence of an incorporeal creature."[8]

"Are not all angels spirits?" rhetorically asks a New Testament writer (Heb. 1:14). Elsewhere we learn that angels are "winds" (Heb. 1:7). This means that in their work of protecting and serving God's people, angels can do amazing things—disappear, reappear, and so on—because they are not limited by physical bodies.

But what about the fact that angels appeared in bodily form in some Bible accounts? Aquinas said angels can *assume* bodies, which they condense from the air by God's power.[9] Angels need bodies "not for themselves, but on our account; that by conversing familiarly with men they may give evidence of that intellectual companionship which men expect to have with them in the life to come."[10]

Who is right? I believe Scripture leans on the side of those who argue for purely spiritual creatures, primarily because angels are termed "spirits" (Heb. 1:14).

As a footnote to the question, in C. S. Lewis's *Out of the Silent Planet*, the first novel of his space trilogy, the traveler Ransom encounters creatures on Mars called *eldila*. This is his term for angels, and Lewis's telling sug-

Daniel in the den of lions

gests what spiritual creatures may be like. Ransom is puzzled at first by his companions' talking with them, for the *eldila* lie just beyond the edge of normal human comprehension. Ransom "seemed to hear, against the background of morning silence, a faint, continual agitation of silvery sound—hardly a sound at all, if you attended to it, and yet impossible to ignore." And as for seeing, he made out only "slight variations of light and shade which no change in the sky accounted for. If the air had not been calm and the ground-weed too short and firm to move in the wind, he would have said that a faint breeze was playing with it, and working such slight alterations in the shading as it does in a corn-field on the Earth. Like the silvery noises in the air, these footsteps of light were shy of observation."[11]

How Are Angels Different from Human Beings?

When one man learned I was working on a book about angels, he immediately wanted to tell me about a friend who had encountered an angel. After talking further, however, I found that his friend claimed to entertain the presence of a loved one who had died. This, my friend thought, was an angel.

Many people think that angels are human beings who have died. Cartoons often show *people* in heaven with wings and harps. But angels are not glorified human beings. In Matthew 22:30, Jesus says that believers in heaven will be *like* the angels, not that we will *be* angels. Hebrews 12:22–23

talks about the heavenly Jerusalem and specifically distinguishes between the "innumerable angels in festal gathering" and the "spirits of the righteous made perfect" (believers). Psalm 8 says that God has made humankind "a little lower than the angels," (Ps. 8:5 KJV; Heb. 2:7), and the New Testament makes the intriguing, mysterious statement that we will, in our glorified state, "judge angels" (1 Cor. 6:3).

Angels are quite different from human beings in significant ways. They are "greater in might and power" (2 Peter 2:11). An angel opened locked prison doors (Acts 5:17–20). An angel rolled back the stone of the crucified Jesus' tomb (Matt. 28:2)—no mean feat. Angels are less limited by constraints of space and are able to move swiftly. In Zechariah 1:11 an angel speaks of "patrolling the earth."

I like the story told by a pediatric nurse and member of an evangelical Lutheran convent. It took place in 1945 in Germany, after Russian troops had overrun many German towns. Local women were being abused, and night was particularly terrifying. Nurses gathered as many women and children as they could and sheltered them in a small, makeshift school. They often worked late at night, and since theirs was the only lighted building, they were in danger, too. Yet the people called the sisters' building "the island of peace," because harm never seemed to befall it.

One day, a woman brought her children and begged the nurse to take them. That evening, as the community held a worship service, the new boy, instead of holding his hands with the rest, stared into the distance with

wide eyes. The community sang a familiar song, asking God to send angels to "place golden weapons around our beds."

"When we said 'Amen,' " the nurse recounted, "the boy came up to me and drew me out of the building. He kept tapping his breastbone and saying, 'Up to here. It came up to here on them.' "

"What do you mean?" she asked. Pointing to the gutter on the roof on the building, he repeated his statement. "The gutter came up to here on them."

The child then told her that while everyone had been singing, he had seen "men" ablaze with light at every corner of the building. They were so tall that they towered above the roof.

"Now it was clear to me," the nurse said, "why this house was called the 'island of peace.' "[12]

Such differences between angels and us are all to our good. Their superhuman strength saves us from untold harm. Said Martin Luther, "The angels are near to us, to those creatures whom by God's commands they are to preserve, to the end we receive no hurt of the devil. . . . Therefore when the devil intends to hurt us, then the loving holy angels resist and drive him away; for the angels have long arms, and although they stand before the face and in the presence of God and his son, Christ, yet they are hard by and about us in those affairs."[13]

How Many Angels Are There?

Saint Albert the Great (A.D. 1206–1280) calculated that there were 399,920,004 angels. Rabbinic lore suggested that every blade of grass had its guardian angel coaxing it to grow. So numerous are "the blessed armies of transcendent intelligent beings," said Pseudo-Dionysius, "that they surpass the fragile and limited realm of our physical numbers."[14] Arriving at a number is somehow far less a preoccupation for moderns than it was for medieval scholastics.

We will never know exact numbers. But we know angels form a mighty multitude. Elisha's servant, for example, had his eyes opened once to see a mountain encamped with the hosts of heaven, "full of horses and chariots of fire all around Elisha" (2 Kings 6:17).

Daniel 7:9–10 records this vision:

> As I watched,
> thrones were set in place,
>   and an Ancient One took his throne, . . .
> his throne was fiery flames,
>   and its wheels were burning fire.
> A stream of fire issued and flowed out from his presence.
> A thousand thousands served him,
>   and ten thousand times ten thousand stood attending
>   him.

Revelation later echoed Daniel's vision, with a depiction of "myriads of myriads and thousands of thousands" of angels surrounding the throne, saying "Worthy is the Lamb that was slaughtered" (Rev. 5:12).

What does it mean that, as Milton's Adam said, "Millions of spiritual creatures walk the earth / Unseen, both when we wake, and when we sleep"?[15] If one angel can in one night destroy Assyrian King Sennacherib's army (2 Kings 19:35), what can legions and uncounted multitudes do? English poet and pastor John Donne once commented, "I consider thy plentiful goodness, O my God, in employing angels more than one, in so many of thy remarkable works." Donne recited instance after instance in Scripture where we read not of a single angel, but many—from the angels ascending and descending on Jacob's ladder to the chorus that proclaimed Christ's birth to the shepherds. "From the first to their last, are angels, angels in the plural, in every service angels associated with angels."[16]

CAN ANGELS FALL FROM GRACE TODAY?

Angels were created by a perfect God, and because God pronounced all of creation good and holy, they were good and holy. Some, however, apparently fell from grace and became the fallen angels we know as demons. But can good angels still fall? Most Christian thinkers have said they cannot.

God's angels are called "elect" in 1 Timothy 5:21. That implies not only that they are called and chosen by God, but enabled by God to continue in grace. Once they decided whether to remain loyal to God or to rebel with

Satan, their decision seems to have been permanent. The angels evidently received, writes Reformed theologian Louis Berkhof, "a special grace of perseverance, by which they were confirmed in their position." Protestants have been reluctant to say much more, he says, but have been "generally satisfied with the knowledge that the good angels retained their original state, were confirmed in their position, and are now incapable of sinning."[17]

This helps us understand why the writer of the book of Hebrews in the New Testament wrote, "it is clear that [Christ] did not come to help angels, but the descendants of Abraham" (Heb. 2:16). Angels' state—elect and good, or fallen and evil—seems to have an awesome irrevocability. Christ came to win our salvation, but, for reasons we cannot fully see, not that of the fallen angels.

John Calvin once noted that some grumble that Scripture does not tell us more about the fall of the angels. But that is to our advantage, he says. "It did not befit the Holy Spirit to feed our curiosity with empty histories to no effect. And we see that the Lord's purpose was to teach nothing in his sacred oracles except what we should learn to our edification."[18]

What Do Angels Look Like?

No single description fits angels. In the Bible they may take on ordinary guise, appear in radiant white, or even bear wings (as in the case of the cherubim and seraphim). Another question arises: If angels are bodiless,

spiritual beings, are they in their natural state invisible? How do any of us see them at all? In one Old Testament story, Balaam the diviner could not see an angel that his donkey saw, until the Lord "opened" his eyes (Num. 22:22, 31).

On the other hand, Billy Graham speculates that angels "have a beauty and variety that surpass anything known to men."[19] Like a character supposes in Reynolds Price's novel, *The Tongues of Angels*, perhaps angels have an indescribable glory:

> All my life, not just since [my father died], I'd been fascinated by the fairly worldwide idea of angels. . . . In special moments, like tonight here alone, I'd try to set down quickly and with a minimum of forethought guess at the face of an angelic messenger. . . . Even in the night like this, I could only think of angels in color. Every color on any known prism. That was why, in dark thick as tar, I had my rainbow pencils in hand. . . . In a few more minutes, I switched on my flashlight again and turned to my book. And in maybe five minutes, I'd finished a face so filled with news, and all of it good, that I thought at once I'd finished nothing better since Father died. Again I doused the light, but the face still burned before me. Its eyes were wider than human eyes. Other-

wise it looked like your finest friend, tuned to perfection in every cell.[20]

When angels appear, they often appear in human form. They are frequently mistaken for people. For this very reason we should show hospitality to strangers, the writer of Hebrews cautioned, "for by doing that some have entertained angels without knowing it" (13:2). This verse may well echo Abraham's encounter with angels, when he welcomed three "men" while standing by the door of his tent (Gen. 18:1–18).

In the Bible angels tend to appear as males, but since we are never told that angels are male and female, I see this as a concession to cultural expectations (or biases). One exception may be Zechariah 5:9, where we read of "two women coming forward. The wind was in their wings."

For all their look of humanness, angels also appear sometimes as vividly unusual—even overwhelming—beings. When an angel appeared to the two Marys at Jesus' empty tomb, the women were clearly frightened. The angel's "appearance was like lightning, and his clothing white as snow. For fear of him the guards shook and became like dead men" (Matt. 28:1–4).

Such vivid stories have influenced angel art and literature through the centuries. In the earliest artistic efforts, no distinguishing marks stand out. In a large catacomb in Rome dated about A.D. 300, we find what are probably the first Christian depictions of angels. Abraham is seen receiving the three stangers under the oaks of Mamre, and, says one writer, "they are

The women at the empty tomb

shown as Abraham is said to have seen them, simply as three men. . . . There are no wings, no halos or other distinguishing features."[21]

That soon changed. Toward the end of the fourth century halos and wings begin to appear. Soon the halo was never omitted from the angel's head. Wings likewise became ubiquitous.

Do angels really have such physical features? What about, for example, the halo? Its use by artists predates Christianity; it is found in ancient Buddhist art and was used by Greeks and Romans to designate gods and heroes. Sometime in the fourth century, Christian artists began to use a halo to grace the head of Jesus, saints, and angels. It symbolized sanctity and supernatural radiance.

But the word *halo* does not appear in the Bible. Nothing suggests angels really have them. As a reminder of angels' heavenly bearing and aura of purity, the halo makes a fine symbol. And because many angel appearances in the Bible seemed to involve radiance and startling light, the halos of the artists remind us that angels are not ordinary creatures.

Do angels have wings? Art and literature have burned them into our imaginations even more than halos. Dante Alighieri's classic, *The Divine Comedy (Purgatory)*, describes a boat in which the spirits are brought over the sea to the shores of Purgatory, with an angel at the helm. The angel's wings are stretched up toward heaven to act as sails, and Dante calls him "the Bird of God."[22] Wings seem inseparable from angels, whether in Renaissance art, in Christmas decorations, or even in popular movies such as

Frank Capra's *It's a Wonderful Life*, in which Clarence, an "angel second class" earns his wings by helping the protagonist George Bailey.[23] It is difficult for some to think of angels in any other way.

To many people's great surprise, however, angels only occasionally appeared with wings in Scripture. In many cases, angels seemed so unremarkable in appearance that men and women often did not immediately realize they were in heavenly company. In the clear cases where angels have wings, something besides pure physical description seems to be at work. The Old Testament prophet Isaiah, for example, tells us of seraphim—angelic beings who stood above the throne of God. These awesome creatures had *six* wings (Is. 6:2); with two they covered their faces, with two their feet, and with two they flew. Here, however, the wings do more than simply allow the being to defy gravity; the wings covering their faces and feet symbolize reverence before a holy God. They allow the angels to wait properly in the presence of a being of overwhelming goodness.

Almost two centuries later, Ezekiel had a vision of a windstorm coming out of the north—"a great cloud with brightness around it and fire flashing forth continually, and in the middle of the fire . . . was something like four living creatures. This was their appearance: they were of human form. Each had four faces, and each of them had four wings. . . . Their wings were spread out above; each creature had two wings, each of which touched the wing of another, while two covered their bodies" (Ezek. 1:4–6, 11). We know from later in the book (Ezek. 10:1–2) that Ezekiel understood these

to be cherubim. But again, so much of Ezekiel's vision (as well as the entire book) is fraught with symbolic significance. The wings in this case may simply communicate power, grace, and alert readiness to move at God's injunction.

What of occasions in Scripture where we read of angels flying? In Daniel 9:21 Gabriel came to Daniel in "swift flight." He is again said to fly in Revelation 14:6–7. But these passages do not mention *wings*.

For all their abundance in Renaissance and modern art, in literature and cinema, wings do not appear necessary for angel work. They may be a concession to us on God's part—a feature important for what is communicated, but not for angels in themselves. However we solve the question, the picture of angel wings reminds us that angels are always ready to help with incredible swiftness, should circumstances require it.

One further note on angel art. Very often angels are portrayed playing the lute or some other musical instrument (sometimes a stringed instrument, sometimes a woodwind), although never in Scripture do we see angels doing such. (Even the fact of their singing is unclear. Many translations render Revelation 5:12 to read that the angels around the throne *sang* their praises to the Lamb. But in the original Greek the word literally means *said*.)[24] The portrait of angels singing and playing instruments, however, richly suggests their overflowing desire to praise and adore their Lord.

Beyond the controversies and questions are a number of short, clear statements about angels we can make with confidence. These affirmations

do more than describe angels; they also point us to truths about God's creative constancy and handiwork.

Grasping the profoundly simple

Briefly, then, are eight intriguing notes about what angels are like.

ANGELS EXPERIENCE EMOTIONS

Struck by God's power and wisdom, the "heavenly beings shouted for joy" at the creation of the world (Job 38:7). Angelic seraphim worship God with a hushed sense of awe and reverence, crying, "Holy, holy, holy" (Isa. 6:3). And we read of "joy in the presence of the angels of God over one sinner who repents" (Luke 15:10). Angels, like God, are not cold and impassive.

ANGELS ARE MIGHTY

Angels are described as "mighty ones" in Psalm 103:20. Even the names for angels (powers, dominions, principalities) suggest this. Their actions, their occasional appearance in Scripture as "heavenly hosts," and the fear their coming sometimes elicits all testify to their might. They have the power to communicate vividly with one another and with other minds, and they can produce tangible effects in the world. They even seem capable of affecting the forces of nature; John in Revelation had a vision of "four angels standing at the four corners of the earth, holding back the four winds of the earth so that no wind could blow on earth or sea or against any tree"

(Rev. 7:1). Their power is nevertheless subject to the limitations of all creatures. They seem, for example, unable to create, change the composition of substances, revise the laws of nature, or search the heart of human beings, for these are "prerogatives peculiar to God," as theologian Charles Hodge argued in his *Systematic Theology*.[25] But angels are not daunted by the things that frighten us. That should encourage us.

ANGELS ARE IMMORTAL

While as created beings they certainly had a beginning, Scripture declares that they live eternally. The most compelling support for this comes from Jesus, when he tells his disciples in Luke 20:36 that believers in heaven "cannot die anymore, because they are like angels." Angels never die or retire. They are always alive to serve God and, as he wills, serve us.

ANGELS ARE INTELLIGENT

They must be, for they communicate intelligently. And they are curious. They are anxious to learn about our salvation in Christ (1 Peter 1:12). Scripture makes explicit reference to their wisdom in passages like 2 Samuel 14:17, where a visitor to King David likens him to "the angel of God, discerning good and evil," and Ephesians 3:10, where it is said that "the wisdom of God in its rich variety" is made known to angels. They are not omniscient, however; they do not know the day or the hour of Christ's return, for example (Matt. 24:36).

Angels Number Beyond Our Counting

As we have noted, we never find in the Bible precise information on the number of angels, but they are clearly a mighty army. "With [God] were myriads of holy ones; at his right, a host of his own" (Deut. 33:2). And in a passage wonderfully suggestive of ineffable glories, we read of "innumerable angels in festal gathering" in Hebrews 12:22. There is no shortage of God's messengers and servants.

Angels Have a Certain Humility

They are not arrogant or reckless. An intriguing verse in the New Testament observes that "when the archangel Michael contended with the devil and disputed about the body of Moses, he did not dare to bring a condemnation of slander against him, but said, 'The Lord rebuke you!'" (Jude 9). The angels, for all their power, as Fred Dickason writes, "are sometimes taxed in the accomplishment of their duties, as in the struggle of elect with evil angels (Rev. 12:7), and stand in need of assistance (Dan. 10:13)."[26] If angels, who daily see God, know their place, must we not remember ours?

Angels Are Not Above Christ

They are indeed subservient to Christ. Christ is God's "only begotten Son," and angels stand ready to serve. They "long to look" (1 Pet. 1:12) into the salvation Christ brings, but apparently are kept from seeing it fully. Christ sits at the "right hand of the Majesty on high, having become as

much superior to angels as the name he has inherited is more excellent than theirs" (Heb. 1:3–4). In what many scholars believe to be a hymn, early Christians sang that God gave Christ

> the name that is above every name,
> so that at the name of Jesus
> every knee should bend,
> in heaven and on earth (Phil. 2:9–10).

Knowing what angels are like leads to another intriguing question: How will we recognize an angel if we meet one? The next chapter will help us find out.

Chapter 8

Was That an Angel?

*Thousands of things do thee employ / In ruling all
This spacious globe: Angels must have their joy,
Devils their rod, the sea his shore, / The winds their stint:
and yet when I did call, / Thou heardst my call, and more.*

George Herbert

$\mathscr{I}$ *think* it's an angel story." So began a call-in listener on a radio program on angels. It was in 1977, he said. "I was about nineteen years old. I didn't know Christ yet. I was sound asleep on the couch in the late afternoon. . . . I was awakened by a knock at the door." When the man answered the door, he found a man in black jeans, white T-shirt, and crewcut at the door. He had "strange eyes."

The peculiar visitor said only one thing: "Do you believe Jesus is the Son of God?"

"Out of my startled sleep," the caller continued, "I blurted 'yes.' "

The man at the door said, "Good. If you didn't, you'd fall through the grate and burn in hell on a hot coal."

Then the doorstep visitor turned and walked away. "I was kind of scared," recalled the man on the program. "So I closed the door and peeked through the drapes. He didn't stop at any other house and walked out of sight. I forgot about this story till three years ago, when I accepted Christ. Was God trying to get a hold of me then?"[1]

The program's featured guest appeared to accept this as an angel visit. She noted how angels sometimes appear as more than incurably nice beings. True enough. But I was not convinced the caller had seen an angel. His account qualified as an odd story, to be sure. But an angel story?

In our culture, stories of the seemingly unexplainable abound. Whole television series are devoted to "unsolved mysteries." People claim to have

experiences with anything from extraterrestrials to telepathy. Many of these stories rank as superstition or silliness. Still, who of us hasn't encountered something odd or out of the ordinary? We awake in the night and *know* a loved one is in danger, only to get a call the next morning confirming our awful hunch. We ask someone to pray for us, and they have uncanny clarity about our situation. Chemistry and psychology and sociology by themselves cannot account for all we experience.

As we have seen, angels sometimes play a part in the "seemingly unexplainable." Biblical figures, the faithful through the centuries, and modern-day believers have attested to that. But that does not mean we should rush to explain everything strange by references to angels. It seems that in some circles the old "God of the gaps" theory, which explained any unaccounted-for action or effect by reference to the divine, has given way to the "angels of the gaps" theory. People turn to angels to explain anything good or beneficial. They credit them too much, forgetting poet George Herbert's prayer that "thousands of things do thee employ."

How can we tell if an angel has indeed appeared? What helps us sort out the natural from the supernatural? How can we be discerning, yet open?

Such questions are not merely for theologians or for the incurably curious. I find great spiritual significance in these questions. Some of what people peg as an angelic encounter, for example, may represent the action of God himself, or it may spring from subterranean currents of the person's

Jacob wrestling with the angel until dawn

own psychology. Of greater concern, however, is if the encounter may represent a brush not with supernatural forces of good, but of *evil*.

It is no accident that the New Testament tells how some in the church possess a gift of "discernment of spirits" (1 Cor. 12:10). This reminds us that not all spirits are benign. Not everything that sounds spiritually dramatic is godly. So we need to sort and sift and test each experience.

How can we tell the difference? What guides us in determining if an experience we or someone else has is angelic? And how do we know if we have come face to face with a heavenly creature or an earthly one? The answers are not easily reduced to formulae. But several questions and guidelines will take us far.

Angelic or human?

We should first ask, Could the encounter have been human rather than angelic? Even if circumstances seemed unusual, we may have seen not a celestial being, but a flesh-and-blood person.

We need to emphasize this because more good is wrought through simple human action than many realize. Paul reminded the poor and largely uneducated believers in first-century Corinth that God "chose what is weak in the world to shame the strong; God chose what is low and despised" (1 Cor. 1:27–28). The Bible often tells of God using tiny things, linked with human efforts, to accomplish big ends: Samson with a jawbone of a donkey (Judg. 15:15); David with five smooth stones (1 Sam. 17:40); a widow's two

small copper coins (Luke 21:2); or a little boy's five barley loaves and two fish (John 6:9). Many of us underestimate the profound good human beings can do in their daily settings. When I worked with pollster George Gallup, Jr., on our book *The Saints Among Us,* what impressed me was how much the influence of the "saints" we profiled was persistently expressed in everyday arenas. They went about changing their world not by preaching to thousands, but through the tiny touches, by working in the ordinary settings of office buildings, neighborhood fences, kitchens, and classrooms.[2] Says Paul the apostle, "If I speak in the tongues of mortals and of angels, but do not have love, I am a noisy gong or a clanging cymbal" (1 Cor. 13:1). God uses angels, but he also uses *me.* What seems to be an angel on a mission of help, then, may simply be a friend or stranger with God-inspired timing.

We should also not forget that God sometimes endues people with superhuman power. The early church in Acts amazed spectators by the "many signs and wonders . . . done among the people through the apostles" (Acts 5:12). Life in the early church included an occasional angel encounter (as in Philip's story in Acts 8:26), but much more often it was *people,* called and empowered by the Holy Spirit, who furthered Christ's kingdom. At times since, including today, ordinary followers of Christ have carried on God's work in winsome, wonderful ways that sometimes astound us.

In fact, I believe God will typically send a person to help rather than an angel. Many contemporary angel stories—of tow-truck drivers showing up

suddenly to stranded motorists, of someone showing up with just the right message of encouragement—sound distinctly human. The encounters remind us powerfully of God's care, but they do not thereby suggest direct angelic intervention. These people may have entertained angels unawares, but I would also not be surprised if some of the stories I have included in this book involved *people* acting under unusual conditions. My faith will not suffer if I were to find that some of these stories involved human agency. God is still gracious however he scatters across our lives the reminders of his goodness.

I recently read a moving story told by a mother of a young child. Laura Sowers's account demonstrates powerfully how what some call angelic may have much to do with the human, how it all may ultimately be beyond our knowing:

My preschooler son Marc and I were shopping in a large department store. On our way down to the main floor, Marc hopped on the escalator. I followed. Suddenly Marc screamed. I'd never heard a sound like that before. " Mama! my foot!"

Marc's right foot was wedged between the side of the moving step and the escalator's wall. His body was twisted toward me. He screamed again. The escalator continued downward.

In the panic of the moment, the danger at the bottom of the escalator flashed before me, the thought of the foot being severed—

"Turn off the escalator!" I screamed. "Somebody help!" And then, "Oh, dear God, dear God, help us!"

Several people at the base of the escalator began a flurry of activity. The escalator stopped! Someone had pushed an emergency button at the bottom of the steps.

Thank you, Father, I prayed.

Marc clutched my arm and cried while I struggled to get a better look at his foot. A chill raced up my spine when I saw the tiny space in which his foot was trapped. It looked no more than a quarter of an inch wide. All I could see of his foot was his heel. The rest had disappeared into the jaws of the machine.

"Someone call the fire department!" I shouted.

Marc looked up at me desperately. "Mama," he said, "pray!"

I crouched next to him, holding him. I prayed. For a moment he quieted. Soon, though, he began crying again. "Daddy! Daddy!" he called out. I shouted out our business phone number, hoping someone would call my husband.

The two of us sat waiting. . . . As the minutes passed I could see dark images of crutches and wheelchairs. . . .

Marc looked up at me and said, "Mama, my bones feel broken and bleedy."

I clutched his blond head tighter to me, but now it was I who was feeling faint. *I can't faint, Lord,* I prayed. *Marc needs me—O Lord, I know you're here! Where? Help me!*

At that moment I felt warm soft arms enfolding me from behind. A woman's soothing voice said quietly in my ear, "Jesus is here, Jesus is here."

The woman had come down the escalator and sat on the step above me. She gently rocked me from side to side, surrounding my shaking body with a calm embrace. "Tell your son his foot is all right," she said in my ear. There was an assurance in her voice.

"Marc," I said into his ear. "Your foot is all right."

"Tell him you'll buy him a new pair of shoes—whatever kind he wants."

"I'll buy you a new pair of shoes. Any kind you like."

Marc's crying stopped. "Cowboy boots? Like

Daddy's?" We were talking about new shoes for two healthy feet! For the first time since the ordeal began, I felt hope. Maybe, just maybe, his foot would be all right.

"Tell him there are no broken bones," she said.

I did.

The firemen arrived. Two men with crowbars pried the step away from the escalator wall, freeing Marc's foot at last. His shoe was in tatters. It took all my courage to watch as the men pulled the shredded sock off Marc's foot, but when they did, they revealed a red, bruised, but whole foot.

I turned to share my joy with my wonderful friend, but all I saw was her leg as she turned the corner at the top of the escalator. I never even saw her face.

My husband, Craig, arrived just as the firemen were setting Marc down on the floor. He was still sobbing, but he could wiggle his toes. Later, X rays confirmed what I already knew: no broken bones, only bruises and swelling.

To this day I do not know who the woman who helped me was, the woman who knew that Jesus was there with us. . . . Many people have suggested that

the woman was an angel of the Lord. I can't be sure
about that, but of this I am certain: She was heaven-
sent.[3]

God *may* have dispatched an angel to a terrified mother and hurting
son. But why not also leave open the possibility that God simply sent a
Spirit-endued *woman* to show compassion and blessed encouragement? I do
not see in the story unmistakable hallmarks of angelic presence. I do not
see why God could not have used a person as easily as an angel. And I see
nothing in the Bible to suggest that God prefers sending angels over having
us do the work he calls us to. He probably sends people at least as often as
angels. That should make us pause before too quickly concluding we have
met an angel.

Sensible or illogical?

Next, we use common sense. Whether with our own or another's account, we must ask discerning questions, weigh carefully what we see and
hear. We do not always accept at face value an impression just because we
sense it. Nor do we assume everyone who tells a good story is to be believed. We test and evaluate. We pay attention to what we know of the
world and how God works within it. These same principles of caution and
logic apply to evaluating angel encounters.

We acknowledge, for example, that buried voices or images from our

past can sometimes erupt into our consciousness with great force. Or, God may speak through inner impressions or dreams. We may even have visions. This does not mean we have been visited by an angel.

That people have claimed God or his angels told them to do all manner of terrible or silly things should keep us from assuming that charged "spiritual moments" are always to be accepted at face value. And on the positive side, a wonderfully freeing insight and vivid image may change us, but by itself does not an angel visit make.

This common sense also has a corporate dimension. We need to test our "visions" and promptings with trusted friends or pastors. The church has become individualistic to a fault. We picture faithfulness as a lonely, heroic battle, a transaction between "me and Jesus" alone. But, like many areas of the Christian life, discernment is not a do-it-yourself project. We need the wise counterbalances of the spiritually mature. We should choose carefully with whom we share our experiences, of course, for not everyone is wise or gifted in listening to another. But sharing with another often helps us evaluate the genuineness of an encounter.

An extreme example demonstrates how important this can be. Angel writer Malcolm Godwin describes an eighty-four-year-old widow named Ruth Norman who drives an electric-blue Cadillac with a flying saucer on the roof. She claims to be the Archangel Uriel (mentioned in the apocryphal book of 2 Esdras and in Jewish and Christian folklore). Her four hundred followers seem to agree. Would that someone, somewhere, had gently set

this woman straight! Amazingly, Godwin concludes, "we are no longer in any position to judge whether she is speaking the truth or having a ball at our expense. . . . And who is in the position to say that she is not an archangel or a reincarnation of a supreme being?"[4] Such reasoning is folly parading under the banner of tolerance. While angels are beyond our ability to control or completely comprehend, some claims stretch all that we know to be sane or wise. We are under no obligation to believe something because someone claims spiritual or angelic sanction.

Faithful or counterfeit?

We should also ask if anything in a purported angel encounter goes against the ultimate source of spiritual truth, the Bible. Does it conflict with what we know to be true from God's inspired revelation?

"Even if we or an angel from heaven should proclaim to you a gospel contrary to what we proclaimed to you," said Paul, "let that one be accursed!" (Gal. 1:8). Angels are not in the business of starting new religions. They do not lead us into new revelation. They may upset our preconceptions, of course, but they do not contradict Christian truth.

A case in point is found in the book, *Ask Your Angels*. The authors give instructions on communicating with "celestials" that not only have no precedent in Scripture, but go against biblical prohibitions against divination. The authors give instructions, for example, on conducting "Inner Telephone" exercises. This involves touching certain parts of the head while vi-

sualizing golden spots of light to signify the dimensions of an internal "transmitter and receiver." "Use the Inner Telephone exercise to call your angels when you're hung up about something, or if you just feel like having a heart-to-heart chat," they write.[5]

Compare such practices with these stringent words from Deuteronomy: "No one shall be found among you who . . . practices divination, or is a soothsayer, or an augur, or a sorcerer, or one who casts spells, or who consults ghosts or spirits . . . For whoever does these things is abhorrent to the LORD; it is because of such abhorrent practices that the LORD your God is driving them out before you. You must remain completely loyal to the LORD your God" (Deut. 18:10–13). We need to measure spiritual experiences against the plumb line of tested biblical truth.

Clarifying or confusing?

We must also ask how a seeming angel message or encounter leaves us feeling. Are we renewed, expectant, more resolved to serve God? Or has it left us restive, confused, with a sense of foreboding? Even God's words of judgment, which he may place in an angel message, carry the promise of our redemption and new life. While a message from God may ask changes from us, it does not lead to despair. God is not a God of despondent confusion.

"The wisdom from above" wrote James in the New Testament, "is first pure, then peaceable, gentle, willing to yield, full of mercy and good fruits,

without a trace of partiality or hypocrisy. And a harvest of righteousness is sown in peace for those who make peace" (James 3:17–18). God's communications though human beings or angels are first and foremost pure. They do not violate our freedom of choice. They do not taunt. They compel us by means other than coercion. Philosopher Dallas Willard writes of the calm force of God's communications: "The voice of God speaking in our souls . . . bears in it a characteristic. . . . spirit of exalted peacefulness and confidence, of joy, of sweet reasonableness, of will for the good." It also comes with a certain power. Willard notes that when Jesus in his earthly life spoke, "his words had a weight of authority that opened up the understanding of the hearers and created faith in them. 'He taught them as one having authority, and not as their scribes' " (Matt. 7:29).[6]

Methodist missionary E. Stanley Jones, notes Willard, once addressed the question of how one can distinguish the voice of God from one's own subconscious: "Perhaps the rough distinction is this: The voice of the sub-conscious argues with you, tries to convince you; but the inner voice of God does not argue, does not try to convince you. It just speaks, and it is self-authenticating. It has the feel of the voice of God within it."[7] Angels will not try to cajole or wheedle. They will speak with a dignity that befits their Master and Lord.

A final note: Lest we think discerning the source of a supernatural communication is a trifling matter, we need to remember that Satan and the demons can deceive us into thinking they are good. Satan, the chief of

fallen angels, as we have noted "disguises himself as an angel of light" (2 Cor. 11:14). Why would he come with his cover "blown," with serpent-like hissing or blatant appeals to livid evil? He is more subtle. He majors in confusion, in questioning what is true. "Did God say . . . ?" he asked Eve in the Garden when provoking her to eat the forbidden fruit (see Genesis 3:1). Our discernment must be prayerfully based in truth.

God-glorifying or angel-centered?

An angel appearance should always ultimately strengthen us for good, pointing us to the God revealed in Christ. So we should always ask, does this purported angel encounter magnify God?

As we have seen, genuine angels do not draw attention to themselves. They point a way to the Lord who has sent them as his messengers and witnesses. And they help us pull our attention away from ourselves to glorify God alone. An angel will never ask you to worship him. An angel will never appear more attractive or interesting than God himself. If we find ourselves thinking for days about the beauty of the angel, with little thought for God, the experience should give us pause. Indeed, many experiences people ascribe to angels should probably be credited to God's direct, gracious action.

Apparently this was an issue in New Testament times. Paul faced off against a budding heresy that would allow God to be worshipped only in the form of his angel intermediaries: "Do not let anyone disqualify you, insisting on self-abasement and worship of angels, dwelling on visions, puffed

up without cause by a human way of thinking, and not holding fast to the head [Christ], from whom the whole body, nourished and held together by its ligaments and sinews, grows with a growth that is from God" (Col. 2:18–19). The goodness and fullness of God was not shared by a series of intermediaries, Paul was saying; God himself, revealed in Christ, is the source of all revelation and goodness.

An intriguing story in the Old Testament suggests this. The unnamed wife of an Israelite named Manoah was visited by an angel and told, "although you are barren, having borne no children, you shall conceive and bear a son" (Judg. 13:3). She was told her son (to be named Samson) would deliver Israel from their enemies the Philistines (which he went on to do). When she told her husband, Manoah, about the angel, he wanted to see and hear it all for himself. The angel appeared, and the woman went to get her husband. Manoah had his own questions, most of which the angel answered. But when Manoah wanted to prepare a meal for the heavenly visitor, the angel said to prepare instead a "burnt offering" to the Lord. And one question the angel would not answer: When Manoah asked the angel his name, "so that we may honor you when your words come true," the heavenly messenger would not give it (Judg. 13:18). Was it angelic modesty? It certainly represented an unwillingness to see the focus taken off what God was about to do. That will be the hallmark of all true angel activity.

Unexpected or forced?

We should also be wary of angel visits that seem to come from someone's prompting or conjuring. Any visit that comes out of someone's effort to summon an angel is likely counterfeit. We are not to seek to "attune" ourselves to angels' "wavelengths," as some counsel; we are to be faithful. If God determines we need an angel's help, we can trust he will send it.

We should also ask, Was the supposed angel visitation a surprise? Angels in the Bible caught the subjects of their visits off guard. An angel visit that seemed to come out of the blue stands a better chance of being authentic.

We should note that God may work through angels with people who do not believe in angels. He may break through the mental routines of skeptics. This happened to Balaam, a diviner mentioned in the Old Testament book of Numbers. Balaam was ordered by Balak, a Moabite king at war with Israel, to put a curse on the Israelite army. Balak was afraid of Israel's military might, and the king, in common with most ancient peoples, believed that blessings and curses had great power.

Balaam was forbidden by God, however, to curse Israel. Even so, Balaam accepted the Moabite king's invitation to come and talk more about the curse. Numbers tells us, "God's anger was kindled because [Balaam] was going, and the angel of the LORD took his stand in the road as his adversary. Now [Balaam] was riding on the donkey, and his two servants were with

The angel appearing to Balaam

him. The donkey saw the angel of the LORD standing in the road, with a drawn sword in his hand; so the donkey turned off the road, and went into the field; and Balaam struck the donkey, to turn it back onto the road" (Num. 22:22–23). Two more times the donkey saw the angel, while Balaam, internationally known prophet, diviner, and "holy man" saw nothing. "Then the LORD opened the eyes of Balaam, and he saw the angel of the LORD standing in the road, with his drawn sword in his hand; and he bowed down, falling on his face" (Num. 22:31). The angel allowed Balaam to go with Balak's messengers, but said, "speak only what I tell you to speak" (Num. 22:35).

Balaam, in spite of himself, ended up speaking a blessing on Israel. God sent an angel not because Balaam was holy (the Bible repeatedly refers to him as corrupt), but because God chose to. God may surprise us or someone we know that way again.

This seems to have happened with a mother and her young daughter. Her account appeared in *Ladies' Home Journal*:

> *P*lease, somebody help me! My baby's not breathing!" screamed Carole Moore (the name has been changed) as she ran into the hallway of her apartment building. Why wasn't anyone answering?
>
> Just a few minutes earlier, the magazine editor had been sitting peacefully in her living room in New

York trying to amuse her daughters: Julie, almost three, and Allison, eighteen months. Allison was uncharacteristically fussy and cried in spite of her mother's efforts to comfort her. The toddler's wails grew louder and louder—then suddenly stopped.

Allison slumped over, her lips turning blue from lack of oxygen. Carole frantically started pounding her on the back. "Breathe, Allison! Breathe!" She grabbed the limp child and headed for the hallway. "Can't somebody help me?"

Carole, who describes herself as "not particularly religious," wasn't looking for divine intervention—just someone who knew first aid. But although there were usually plenty of people in the neighboring apartments, on this particular day in the spring of 1990, no one answered her cries.

Suddenly Carole felt a deep calm settle over her. "Relax, Carole," she said to herself. "You took a class in child safety last year. You know what to do." As Julie watched, wide-eyed, from the doorway, Carole lay Allison on the hall floor, leaned over her and began mouth-to-mouth resuscitation. The child soon responded. "My terror just disappeared," Carole says.

"Something took over, and it was almost like I had stepped outside myself. I could see myself doing what I had to do."

That night, after the doctor had diagnosed Allison's illness as croup and the baby was sleeping peacefully, Julie crawled into her mother's lap. "Mommy," she asked quietly, "who was that man who had his hand on your shoulder?"

"What man, honey?" Carole asked. . . .

Although Julie couldn't describe the stranger . . . he'd obviously made a big impression on her. After six weeks of questioning her mother daily, the little girl burst into tears of frustration. "Mommy, why can't you tell me about the man?" she asked, sobbing. Carole hugged her daughter close. "I didn't see the man, honey," she said. "That's why I can't explain him to you. I'm so sorry."

Two years later, the experience still amazes Carole. . . . "My husband and I have never read stories to the children about Jesus or God, and I never heard any of Julie's friends talk about religious topics. . . ." Carole adds, . . . "I've always felt that [spiritual] things like this can happen, and it makes me feel good that it has happened to Julie. . . . It's also made

me believe more strongly in the afterlife. . . . Now I feel that there is something beyond death."[8]

Good fruit or bad?

Finally, we need to ask how a purported angel appearance affected someone's life (or our own). Did what happened lead further into faithfulness?

People are free to turn aside from what God says or does, of course. Someone's unfaithful response to an angel visit does not negate its reality. But usually we can expect that a true angel visit will turn a person around for the good. What Jesus said of false prophets applies to people's claims of entertaining angels: "You will know them by their fruits. Are grapes gathered from thorns, or figs from thistles? In the same way, every good tree bears good fruit, but the bad tree bears bad fruit" (Matt. 7:16–17). A visit from a good angel should bear good fruit in someone's choices and direction. Sitting in the presence of the holy tends to make us holy.

So we ask, Does this encounter help us "set [our] minds on things above," as Paul says in Colossians 3:2? Does it quicken our hope for the things of God? Does it reorient our focus toward Christ?

This happened in a story told by fourth- and fifth-century biographer Paulinus. Writing of Bishop Ambrose, Paulinus recounts, "There was a certain man of the Arian heresy, violent beyond measure as a disputant and harsh and immovable as regards the Catholic faith. This man was in the

church one day during a sermon by the bishop [Ambrose]. Later, he himself related that he saw an angel there, speaking into the ears of the bishop as he preached, so that the bishop seemed to be proclaiming to the people the words of the angel. By this sight he was converted, and the faith which he formerly attacked he himself now began to defend."[9]

If you experience an angel visit, the result should be more focus, more faithfulness, more centeredness on God. Angels may awaken our spiritual longing, but they cannot satisfy it. We should find ourselves more hungry for God, who alone can nourish and fill us. "You called and cried out loud," wrote Augustine in a prayer to God, "and shattered my deafness. You were radiant and resplendent, you put to flight my blindness. You were fragrant, and I drew in my breath and now pant after you. I tasted you, and I feel but hunger and thirst for you. You touched me, and I am set on fire to attain the peace that is yours."[10]

Living with uncertainty

Even after we have prayerfully asked these discerning questions, we may still not have determined if what we encountered was an angel. Sometimes saying "I don't know for sure" can be a faithful response. We cannot settle the nature of every specific instance beyond a glimmer of doubt. More important is discovering the larger role angels play in God's scheme of things—and our lives. The last chapter, to which we now turn, will help us do so.

Chapter 9

Angels and Your Everyday Life

Many mysteries ascribed to our inventions, have been the courteous revelations of Spirits; for those noble essences in heaven bear a friendly regard unto their fellow-natures on earth.

Sir Thomas Browne

*W*hat about angels and *us*? In the many months of writing this book, I have often wondered: Will I ever, this side of heaven, see the curtain of this world drawn back, for even a moment, so that I glimpse an angel in his glory? Will I ever say, as have many I have talked with, "Yes, an angel unmistakably crossed my path"?

I do not know. Who can?

And I wonder, Why do angels sometimes seem to show up, when in countless other instances there is no sign to be seen? "The question is," wonders playwright Tony Kushner in a *Time* magazine cover story on angels, "why are you saved with your guardian angel and not the woman who was shot to death shielding her children in Brooklyn three weeks ago? That suggests a capricious divine force. If there is a God, he can't possibly work that way."[1] But God can work that way. I have come to a couple of conclusions that help me make sense of such questions.

First, I must learn to trust God, whether angels show up or not. Much of life requires faith. Much we cannot understand. Why do angelic guardians catch some children falling off their bikes while other children are mown down in drive-by shootings? I do not know. Just as I do not know why God seems to answer directly and dramatically some prayers for healing while seeming to ignore others.

The Irish dramatist, poet, and playwright Oscar Wilde once said that there was enough suffering in any London lane to show God's love is fancy, not fact. Yet belief in God and his angels does not guarantee a benign uni-

verse where enemy shellings, unspeakable tortures, and starving people suddenly disappear. God stands with us, even when life hurts. Angels go with us even when we do not see them or sense them. Suffering does not mean that God does not exist or care.

I am struck by the fact that the one chapter in the Bible that seems to talk most about faith and heaven also unflinchingly describes suffering as part of the believer's lot. "Faith," Hebrews 11 in the New Testament begins, "is the assurance of things hoped for, the conviction of things not seen." We immediately read about Abel, Noah, Abraham, Joseph—a veritable pantheon. "And what more should I say?" the writer continues. "For time would fail me to tell of Gideon, Barak, Samson, Jephthah, of David and Samuel and the prophets—who through faith conquered kingdoms, administered justice, obtained promises, shut the mouths of lions. . . ." But then we see an altogether different side: "Others were tortured. . . . Others suffered mocking and flogging, and even chains and imprisonment. They were stoned to death, they were sawn in two, they were killed by the sword; they went about in skins of sheep and goats, destitute, persecuted, tormented. . . . Yet all these, though they were commended for their faith, did not receive what was promised." They had to wait until Christ "provided something better" (see Heb. 11). What contrasts, how striking the juxtapositions of faith and longing! In the same breath we hear of conquering and imprisonment, of triumph and humiliation. Angels do not change this picture, however active they are.

"All of these" faithful ones, the writer explains, "died in faith without having received the promises, but from a distance they saw and greeted them. . . . They desire a better country, that is, a heavenly one" (Heb. 11:13, 16). They looked toward the angels' homeland.

This is why C. S. Lewis could speak of pain as something of a good. Suffering helps us to not settle for the notion that this world is all there is. Pain is a wake-up call, a megaphone to rouse an otherwise deaf world and remind us that we live on a fallen planet in need of reconstruction. Pain keeps us from easily viewing this earth as a final home.[2] Angels do not make life a paradise here and now, but they do show up often enough to help us not forget that a heavenly country awaits us. This leads to my second conclusion.

I must cultivate a taste for the heavenly, an openness to God's unexpected ways. I like the title of *Christianity Today* president Harold Myra's book, *Living by God's Surprises.*[3] Because God is beyond our predicting, a life lived with him can never be reduced to the tidy or known. Will we live long lives blessed with radiant health? Will cancer stalk us in middle age? Will our children and their children experience weal or woe, blessing or hardship? Will God visit us with a mystic's rapture? We cannot say.

But I do know that I long for a sensitivity to the things of heaven. There was something in the biblical "greats"—Abraham, Mary, Peter—that conditioned them to recognize the numinous and holy and heavenly when it appeared. Something in them was alert and attuned. Should an angel have

never appeared, they would have lived lives of simple faithfulness, shot through nevertheless with the presence of God, with what C. S. Lewis called the "drippings of grace."

Musing on how the biblical figures seemed to know what to do when an angel appeared, Thomas Howard writes,

> *H*ad Isaiah had a course in angelology? . . . Was Zechariah a priest at the shrine of Saint Michael? No, in every case, the response of these people seems to have been a by-product of a prior humility and goodness. These people loved and served the Lord himself. Hence they recognized holiness when it appeared in angelic form, and their reaction was appropriate. They were accustomed to bowing before the ineffable.[4]

In the byways and slow moments, in the dreams and disappointments that spur me on or hold me back, I want not to miss that humble openness. And I want such familiarity with the things of God that should he or an angel speak, I will know how to listen, I will be quick to recognize his voice, I will be ready to respond.

Notes

Part 1 Epigraph: Martin Luther, **Table Talk of Martin Luther**, Thomas Kepler, ed. (Grand Rapids: Baker, 1952, 1979), 280.

Chapter 1
Epigraph: William Shakespeare, **Hamlet**, 1:5.

1. Sophy Burnham, **A Book of Angels** (New York: Ballantine, 1990), xii.

2. Mortimer Adler, **The Angels and Us** (New York: Collier/Macmillan, 1982), xii–xiii.

3. Nancy Gibbs, "Angels Among Us," **Time**, Dec. 27, 1993, 56.

4. Peter Lamborn Wilson, **The Little Book of Angels** (Rockport, Mass.: Element, 1993), 50.

5. John Calvin, **Calvin: Institutes of the Christian Religion**, Vol. 1, ed. by John T. McNeill (Philadelphia: Westminster, 1960), 162.

6. Billy Graham, **Angels** (Waco, Texas: Word, 1975), 17.

7. Richard Baxter, **The Certainty of the Worlds of Spirits** (London: T. Parkhurst, 1691), 17.

8. G. K. Chesterton, quoted in Elisabeth Eliot, **A Slow and Certain Light** (Waco, Texas: Word, 1973), 82.

Chapter 2

Epigraph: Richard Hooker, **Lawes** 1.4, quoted in **A Dictionary of Biblical Tradition in English Literature**, David Lyle Jeffrey, gen. ed. (Grand Rapids, Michigan: William B. Eerdmans, 1992), 40.

1. Ignatius Meimaris, "The Subway," **SBC Life**, Summer 1993, 12. Used by permission.

2. John Calvin, **Calvin: Institutes of the Christian Religion**, Vol. 1, John T. McNeill, ed. (Philadelphia: Westminster, 1960), 166.

3. Elisabeth Elliot, **A Slow and Certain Light** (Waco, Texas: Word, 1973), 81.

4. Reynolds Price, "The Gospel According to John," in **Incarnation**, Alfred Corn, ed. (New York: Viking Penguin, 1990), 72.

5. Philip Yancey, "Do I Matter? Does God Care?" **Christianity Today**, November 22, 1993, 22.

6. Quoted in Dallas Willard, **In Search of Guidance** (San Francisco: HarperSanFrancisco, 1993), 28–29.

7. Theodora Ward, **Men and Angels** (New York: Viking, 1969), 15.

8. Martin Luther, **The Table Talk of Martin Luther**, Thomas S. Kepler, ed. (Grand Rapids, Michigan: Baker, 1979), 279.

9. Judith MacNutt, "The Ring," **Charisma**, February 1993, 52–53. Reprinted with permission by **Charisma** magazine, Strang Communications Co.

10. Reynolds Price, **A Palpable God** (New York: Atheneum, 1978).

11. **The Book of Common Prayer**, (New York: The Seabury Press, 1979), 244.

12. C. Fred Dickason, **Angels Elect and Evil** (Chicago: Moody Press, 1975), 12.

13. William Shakespeare, **Hamlet**, I.4.

14. Don and Caffy Whitney, "The Pickup Truck," **SBC Life**, Summer 1993, 10. Used by permission.

15. Euphie Eallonardo, "The Fourth Man," **His Mysterious Ways** (Carmel, NY: Guideposts, 1989), 23–24. Reprinted with permission from **Guideposts Magazine**. Copyright © 1982 by Guideposts Associates, Inc., Carmel, NY 10512.

16. William Shakespeare, **The Life of King Henry the Fifth**, Prologue.

17. John Henry Newman, quoted in **The Company of Heaven** (London: Longman, Green, and Company, 1903), 8–9.

18. Judith MacNutt, "The Ring," 52–53.

Chapter 3

Epigraph: Nancy Gibbs, "Angels Among Us," **Time**, December 27, 1993, 65.

1. Lily Tomlin, quoted in Dallas Willard, **In Search of Guidance** (San Francisco: HarperSanFrancisco/Grand Rapids: Zondervan, 1993), 6.

2. Daniel 7:15–27 and 8:13–26; Revelation 1:1 and 22:6, 8.

3. Hebrews 2:2; Galatians 3:19; Acts 7:53.

4. Luke 1:26–38; Matthew 28:1–7; Acts 1:10–11.

5. John Milton, **Paradise Lost** and **Paradise Regained** (VII: 569–573), (New York: Penguin/New American Library, 1968), 214.

6. As told in Myrna Grant, **Vanya** (Carol Stream, Illinois: Creation House, 1974), 51–52.

7. Sam Cathey, "The Stewardess," **SBC Life**, Summer 1993, 10–11. Used by permission.

8. Thomas Torrance, "The Spiritual Significance of Angels," in **Alive to God**, J. I. Packer and Loren Wilkinson, eds. (Downers Grove, Illinois: InterVarsity Press, 1993), 136–137.

9. Eugene Peterson, **The Message** (Colorado Springs, Colorado: NavPress, 1993), 114–115.

10. Walter Wangerin, "Painting Christmas," **Christianity Today**, December 13, 1993, 30.

11. Eileen Elias Freeman, **Touched by Angels** (New York: Warner, 1993), 26.

12. John Calvin, **Institutes**, Vol. 1, 164.

13. Peter Lamborn Wilson, **The Little Book of Angels**, 50–51.

14. Quoted in Kristin Szremski, "Talking with Your Angel," **The Carol Stream** [Ill.] Press, October 14, 1993, 13.

15. Quoted in Theodora Ward, **Men and Angels** (New York: Viking Press, 1969), 147.

16. Dallas Willard, **In Search of Guidance**, 21.

17. Ibid.

18. Kenneth Woodward, "Talking to God," **Newsweek**, January 6, 1992, 44.

19. Dallas Willard, **In Search of Guidance**, 92.

Chapter 4

Epigraph: Evagrius, in **The Syriac Fathers on Prayer and the Spiritual Life**, Sebastian Brock, Kalamazoo, trans. (Kalamazoo, Michigan: Cistercian Publications, 1987), 72–73.

1. Quoted in Jaroslav Pelikan, **The Melody of Theology** (Cambridge, Massachusetts: Harvard University Press, 1988), 1.

2. Edmund Spenser, "The Fairie Queen," **The Complete Poetical Works of Edmund Spenser** (Boston and New York: Hougton Mifflin Company, 1908), 280.

3. Madeleine L'Engle, quoted in **Draper's Book of Quotations for the Christian World** (Wheaton, Illinois: Tyndale House, 1992), 18.

4. Milton, **Paradise Lost** and **Paradise Regained**, VI:897–900, 198.

5. John Calvin, **Institutes**, Vol. 1, 175.

6. Martin Luther, **The Table Talk of Martin Luther**, 280–281.

7. Corrie ten Boom, **A Prisoner—And Yet!** (Toronto, Canada: Evangelical Publishers, 1947), 85–87.

8. Clara Erskine Clement, **Angels in Art** (Boston: L. C. Page, 1898), 24.

9. Frank E. Peretti, **This Present Darkness** (Westchester, Illinois: Crossway Books, 1989), 143.

10. Thomas Merton, **The Ascent to Truth** (San Diego: Harcourt Brace Javonovich, 1951, 1979), 69.

11. Martin Luther, quoted in **Prayers Across the Centuries** (Carol Stream, Illinois: Harold Shaw, 1993), 87.

12. Luci Shaw, **Polishing the Petoskey Stone** (Carol Stream, Illinois: Harold Shaw, 1990), 155.

13. Billy Graham, **Angels**, 3–4.

14. Richard Baxter, **The Certainty of the Worlds of Spirits** (London: T. Parkhurst, 1691), 4.

15. Liturgy of St. James, quoted in Theodora Ward, **Men and Angels** (New York: Viking Press, 1969), 25.

16. Ibid.

17. C. S. Lewis, **The Lion, the Witch and the Wardrobe** (New York: Collier/Macmillan, 1950), 123.

18. Josephus, quoted in **The NIV Study Bible**, Kenneth Barker, gen. ed., note on Acts 12:21 (Grand Rapids: Zondervan, 1985), 1669.

19. Billy Graham, **Angels**, 26.

Chapter 5
Epigraph: Augustine, quoted in Dick Eastman, **Celebration of Praise** (Grand Rapids, Michigan: Baker, 1984), 9.

1. John Donne, **John Donne's Sermons on the Psalms and Gospels**, Evelyn M. Simpson, ed. (Berkeley and Los Angeles: University of California Press, 1967), 226.

2. Francis Thompson, "The Kingdom of Heaven," in **Francis Thompson: Poems and Essays** (Freeport, New York: Books for Libraries Press, 1969), 226.

3. Frederick Buechner, **Wishful Thinking** (New York: Harper & Row, 1973), 1–2.

4. V. Raymond Edman, "I, Too, Saw an Angel," **Bulletin of Wheaton College**, December 1959, n.p.

5. Thomas Howard, "The Parts Angels Play," **Christianity Today**, December 12, 1980, 21.

6. Augustine, **Confessions**, Henry Chadwick, trans. (Oxford: Oxford University Press, 1991), 3.

7. Diane M. Komp, **A Window to Heaven** (Grand Rapids, Mich.: Zondervan, 1992), 28–29.

8. Olive Fleming Liefeld, **Unfolding Destinies** (Grand Rapids, Michigan: Zondervan, 1992), 235–239.

9. Augustine, quoted in Dick Eastman, **Celebration of Praise**, 9.

10. **Westminster Shorter Catechism**, a confession of faith commonly used by those in the Protestant Reformed tradition.

11. Augustine, **Confessions**, 125.

12. Quoted in Brock, **The Syriac Fathers on Prayer and the Spiritual Life**, 204–205.

13. Ibid., 202–203.

14. Milton, **Paradise Lost**, (IV 677–678), 139.

15. Ibid., (IV 681–686).

16. Quoted in Thomas Torrance, "The Spiritual Significance of Angels," 131–132.

PART 2 Epigraph: quoted in Joan Wester Anderson, **Where Angels Walk** (New York: Ballentine, 1992), 227.

Chapter 6
Epigraph: Karl Barth, **Church Dogmatics Vol. III**, (Edinburgh: T. & T. Clark, 1960), 380.

1. Karen Goldman, **The Angel Book** (New York: Simon & Schuster, 1988, 1992), 12, 56.

2. Quoted in Peter Steinfels, "Beliefs," **New York Times**, December 11, 1993, 12.

3. Karen Goldman, **The Angel Book**, 11.

4. Alma Daniel, Timothy Wyllie, Andrew Ramer, **Ask Your Angels** (New York: Ballantine, 1992), 5.

5. Karen Goldman, **The Angel Book**, 24.

6. Malcolm Godwin, **Angels** (New York: Simon & Schuster, 1990), 7.

7. Eutychus, "How Many Angels," **Christianity Today**, December 20, 1974, 15.

8. Meridith L. Young-Sowers, Angel Messenger Cards (Walpole, New Hampshire: Stillpoint Publishers, n.d.)

9. Peter Steinfels, "Beliefs," 12.

10. Alma Daniel, Timothy Wyllie, Andrew Ramer, **Ask Your Angels**, 56.

11. John Calvin, **Institutes**, Vol. 1, 166.

12. Quoted in Jean Danielou, **The Angels and Their Mission** (Westminster, Maryland: The Newman Press, n.d.), 69.

13. Ibid.

14. St. Thomas Aquinas, **Summa Theologica** Q. 113 Art. 1, 2 (New York: Benzinger Brothers, 1947), 550–551.

15. John Calvin, **Institutes**, Vol. 1, 167.

16. Mortimer Adler, **The Angels and Us**, 44.

17. C. Fred Dickason, **Angels Elect and Evil**, 62.

18. Alma Daniel, Timothy Wyllie, Andrew Ramer, **Ask Your Angels**, 9.

19. Peter Lamborn Wilson, **The Little Book of Angels**, 1993, 23.

20. John Calvin, **Institutes**, Vol. 1, 170.

21. J. I. Packer, **Keep in Step with the Spirit** (Old Tappan, New Jersey: Revell, 1984), 66.

Chapter 7
Epigraph: John Henry Newman, quoted in David Connolly, **In Search of Angels** (New York: Perigee/Putnam, 1993), 32.

1. Thomas Howard, "The Parts Angels Play," **Christianity Today**, December 12, 1980, p. 20.

2. Gregory of Nazianzus, quoted in Thomas Torrance, "The Spiritual Significance of Angels," 123.

3. Quoted in Karl Barth, **Church Dogmatics** (Edinburgh: T. & T. Clark, 1960), 371.

4. Augustine, **The City of God**, Vernon J. Bourke, ed. (New York: Image/Doubleday, 1958), 215–217.

5. John Calvin, **Institutes,** Vol. 1., 164.

6. C. S. Lewis, **A Preface to Paradise Lost** (London: Oxford University Press, 1942), 109.

7. John Milton, **Paradise Lost** (VIII, 622–625), 233–234.

8. St. Thomas Aquinas, Q. 50, **Summa Theologica**, 259.

9. Ibid., Q. 51, 266.

10. Ibid., 265.

11. C. S. Lewis, **Out of the Silent Planet** (New York: Macmillan, n.d.), 117.

12. Basilea Schlink, **The Unseen World of Angels and Demons** (Old Tappan, New Jersey: Chosen Books, 1986), 137, quoted in Joan Wester Anderson, **Where Angels Walk** (Sea Cliff, New York: Barton & Brett, 1992), 148–149.

13. Martin Luther, **Table Talk of Martin Luther**, 279–280.

14. Pseudo-Dionysius, **The Complete Works**, Colm Luibheid, trans. (New York: Paulist Press, 1987), 181.

15. John Milton, **Paradise Lost** (IV, 677–678), 139.

16. John Donne, **Devotions** (Ann Arbor: Michigan: University of Michigan Press, 1959), 47–48.

17. L. Berkhof, **Systematic Theology** (Grand Rapids, Mich.: William B. Eerdmans, 1946), 145.

18. John Calvin, **Institutes**, Vol. 1, 175.

19. Billy Graham, **Angels**, 35.

20. Reynolds Price, **The Tongues of Angels** (New York: Ballantine, 1990), 91–92.

21. Theodora Ward, **Men and Angels** (New York: Viking Press, 1969), 83.

22. Dante Alighieri, **Purgatory**, Canto 2, 38.

23. Frank Capra, **It's a Wonderful Life**, Republic Pictures Corporation, 1948, 1993.

24. See Andrew Bandstra, "A Job Description for Angels," **Christianity Today**, April 5, 1993, 21.

25. Charles Hodge, **Systematic Theology** (Grand Rapids, Michigan: Eerdmans, 1946), 668.

26. C. Fred Dickason, **Angels**, 27.

Chapter 8
Epigraph: George Herbert, "Praise (III)" in **George Herbert: The Country Parson**, The Temple, John N. Wall, ed. (New York: Paulist, 1981), 283.

1. Dick Staub, interviewer, "Chicago Talks," WYLL Chicago, Illinois, July 23, 1990.

2. George H. Gallup, Jr. and Timothy Jones, **The Saints Among Us** (Ridgefield, Connecticut: Morehouse, 1992).

3. Laura Z. Sowers, "The Woman from Nowhere," **His Mysterious Ways** (Carmel: Guideposts, 1989), 31–34. Reprinted with permission from **Guideposts Magazine**. Copyright © 1982 by Guideposts Associates, Inc., Carmel, NY 10512.

4. Malcom Godwin, **Angels**, 204–205.

5. Alma Daniel, Timothy Wyllie, and Andrew Ramer, **Ask Your Angels**, 222.

6. Dallas Willard, **In Search of Guidance**, 188, 190.

7. E. Stanley Jones, **A Song of Ascents**, quoted in Dallas Willard, ibid., 188.

8. As told by Andrea Gross, "I Met an Angel," **Ladies' Home Journal**, December 1992, 60, 63. Copyright 1992, Meredith Corporation. All rights reserved. Reprinted from **Ladies' Home Journal** magazine with permission of the authors.

9. Paulinus, "Life of St. Ambrose, Bishop of Milan," **The Fathers of the Church**, 1952, 43.

10. Augustine, **Confessions**, 201.

Chapter 9

Epigraph: Sir Thomas Browne, **Religio Medici** [1634/35], 71–72, quoted in **A Dictionary of Biblical Tradition in English Literature**, David Lyle Jeffrey, gen. ed. (Grand Rapids, Michigan: William B. Eerdmans, 1992), 40.

1. Quoted in Nancy Gibbs, "Angels Among Us," 65.

2. C. S. Lewis, **The Problem of Pain** (New York: Collier/Macmillan, 1962), 115.

3. Harold Myra, **Living by God's Surprises** (Waco, Texas: Word, 1988).

4. Thomas Howard, "The Parts Angels Play," **Christianity Today**, December 12, 1980, 20.

TO HAVE OR TO BE?

WORLD PERSPECTIVES

Volumes already published

WORLD PERSPECTIVES *Volume Fifty*

Planned and Edited by **RUTH NANDA ANSHEN**

TO HAVE
OR TO BE?

ERICH FROMM

HARPER & ROW, PUBLISHERS

New York, Hagerstown, San Francisco, London

FIRST EDITION

Library of Congress Cataloging in Publication Data

Fromm, Erich, date
  To have or to be?
  (World perspectives; v. 50)
  Bibliography: p.
  1. Personality. 2. Ontology. I. Title.
BF698.F746   1976   128   73-130449
ISBN 0-06-011379-0

76 77 78 79 80 10 9 8 7 6 5 4 3 2 1

Contents

PART THREE   THE NEW MAN AND THE NEW
SOCIETY

World Perspectives
What This Series Means

It is the thesis of *World Perspectives* that man is in the process of developing a new consciousness which, in spite of his apparent spiritual and moral captivity, can eventually lift the human race above and beyond the fear, ignorance, and isolation which beset it today. It is to this nascent consciousness, to this concept of man born out of a universe perceived through a fresh vision of reality, that *World Perspectives* is dedicated.

My Introduction to this Series is not of course to be construed as a prefatory essay for each individual book. These few pages simply attempt to set forth the general aim and purpose of the Series as a whole. They try to point to the principle of permanence within change and to define the essential nature of man, as presented by those scholars who have been invited to participate in this intellectual and spiritual movement.

Man has entered a new era of evolutionary history, one in which rapid change is a dominant consequence. He is contending with a fundamental change, since he has intervened in the evolutionary process. He must now better appreciate this fact and then develop the wisdom to direct the process toward his fulfillment rather than toward his destruction. As he learns to apply his understanding of the physical world for practical purposes, he is, in reality, extending his innate capacity and augmenting his ability and his need to communicate as well as his ability to think and to create. And as a result, he is substituting a goal-directed evolutionary process in his struggle against environmental hardship for the slow, but effective, biological evolution which produced modern man through mutation and natural selection. By intelligent intervention in the evolutionary process man has greatly accelerated and greatly expanded the range of his possibilities. But he has not changed the basic fact that it remains a trial and error process, with the danger of taking paths that lead to sterility of mind and heart, moral apathy and intellectual inertia; and even producing social dinosaurs unfit to live in an evolving world.

Only those spiritual and intellectual leaders of our epoch who have a paternity in this extension of man's horizons are invited to participate in the Series: those who are aware of the truth that beyond the divisiveness among men there exists a primordial unitive power since we are all bound together by a common humanity more fundamental than any unity of dogma; those who recognize that the centrifugal force which has scattered and atomized mankind must be replaced by an integrating structure and process capable of bestowing meaning and purpose on existence; those who realize that science itself, when not inhibited by the limitations of its own methodology, when chastened and humbled, commits man to an indeterminate range of yet undreamed consequences that may flow from it.

Virtually all of our disciplines have relied on conceptions which are now incompatible with the Cartesian axiom, and with the static world view we once derived from it. For underlying the new ideas, including those of modern physics, is a unifying order, but it is not causality; it is purpose, and not the purpose of the universe and of man, but the purpose *in* the universe and *in* man. In other words, we seem to inhabit a world of dynamic process and structure. Therefore we need a calculus of potentiality rather than one of probability, a dialectic of polarity, one in which unity and diversity are redefined as simultaneous and necessary poles of the same essence.

Our situation is new. No civilization has previously had to face the challenge of scientific specialization, and our response must be new. Thus this Series is committed to ensure that the spiritual and moral needs of a man as a human being and the scientific and intellectual resources at his command for *life* may be brought into a productive, meaningful and creative harmony.

In a certain sense we may say that man now has regained his former geocentric position in the universe. For a picture of the Earth has been made available from distant space, from the lunar desert, and the sheer isolation of the Earth has become plain. This is as new and as powerful an idea in history as any that has ever been born in man's consciousness. We are all becoming seriously concerned with our natural environment. And this concern is not only the result of the warnings given by biologists, ecologists and conservationists. Rather it is the result of a deepening awareness that something new has happened, that the planet Earth is a unique and precious place. Indeed, it may not be a mere coincidence that this awareness should have been born at the exact moment when man took his first step into outer space.

This Series endeavors to point to a reality of which scientific theory has revealed only one aspect. It is the commitment to this reality that lends universal intent to a scientist's most original and solitary thought. By acknowledging this frankly we shall restore science to the great family of human aspirations by which men hope to fulfill themselves in the world community as thinking and sentient beings. For our problem is to discover a principle of differentiation and yet relationship lucid enough to justify and to purify scientific, philosophic and all other knowledge, both discursive and intuitive, by accepting their interdependence. This is the crisis in consciousness made articulate through the crisis in science. This is the new awakening.

Each volume presents the thought and belief of its author and points to the way in which religion, philosophy, art, science, economics, politics and history may constitute that form of human activity which takes the fullest and most precise account of variousness, possibility, complexity and difficulty. Thus *World Perspectives* endeavors to define that ecumenical power of the mind and heart which enables man through his mysterious greatness to re-create his life.

This Series is committed to a re-examination of all those sides of human endeavor which the specialist was taught to believe he could safely leave aside. It attempts to show the structural kinship between subject and object; the indwelling of the one in the other. It interprets present and past events impinging on human life in our growing World Age and world consciousness and envisages what man may yet attain when summoned by an unbending inner necessity to the quest of what is most exalted in him. Its purpose is to offer new vistas in terms of world and human development while refusing to betray the intimate correlation between universality and individuality, dynamics and form, freedom and destiny. Each author deals with the increasing realization that spirit and nature are not separate and apart; that intuition and reason must regain their convergence as the means of perceiving and fusing inner being with outer reality.

World Perspectives endeavors to show that the conception of wholeness, unity, organism is a higher and more concrete conception than that of matter and energy. Thus an enlarged meaning of life, of biology, not as it is revealed in the test tube of the laboratory but as it is experienced within the organism of life itself, is attempted in this Series. For the principle of life consists in the tension which connects spirit with the realm of matter, symbiotically joined. The element of life is dominant in the very texture of nature, thus rendering life, biology, a transempirical science. The laws of life have their origin beyond their mere physical manifestations and compel us to consider their spiritual source. In fact, the widening of the conceptual framework has not only served to restore order within the respective branches of knowledge, but has also disclosed analogies in man's position regarding the analysis and synthesis of experience in apparently separated domains of knowledge, suggesting the possibility of an ever more embracing objective description of the meaning of life.

Knowledge, it is shown in these books, no longer consists in a manipulation of man and nature as opposite forces, nor in the reduction of data to mere statistical order, but is a means of liberating mankind from the destructive power of fear, pointing the way toward the goal of the rehabilitation of the human will and the rebirth of faith and confidence in the human person. The works published also endeavor to reveal that the cry for patterns, systems and authorities is growing less insistent as the desire grows stronger in both East and West for the recovery of a dignity, integrity and self-realization which are the inalienable rights of man who may now guide change by means of conscious purpose in the light of rational experience.

The volumes in this Series endeavor to demonstrate that only in a society in which awareness of the problems of science exists, can its discoveries start great waves of change in human culture, and in such a manner that these discoveries may deepen and not erode the sense of universal human community. The differences in the disciplines, their epistemological exclusiveness, the variety of historical experiences, the differences of traditions, of cultures, of languages, of the arts, should be protected and preserved. But the interrelationship and unity of the whole should at the same time be accepted.

The authors of *World Perspectives* are of course aware that the ultimate answers to the hopes and fears which pervade modern society rest on the moral fibre of man, and on the wisdom and responsibility of those who promote the course of its development. But moral decisions cannot dispense with an insight into the interplay of the objective elements which offer and limit the choices made. Therefore an understanding of what the issues are, though not a sufficient condition, is a necessary prerequisite for directing action toward constructive solutions.

Other vital questions explored relate to problems of international understanding as well as to problems dealing with prejudice and the resultant tensions and antagonisms. The growing perception and responsibility of our World Age point to the new reality that the individual person and the collective person supplement and integrate each other; that the thrall of totalitarianism of both left and right has been shaken in the universal desire to recapture the authority of truth and human totality. Mankind can finally place its trust not in a proletarian authoritarianism, not in a secularized humanism, both of which have betrayed the spiritual property right of history, but in a sacramental brotherhood and in the unity of knowledge. This new consciousness has created a widening of human horizons beyond every parochialism, and a revolution in human thought comparable to the basic assumption, among the ancient Greeks, of the sovereignty of reason; corresponding to the great effulgence of the moral conscience articulated by the Hebrew prophets; analogous to the fundamental assertions of Christianity; or to the beginning of the new scientific era, the era of the science of dynamics, the experimental foundations of which were laid by Galileo in the Renaissance.

An important effort of this series is to re-examine the contradictory meanings and applications which are given today to such terms as democracy, freedom, justice, love, peace, brotherhood and God. The purpose of such inquiries is to clear the way for the foundation of a genuine *world* history not in terms of nation or race or culture but in terms of man in relation to God, to himself, his fellow man and the universe, that reach beyond immediate self-interest. For the meaning of the World Age consists in respecting man's hopes and dreams which lead to a deeper understanding of the basic values of all peoples.

World Perspectives is planned to gain insight into the meaning of man, who not only is determined by history but who also determines history. History is to be understood as concerned not only with the life of man on this planet but as including also such cosmic influences as interpenetrate our human world. This generation is discovering that history does not conform to the social optimism of modern civilization and that the organization of human communities and the establishment of freedom and peace are not only intellectual achievements but spiritual and moral achievements as well, demanding a cherishing of the wholeness of human personality, the "unmediated wholeness of feeling and thought," and constituting a never-ending challenge to man, emerging from the abyss of meaninglessness and suffering, to be renewed and replenished in the totality of his life.

Justice itself, which has been "in a state of pilgrimage and crucifixion" and now is being slowly liberated from the grip of social and political demonologies in the East as well as in the West, begins to question its own premises. The modern revolutionary movements which have challenged the sacred institutions of society by protecting injustice in the name of social justice are here examined and re-evaluated.

In the light of this, we have no choice but to admit that the *un*freedom against which freedom is measured must be retained with it, namely, that the aspect of truth out of which the night view appears to emerge, the darkness of our time, is as little abandonable as is man's subjective advance. Thus the two sources of man's consciousness are inseparable, not as dead but as living and complementary, an aspect of that "principle of complementarity" through which Niels Bohr has sought to unite the quantum and the wave, both of which constitute the very fabric of life's radiant energy.

There is in mankind today a counterforce to the sterility and danger of a quantitative, anonymous mass culture; a new, if sometimes imperceptible, spiritual sense of convergence toward human and world unity on the basis of the sacredness of each human person and respect for the plurality of cultures. There is a growing awareness that equality may not be evaluated in mere numerical terms but is proportionate and analogical in its reality. For when equality is equated with interchangeability, individuality is negated and the human person transmuted into a faceless mask.

We stand at the brink of an age of a world in which human life presses forward to actualize new forms. The false separation of man and nature, of time and space, of freedom and security, is acknowledged, and we are faced with a new vision of man in his organic unity and of history offering a richness and diversity of equality and majesty of scope hitherto unprecedented. In relating the accumulated wisdom of man's spirit to the new reality of the World Age, in articulating its thought and belief, *World Perspectives* seeks to encourage a renaissance of hope in society and of pride in man's decision as to what his destiny will be.

Man has certainly contrived to change the environment, but subject to the new processes involved in this change, the same process of selection continues to operate. The environment has changed partly in a physical and geographical sense, but more particularly from the knowledge we now possess. The Biblical story of Adam and Eve contains a deep lesson, which a casual reading hardly reveals. Once the "fruit of the Tree of Knowledge" has been eaten, the world is changed. The new world is dictated by the knowledge itself, not of course by an edict of God. The Biblical story has further interest in that the new world is said to be much worse than the former idyllic state of ignorance. Today we are beginning to wonder whether this might not also be true. Yet we are uneasy, apprehensive, and our fears lead to the collapse of civilizations. Thus we turn to the truth that knowledge and life are indivisible, even as life and death are inseparable. We *are* what we know and think and feel; we are linked with history, with the world, with the universe, and faith in *Life* creates its own verification.

World Perspectives is committed to the recognition that all great changes are preceded by a vigorous intellectual re-evaluation and reorganization. Our authors are aware that the

sin of *hubris* may be avoided by showing that the creative
process itself is not a free activity if by free we mean arbitrary,
or unrelated to cosmic law. For the creative process in the
human mind, the developmental process in organic nature
and the basic laws of the inorganic realm may be but varied
expressions of a universal formative process. Thus *World Perspectives* hopes to show that although the present apocalyptic
period is one of exceptional tensions, there is also at work an
exceptional movement toward a compensating unity which
refuses to violate the ultimate moral power at work in the
universe, that very power upon which all human effort must
at last depend. In this way we may come to understand that
there exists an inherent interdependence of spiritual and
mental growth which, though conditioned by circumstances,
is never determined by circumstances. In this way the great
plethora of human knowledge may be correlated with an insight into the nature of human nature by being attuned to the
wide and deep range of human thought and human experience.

Incoherence is the result of the present disintegrative processes in education. Thus the need for *World Perspectives* expresses itself in the recognition that natural and man-made
ecological systems require as much study as isolated particles
and elementary reactions. For there is a basic correlation of
elements in nature as in man which cannot be separated,
which compose each other and alter each other mutually.
Thus we hope to widen appropriately our conceptual framework of reference. For our epistemological problem consists
in our finding the proper balance between our lack of an
all-embracing principle relevant to our way of evaluating life
and in our power to express ourselves in a logically consistent
manner.

Our Judeo-Christian and Greco-Roman heritage, our Hel-
lenic tradition, has compelled us to think in exclusive categories. But our *experience* challenges us to recognize a totality
richer and far more complex than the average observer could

have suspected—a totality which compels him to think in ways which the logic of dichotomies denies. We are summoned to revise fundamentally our ordinary ways of conceiving experience, and thus, by expanding our vision and by accepting those forms of thought which also include nonexclusive categories, the mind is then able to grasp what it was incapable of grasping or accepting before.

Nature operates out of necessity; there is no alternative in nature, no will, no freedom, no choice as there is for man. Man must have convictions and values to live for, and this also is recognized and accepted by those scientists who are at the same time philosophers. For they then realize that duty and devotion to our task, be it a task of acting or of understanding, will become weaker and rarer unless guidance is sought in a metaphysics that transcends our historical and scientific views or in a religion that transcends and yet pervades the work we are carrying on in the light of day.

For the nature of knowledge, whether scientific or ontological, consists in reconciling *meaning* and *being*. And *being* signifies nothing other than the actualization of potentiality, self-realization which keeps in tune with the transformation. This leads to experience in terms of the individual; and to organization and patterning in terms of the universe. Thus organism and world actualize themselves simultaneously.

And so we may conclude that organism is *being* enduring in time, in fact in eternal time, since it does not have its beginning with procreation, nor with birth, nor does it end with death. Energy and matter in whatever form they may manifest themselves are transtemporal and transspatial and are therefore metaphysical. Man as man is summoned to know what is right and what is wrong, for emptied of such knowledge he is unable to decide what is better or what is worse.

World Perspectives hopes to show that human society is different from animal societies, which, having reached a certain stage, are no longer progressive but are dominated by routine and repetition. Thus man has discovered his own nature, and with this self-knowledge he has left the state of nonage and entered manhood. For he is the only creature who is able to say not only "no" to life but "yes" and to make for himself a life that is human. In this decision lie his burden and his greatness. For the power of life or death lies not only in the tongue but in man's recently acquired ability to destroy or to create life itself, and therefore he is faced with unlimited and unprecedented choices for good and for evil that dominate our time. Our common concern is the very destiny of the human race. For man has now intervened in the process of evolution, a power not given to the pre-Socratics, nor to Aristotle, nor to the Prophets in the East or the West, nor to Copernicus, nor to Luther, Descartes, or Machiavelli. Judgments of value must henceforth direct technological change, for without such values man is divested of his humanity and of his need to collaborate with the very fabric of the universe in order to bestow meaning, purpose, and dignity upon his existence. No time must be lost since the wavelength of change is now shorter than the life-span of man.

In spite of the infinite obligation of men and in spite of their finite power, in spite of the intransigence of nationalisms, and in spite of the homelessness of moral passions rendered ineffectual by the technological outlook, beneath the apparent turmoil and upheaval of the present, and out of the transformations of this dynamic period with the unfolding of a world-consciousness, the purpose of *World Perspectives* is to help quicken the "unshaken heart of well-rounded truth" and interpret the significant elements of the World Age now taking shape out of the core of that undimmed continuity of the creative process which restores man to mankind while deepening and enhancing his communion and his symbiotic relationship with the universe.

RUTH NANDA ANSHEN

The Way to do is to be.

LAO-TSE

People should not consider so much what they are to *do*, as what they *are*.

MASTER ECKHART

The less you *are* and the less you express of your life—the more you *have* and the greater is your alienated life.

KARL MARX

Foreword

This book follows two trends of my previous writings. First, it extends the development of my work in radical-humanistic psychoanalysis, concentrating on the analysis of selfishness and altruism as two basic character orientations. The last third of the book, Part Three, then carries further a theme I dealt with in *The Sane Society* and *The Revolution of Hope:* the crisis of contemporary society and possibilities for its solution. Repetitions of previously expressed thoughts have been unavoidable, but I hope the new viewpoint from which this small work is written and its extended concepts will compensate even readers who are familiar with my previous writings.

Actually, the title of this book and two earlier titles are almost identical: Gabriel Marcel, *Being and Having,* and Balthasar Staehelin, *Haben und Sein* (Having and Being). All three books are written in the spirit of humanism, but approach the subject in very different ways: Marcel writes from a theological and philosophical standpoint; Staehelin's book is a constructive discussion of materialism in modern science and a contribution to *Wirklichkeitsanalyse;* this volume deals with an empirical psychological and social analysis of the two modes of existence. I recommend the books by Marcel and Staehelin to readers who are sufficiently interested in the topic. (I did not know of the existence of a published English translation of Marcel's book until recently and read it instead in an excellent English translation prepared for my private use by Beverley Hughes. The published version is the one cited in the Bibliography.)

In the interest of a making this a more readable book, its footnotes were reduced to a bare minimum, both in number and in length. While some book references appear in parentheses in the text, exact references are to be found in the Bibliography.

Another point of style that I want to clarify concerns the use of generic "man" and "he." I believe I have avoided all "male-oriented" language, and I thank Marion Odomirok for convincing me that the use of language in this respect is far more important than I used to think. On one point only have we been unable to agree in our approach to sexism in language, namely in respect to the word "man" as the term of reference for the species *Homo sapiens.* The use of "man" in this context, without differentiation of sex, has a long tradition in humanist thinking, and I do not believe we can do without a word that denotes clearly the human species character. No such difficulty exists in the German language: one uses the word *Mensch* to refer to the nonsex-differentiated being. But even in English the word "man" is used in the same sex-undifferentiated way as the German *Mensch,* as meaning human being or the human race. I think it is advisable to restore its nonsexual meaning to the word "man," rather than substituting awkward-sounding words. In this book I have capitalized "Man" in order to clarify my nonsex-differentiated use of the term.

There remains now only the pleasant task of expressing my thanks to the several persons who have contributed to the content and style of this book. First of all, I want to thank Rainer Funk, who was of great help to me in more than one respect: in long discussions he helped my understanding of fine points of Christian theology; he was untiring in pointing to literature in the field of theology; he read the manuscript several times and his excellent constructive suggestions as well as his critique helped greatly to enrich the manuscript and to eliminate some errors. I am most grateful to Marion Odomirok for greatly improving this book by her sensitive editing. My thanks also go to Joan Hughes, who conscientiously and patiently typed and retyped the numerous versions of the manuscript and made many excellent suggestions as to style and language. Finally, I thank Annis Fromm, who read the manuscript in its several versions and always responded with many valuable insights and suggestions.

E.F.

New York
June 1976

Introduction: The Great Promise, Its Failure, and New Alternatives

The End of an Illusion

The Great Promise of Unlimited Progress—the promise of domination of nature, of material abundance, of the greatest happiness for the greatest number, and of unimpeded personal freedom—has sustained the hopes and faith of the generations since the beginning of the industrial age. To be sure, our civilization began when the human race started taking active control of nature; but that control remained limited until the advent of the industrial age. With industrial progress, from the substitution of mechanical and then nuclear energy for animal and human energy to the substitution of the computer for the human mind, we could feel that we were on our way to unlimited production and, hence, unlimited consumption; that technique made us omnipotent; that science made us omniscient. We were on our way to becoming gods, supreme beings who could create a second world, using the natural world only as building blocks for our new creation.

Men and, increasingly, women experienced a new sense of freedom; they became masters of their own lives: feudal chains had been broken and one could do what one wished, free of every shackle. Or so people felt. And even though this was true only for the upper and middle classes, their achievement could lead others to the faith that eventually the new freedom could be extended to all members of society, provided industrialization kept up its pace. Socialism and communism quickly changed from a movement whose aim was a *new* society and a *new* man into one whose ideal was a bourgeois life for all, the *universalized bourgeois* as the men and women of the future. The achievement of wealth and comfort for all was supposed to result in unrestricted happiness for all. The trinity of unlimited production, absolute freedom, and unrestricted happiness formed the nucleus of a new religion, Progress, and a new Earthly City of Progress was to replace the City of God. It is not at all astonishing that this new religion provided its believers with energy, vitality, and hope.

The grandeur of the Great Promise, the marvelous material and intellectual achievements of the industrial age, must be visualized in order to understand the trauma that realization of its failure is producing today. For the industrial age has indeed failed to fulfill its Great Promise, and ever growing numbers of people are becoming aware that:

• Unrestricted satisfaction of all desires is not conducive to *well-being,* nor is it the way to happiness or even to maximum pleasure.

• The dream of being independent masters of our lives ended when we began awakening to the fact that we have all become cogs in the bureaucratic machine, with our thoughts, feelings, and tastes manipulated by government and industry and the mass communications that they control.

• Economic progress has remained restricted to the rich nations, and the gap between rich and poor nations has ever widened.

• Technical progress itself has created ecological dangers and the dangers of nuclear war, either or both of which may put an end to all civilization and possibly to all life.

When he came to Oslo to accept the Nobel Prize for Peace

(1952), Albert Schweitzer challenged the world "to dare to face the situation. . . . Man has become a superman. . . . But the superman with the superhuman power has not risen to the level of superhuman reason. To the degree to which his power grows he becomes more and more a poor man. . . . It must shake up our conscience that we become all the more inhuman the more we grow into supermen."

Why Did the Great Promise Fail?

The failure of the Great Promise, aside from industrialism's essential economic contradictions, was built into the industrial system by its two main psychological premises: (1) that the aim of life is happiness, that is, maximum pleasure, defined as the satisfaction of any desire or subjective need a person may feel *(radical hedonism)*; (2) that egotism, selfishness, and greed, as the system needs to generate them in order to function, lead to harmony and peace.

It is well known that the rich throughout history practiced radical hedonism. Those of unlimited means, such as the elite of Rome, of Italian cities of the Renaissance, and of England and France in the eighteenth and nineteenth centuries, tried to find a meaning to life in unlimited pleasure. But while maximum pleasure in the sense of radical hedonism was the practice of certain groups at certain times, with but a single exception prior to the seventeenth century, it was never the *theory* of well-being expressed by the great Masters of Living in China, India, the Near East, and Europe.

The one exception is the Greek philosopher Aristippus, a pupil of Socrates (first half of the fourth century B.C.), who taught that to experience an optimum of bodily pleasure is the goal of life and that happiness is the sum total of pleasures enjoyed. The little we know of his philosophy we owe to Diogenes Laertius, but it is enough to reveal Aristippus as the only real hedonist, for whom the existence of a desire is the

basis for the right to satisfy it and thus to realize the goal of
life: Pleasure.

Epicurus can hardly be regarded as representative of Aristippus' kind of hedonism. While for Epicurus "pure" pleasure
is the highest goal, for him this pleasure meant "absence of
pain" *(aponia)* and stillness of the soul *(ataraxia)*. According
to Epicurus, pleasure as satisfaction of a desire cannot be the
aim of life, because such pleasure is necessarily followed by
unpleasure and thus keeps humanity away from its real goal
of absence of pain. (Epicurus' theory resembles Freud's in
many ways.) Nevertheless, it seems that Epicurus represented
a certain kind of subjectivism contrary to Aristotle's position,
as far as the contradictory reports on Epicurus' statement
permit a definite interpretation.

None of the other great Masters taught that the *factual
existence of a desire constituted an ethical norm.* They were concerned with humankind's optimal well-being *(vivere bene).* The
essential element in their thinking is the distinction between
those needs (desires) that are only subjectively felt and whose
satisfaction leads to momentary pleasure, and those needs
that are rooted in human nature and whose realization is
conducive to human growth and produces *eudaimonia,* i.e.,
"well-being." In other words, they were concerned with *the
distinction between purely subjectively felt needs and objectively valid
needs*—part of the former being harmful to human growth and
the latter being in accordance with the requirements of human nature.

The theory that the aim of life is the fulfillment of every
human desire was clearly voiced, for the first time since Aristippus, by philosophers in the seventeenth and eighteenth
centuries. It was a concept that would easily arise when
"profit" ceased to mean "profit for the soul" (as it does in the
Bible and, even later, in Spinoza), but came to mean material,
monetary profit, in the period when the middle class threw
away not only its political shackles but also all bonds of love
and solidarity and believed that being *only* for oneself meant

being more rather than less oneself. For Hobbes happiness is the continuous progress from one greed *(cupiditas)* to another; La Mettrie even recommends drugs as giving at least the illusion of happiness; for de Sade the satisfaction of cruel impulses is legitimate, precisely because they exist and crave satisfaction. These were thinkers who lived in the age of the bourgeois class's final victory. What had been the unphilosophical practices of aristocrats became the practice and theory of the bourgeoisie.

Many ethical theories have been developed since the eighteenth century—some were more respectable forms of hedonism, such as Utilitarianism; others were strictly antihedonistic systems, such as those of Kant, Marx, Thoreau, and Schweitzer. Yet the present era, by and large since the end of the First World War, has returned to the practice and theory of radical hedonism. The concept of unlimited pleasure forms a strange contradiction to the ideal of disciplined work, similar to the contradiction between the acceptance of an obsessional work ethic and the ideal of complete laziness during the rest of the day and during vacations. The endless assembly line belt and the bureaucratic routine on the one hand, and television, the automobile, and sex on the other, make the contradictory combination possible. Obsessional work alone would drive people just as crazy as would complete laziness. With the combination, they can live. Besides, both contradictory attitudes correspond to an economic necessity: twentieth-century capitalism is based on maximal consumption of the goods and services produced as well as on routinized teamwork.

Theoretical considerations demonstrate that radical hedonism cannot lead to happiness as well as why it cannot do so, given human nature. But even without theoretical analysis the observable data show most clearly that our kind of "pursuit of happiness" does not produce well-being. We are a society of notoriously unhappy people: lonely, anxious, depressed, destructive, dependent—people who are glad when we have killed the time we are trying so hard to save.

Ours is the greatest social experiment ever made to solve the question whether pleasure (as a passive affect in contrast to the active affect, well-being and joy) can be a satisfactory answer to the problem of human existence. For the first time in history the satisfaction of the pleasure drive is not only the privilege of a minority but is possible for more than half the population. The experiment has already answered the question in the negative.

The second psychological premise of the industrial age, that the pursuit of individual egoism leads to harmony and peace, growth in everyone's welfare, is equally erroneous on theoretical grounds, and again its fallacy is proven by the observable data. Why should this principle, which only one of the great classical economists, David Ricardo, rejected, be true? To be an egoist refers not only to my behavior but to my character. It means: that I want everything for myself; that possessing, not sharing, gives me pleasure; that I must become greedy because if my aim is having, I *am* more the more I *have;* that I must feel antagonistic toward all others: my customers whom I want to deceive, my competitors whom I want to destroy, my workers whom I want to exploit. I can never be satisfied, because there is no end to my wishes; I must be envious of those who have more and afraid of those who have less. But I have to repress all these feelings in order to represent myself (to others as well as to myself) as the smiling, rational, sincere, kind human being everybody pretends to be.

The passion for having must lead to never-ending class war. The pretense of the communists that their system will end class struggle by abolishing classes is fiction, for their system is based on the principle of unlimited consumption as the goal of living. As long as everybody wants to have more, there must be formations of classes, there must be class war, and in global terms, there must be international war. *Greed and peace preclude each other.*

Radical hedonism and unlimited egotism could not have

emerged as guiding principles of economic behavior had not a drastic change occurred in the eighteenth century. In medieval society, as in many other highly developed as well as primitive societies, economic behavior was determined by ethical principles. Thus, for the scholastic theologians, such economic categories as price and private property were part of moral theology. Granted that the theologians found formulations to adapt their moral code to the new economic demands (for instance Thomas Aquinas' qualification to the concept of "just price"); nevertheless, economic behavior remained *human* behavior and, hence, was subject to the values of humanistic ethics. Through a number of steps eighteenth-century capitalism underwent a radical change: economic behavior became separate from ethics and human values. Indeed, the economic machine was supposed to be an autonomous entity, independent of human needs and human will. It was a system that ran by itself and according to its own laws. The suffering of the workers as well as the destruction of an ever-increasing number of smaller enterprises for the sake of the growth of ever larger corporations was an economic necessity that one might regret, but that one had to accept as if it were the outcome of a natural law.

The development of this economic system was no longer determined by the question: *What is good for Man?* but by the question: *What is good for the growth of the system?* One tried to hide the sharpness of this conflict by making the assumption that what was good for the growth of the system (or even for a single big corporation) was also good for the people. This construction was bolstered by an auxiliary construction: that the very qualities that the system required of human beings —egotism, selfishness, and greed—were innate in human nature; hence, not only the system but human nature itself fostered them. Societies in which egotism, selfishness, and greed did not exist were supposed to be "primitive," their inhabitants "childlike." People refused to recognize that these traits were not natural drives that caused industrial society to exist, but that they were the *products* of social circumstances.

Not least in importance is another factor: people's relation to nature became deeply hostile. Being "freaks of nature" who by the very conditions of our existence are within nature and by the gift of our reason transcend it, we have tried to solve our existential problem by giving up the Messianic vision of harmony between humankind and nature by conquering nature, by transforming it to our own purposes until the conquest has become more and more equivalent to destruction. Our spirit of conquest and hostility has blinded us to the facts that natural resources have their limits and can eventually be exhausted, and that nature will fight back against human rapaciousness.

Industrial society has contempt for nature—as well as for all things not machine-made and for all people who are not machine makers (the nonwhite races, with the recent exceptions of Japan and China). People are attracted today to the mechanical, the powerful machine, the lifeless, and ever increasingly to destruction.

The Economic Necessity for Human Change

Thus far the argument here has been that the character traits engendered by our socioeconomic system, i.e., by our way of living, are pathogenic and eventually produce a sick person and, thus, a sick society. There is, however, a second argument from an entirely different viewpoint in favor of profound psychological changes in Man as an alternative to economic and ecological catastrophe. It is raised in two reports commissioned by the Club of Rome, one by D. H. Meadows et al., the other by M. D. Mesarovic and E. Pestel. Both reports deal with the technological, economic, and population trends on a world scale. Mesarovic and Pestel conclude that only drastic economic and technological changes on a global level, according to a master plan, can "avoid major and ultimately global catastrophe," and the data they array as proof of their thesis are based on the most global and systematic research that has been made so far. (Their book has certain methodological advantages over Meadows's report, but that earlier study considers even more drastic economic changes as an alternative to catastrophe.) Mesarovic and Pestel conclude, furthermore, that such economic changes are possible only *"if fundamental changes in the values and attitudes of man occur* [or as I would call it, in human character orientation], *such as a new ethic and a new attitude toward nature"* (emphasis added). What they are saying confirms only what others have said before and since their report was published, that a new society is possible *only if,* in the process of developing it, a new human being also develops, or in more modest terms, if a fundamental change occurs in contemporary Man's character structure.

Unfortunately, the two reports are written in the spirit of quantification, abstraction, and depersonalization so characteristic of our time, and besides that, they neglect completely all political and social factors, without which no realistic plan can possibly be made. Yet they present valuable data, and for the first time deal with the economic situation of the human race as a whole, its possibilities and its dangers. Their conclusion, that a new ethic and a new attitude toward nature are necessary, is all the more valuable because this demand is so contrary to their philosophical premises.

At the other end of the gamut stands E. F. Schumacher, who is also an economist, but at the same time a radical humanist. His demand for a radical human change is based on two arguments: that our present social order makes us sick, and that we are headed for an economic catastrophe unless we radically change our social system.

The need for profound human change emerges not only as an ethical or religious demand, not only as a psychological demand arising from the pathogenic nature of our present social character, but also as a condition for the sheer survival of the human race. Right living is no longer only the fulfillment of an ethical or religious demand. For the first time in history the *physical survival of the human race depends on a radical change of the human heart.* However, a change of the human heart is possible only to the extent that drastic economic and social changes occur that give the human heart the chance for change and the courage and the vision to achieve it.

Is There an Alternative to Catastrophe?

All the data mentioned so far are published and well known. The almost unbelievable fact is that no serious effort is made to avert what looks like a final decree of fate. While in our private life nobody except a mad person would remain passive in view of a threat to our total existence, those who are in charge of public affairs do practically nothing, and those who have entrusted their fate to them let them continue to do nothing.

How is it possible that the strongest of all instincts, that for survival, seems to have ceased to motivate us? One of the most obvious explanations is that the leaders undertake many actions that make it possible for them to pretend they are doing something effective to avoid a catastrophe: endless conferences, resolutions, disarmament talks, all give the impression that the problems are recognized and something is being done to resolve them. Yet nothing of real importance happens; but both the leaders and the led anesthetize their consciences and their wish for survival by giving the appearance of knowing the road and marching in the right direction.

Another explanation is that the selfishness the system generates makes leaders value personal success more highly than social responsibility. It is no longer shocking when political leaders and business executives make decisions that seem to be to their personal advantage, but at the same time are harmful and dangerous to the community. Indeed, if selfishness is one of the pillars of contemporary practical ethics, why should they act otherwise? They do not seem to know that greed (like submission) makes people stupid as far as the pursuit of even their own real interests is concerned, such as their interest in their own lives and in the lives of their spouses and their children (cf. J. Piaget, *The Moral Judgment of the Child*). At the same time, the general public is also so selfishly concerned with their private affairs that they pay little attention to all that transcends the personal realm.

Yet another explanation for the deadening of our survival instinct is that the changes in living that would be required are so drastic that people prefer the future catastrophe to the sacrifice they would have to make now. Arthur Koestler's description of an experience he had during the Spanish Civil War is a telling example of this widespread attitude: Koestler sat in the comfortable villa of a friend while the advance of Franco's troops was reported; there was no doubt that they would arrive during the night, and very likely he would be shot; he could save his life by fleeing, but the night was cold and rainy, the house, warm and cozy; so he stayed, was taken prisoner, and only by almost a miracle was his life saved many weeks later by the efforts of friendly journalists. This is also the kind of behavior that occurs in people who will risk dying rather than undergo an examination that could lead to the diagnosis of a grave illness requiring major surgery.

Aside from these explanations for fatal human passivity in matters of life and death, there is another, which is one of my reasons for writing this book. I refer to the view that we have no alternatives to the models of corporate capitalism, social democratic or Soviet socialism, or technocratic "fascism with a smiling face." The popularity of this view is largely due to the fact that little effort has been made to study the feasibility of entirely new social models and to experiment with them. Indeed, as long as the problems of social reconstruction will not, even if only partly, take the place of the preoccupation of our best minds with science and technique, the imagination will be lacking to visualize new and realistic alternatives.

The main thrust of this book is the analysis of the two basic modes of existence: the *mode of having* and the *mode of being.* In the opening chapter I present some "first glance" observations concerning the difference between the two modes. The second chapter demonstrates the difference, using a number of examples from daily experience that readers can easily relate to in their own personal experience. Chapter III presents the views on having and being in the Old and the New Testaments and in the writings of Master Eckhart. Subsequent chapters deal with the most difficult issue: the analysis of the difference between the having and the being modes of existence in which I attempt to build theoretical conclusions on the basis of the empirical data. While up to this point the book mainly concerns the individual aspects of the two basic modes of existence, the final chapters deal with the relevance of these modes in the formation of a New Man and a New Society and address themselves to the possibilities of alternatives to debilitating individual ill-being, and to catastrophic socioeconomic development of the whole world.

PART ONE

UNDERSTANDING THE DIFFERENCE BETWEEN HAVING AND BEING

I

A First Glance

The Importance of the Difference Between Having and Being

The alternative of *having* versus *being* does not appeal to common sense. *To have,* so it would seem, is a normal function of our life: in order to live we must have things. Moreover, we must have things in order to enjoy them. In a culture in which the supreme goal is to have—and to have more and more—and in which one can speak of someone as "being worth a million dollars," how can there be an alternative between having and being? On the contrary, it would seem that the very essence of being is having; that if one *has* nothing, one *is* nothing.

Yet the great Masters of Living have made the alternative between having and being a central issue of their respective systems. The Buddha teaches that in order to arrive at the highest stage of human development, we must not crave possessions. Jesus teaches: "For whosoever will save his life shall lose it; but whosoever will lose his life for my sake, the same shall save it. For what is a man advantaged, if he gain the whole world, and lose himself, or be cast away?" (Luke 9:24–25). Master Eckhart taught that to have nothing and make oneself open and "empty," not to let one's ego stand in one's way, is the condition for achieving spiritual wealth and strength. Marx taught that luxury is as much a vice as poverty and that our goal should be to *be* much, not to *have* much. (I refer here to the real Marx, the radical humanist, not to the vulgar forgery presented by Soviet communism.)

For many years I had been deeply impressed by this distinction and was seeking its empirical basis in the concrete study of individuals and groups by the psychoanalytic method. What I saw has led me to conclude that this distinction, together with that between love of life and love of the dead, represents the most crucial problem of existence; that empirical anthropological and psychoanalytic data tend to demonstrate that *having and being are two fundamental modes of experience, the respective strengths of which determine the differences between the characters of individuals and various types of social character.*

Examples in Various Poetic Expressions

As an introduction to understanding the difference between the having and being modes of existence, let me use as an illustration two poems of similar content that the late D.T. Suzuki referred to in "Lectures on Zen Buddhism." One is a haiku by a Japanese poet, Basho, 1644–1694; the other poem is by a nineteenth-century English poet, Tennyson. Each poet describes a similar experience: his reaction to a flower he sees while taking a walk. Tennyson's verse is:

> Flower in a crannied wall,
> I pluck you out of the crannies,
> I hold you here, root and all, in my hand,
> Little flower—but *if* I could understand
> What you are, root and all, and all in all,
> I should know what God and man is.

Translated into English, Basho's haiku runs something like this:

> When I look carefully
> I see the *nazuna* blooming
> By the hedge!

The difference is striking. Tennyson reacts to the flower by wanting to *have* it. He "plucks" it "root and all." And while he ends with an intellectual speculation about the flower's possible function for his attaining insight into the nature of God and man, the flower itself is killed as a result of his interest in it. Tennyson, as we see him in his poem, may be compared to the Western scientist who seeks the truth by means of dismembering life.

Basho's reaction to the flower is entirely different. He does not want to pluck it; he does not even touch it. All he does is "look carefully" to "see" it. Here is Suzuki's description:

> It is likely that Basho was walking along a country road when he noticed something rather neglected by the hedge. He then approached closer, took a good look at it, and found it was no less than a wild plant, rather insignificant and generally unnoticed by passersby. This is a plain fact described in the poem with no specifically poetic feeling expressed anywhere except perhaps in the last two syllables, which read in Japanese *kana*. This particle, frequently attached to a noun or an adjective or an adverb, signifies a certain feeling of admiration or praise or sorrow or joy, and can sometimes quite appropriately be rendered into English by an exclamation mark. In the present *haiku* the whole verse ends with this mark.

Tennyson, it appears, needs to possess the flower in order to understand people and nature, and by his *having* it, the flower is destroyed. What Basho wants is to *see,* and not only to look at the flower, but to be at one, to "one" himself with it—and to let it live. The difference between Tennyson and Basho is fully explained in this poem by Goethe:

FOUND

I walked in the woods
All by myself,

To seek nothing,
That was on my mind.

I saw in the shade
A little flower stand,
Bright like the stars
Like beautiful eyes.

I wanted to pluck it,
But it said sweetly:
Is it to wilt
That I must be broken?

I took it out
With all its roots,
Carried it to the garden
At the pretty house.

And planted it again
In a quiet place;
Now it ever spreads
And blossoms forth.

Goethe, walking with no purpose in mind, is attracted by the brilliant little flower. He reports having the same impulse as Tennyson: to pluck it. But unlike Tennyson, Goethe is aware that this means killing the flower. For Goethe the flower is so much alive that it speaks and warns him; and he solves the problem differently from either Tennyson or Basho. He takes the flower "with all its roots" and plants it again so that its life is not destroyed. Goethe stands, as it were, between Tennyson and Basho: for him, at the crucial moment, the force of life is stronger than the force of mere intellectual curiosity. Needless to say that in this beautiful poem Goethe expresses the core of his concept of investigating nature.

Tennyson's relationship to the flower is in the mode of having, or possession—not material possession but the possession of knowledge. Basho's and Goethe's relationship to the flower each sees is in the mode of being. By being I refer to the mode of existence in which one neither *has* anything nor *craves to have* something, but is joyous, employs one's faculties productively, is *oned* to the world.

Goethe, the great lover of life, one of the outstanding fighters against human dismemberment and mechanization, has given expression to being as against having in many poems. His Faust is a dramatic description of the conflict between being and having (the latter represented by Mephistopheles), while in the following short poem he expresses the quality of being with the utmost simplicity:

PROPERTY

I know that nothing belongs to me
But the thought which unimpeded
From my soul will flow.
And every favorable moment
Which loving Fate
From the depth lets me enjoy.

The difference between being and having is not essentially that between East and West. The difference is rather between a society centered around persons and one centered around things. The having orientation is characteristic of Western industrial society, in which greed for money, fame, and power has become the dominant theme of life. Less alienated societies—such as medieval society, the Zuni Indians, the African tribal societies that were not affected by the ideas of modern "progress"—have their own Bashos. Perhaps after a few more generations of industrialization, the Japanese will have their Tennysons. It is not that Western Man cannot fully understand Eastern systems, such as Zen Buddhism (as Jung thought), but that modern Man cannot understand the spirit of a society that is not centered in property and greed. Indeed, the writings of Master Eckhart (as difficult to understand as Basho or Zen) and the Buddha's writings are only two dialects of the same language.

Idiomatic Changes

A certain change in the emphasis on having and being is apparent in the growing use of nouns and the decreasing use of verbs in Western languages in the past few centuries.

A noun is the proper denotation for a thing. I can say that I *have* things: for instance that I have a table, a house, a book, a car. The proper denotation for an activity, a process, is a verb: for instance I am, I love, I desire, I hate, etc. Yet ever more frequently an *activity* is expressed in terms of *having;* that is, a noun is used instead of a verb. But to express an activity by *to have* in connection with a noun is an erroneous use of language, because processes and activities cannot be possessed; they can only be experienced.

Older Observations: Du Marais—Marx

The evil consequences of this confusion were already recognized in the eighteenth century. Du Marais gave a very precise expression of the problem in his posthumously published work *Les Veritables Principes de la Grammaire* (1769). He writes: "In this example, *I have a watch, I have* must be understood in its proper sense; but in *I have an idea, I have* is said only by way of imitation. It is a borrowed expression. *I have an idea* means *I think, I conceive of in such and such a way. I have a longing* means *I desire; I have the will* means *I want,* etc." (my translation; I am indebted to Dr. Noam Chomsky for the reference to Du Marais).

A century after Du Marais observed this phenomenon of the substitution of nouns for verbs Marx and Engels deal with the same problem, but in a more radical fashion, in *The Holy Family.* Included in their critique of Edgar Bauer's "critical critique" is a small, but very important essay on love in which reference is made to the following statement by Bauer: "Love is a cruel goddess, who like all deities, wants to possess the whole man and who is not content until he has sacrificed to her not only his soul but also his physical self. Her cult is suffering; the peak of this cult is self-sacrifice, is suicide" (my translation).

Marx and Engels answer: Bauer "transforms love into a 'goddess,' and into a 'cruel goddess' by transforming the *loving man* or the *love of man* into the *man of love;* he thus separates love as a separate being from man and makes it an independent entity" (my translation). Marx and Engels point here to the decisive factor in the use of the noun instead of the verb. The noun "love," which is only an abstraction for the activity of loving, becomes separated from the man. The loving man becomes the man of love. Love becomes a goddess, an idol into which the man projects his loving; in this process of alienation he ceases to experience love, but is in touch only with his capacity to love by his submission to the goddess Love. He has ceased to be an active person who feels; instead he has become an alienated worshiper of an idol, and he is lost when out of touch with his idol.

Contemporary Usage

During the two hundred years since Du Marais, this trend of the substitution of nouns for verbs has grown to proportions that even he could hardly have imagined. Here is a typical, if slightly exaggerated, example of today's language. Assume that a person seeking a psychoanalyst's help opens the conversation with the following sentence: "Doctor, I *have* a problem; I *have* insomnia. Although I *have* a beautiful house, nice children, and a happy marriage, I *have* many worries." Some decades ago, instead of "I have a problem," the patient probably would have said, "I *am* troubled"; instead of "I *have* insomnia," "I *cannot* sleep"; instead of "I *have* a happy marriage," "I *am* happily married."

The more recent speech style indicates the prevailing high degree of alienation. By saying "I *have* a problem" instead of "I *am* troubled," subjective experience is eliminated: the *I* of

experience is replaced by the *it* of possession. I have transformed my feeling into something I possess: the problem. But
"problem" is an abstract expression for all kinds of difficulties. I cannot *have* a problem, because it is not a thing that can
be owned; it, however, can have me. That is to say, I have
transformed *myself* into "a problem" and am now owned by
my creation. This way of speaking betrays a hidden, unconscious alienation.

Of course, one can argue that insomnia is a physical symptom like a sore throat or a toothache, and that it is therefore
as legitimate to say that one *has* insomnia as it is to say that
one *has* a sore throat. Yet there is a difference: a sore throat
or a toothache is a bodily sensation that can be more or less
intense, but it has little psychical quality. One can *have* a sore
throat, for one has a throat, or an aching tooth, for one has
teeth. Insomnia, on the contrary, is not a bodily sensation but
a state of mind, that of not being able to sleep. If I speak of
"having insomnia" instead of saying "I cannot sleep," I betray my wish to push away the experience of anxiety, restlessness, tension that prevents me from sleeping, and to deal with
the mental phenomenon *as if it were* a bodily symptom.

For another example: To say, "I have great love for you,"
is meaningless. Love is not a thing that one can have, but a
process, an inner activity that one is the subject of. I can love,
I can *be* in love, but in loving, I *have* . . . nothing. In fact, the
less I have, the more I can love.

Origin of the Terms

"To have" is a deceptively simple expression. Every human
being *has* something: a body,* clothes, shelter—on up to the
modern man or woman who has a car, a television set, a

*It should be mentioned here, at least in passing, that there also exists a being
relationship to one's body that experiences the body as alive, and that can be expressed by saying "I am my body," rather than "I have my body"; all practices of
sensory awareness attempt this being experience of the body.

washing machine, etc. Living without having something is virtually impossible. Why, then, should having be a problem? Yet the linguistic history of "having" indicates that the word is indeed a problem. To those who believe that to have is a most natural category of human existence it may come as a surprise to learn that many languages have no word for "to have." In Hebrew, for instance, "I have" must be expressed by the indirect form *jesh li* ("it is to me"). In fact, languages that express possession in this way, rather than by "I have," predominate. It is interesting to note that in the development of many languages the construction "it is to me" is followed later on by the construction "I have," but as Emile Benveniste has pointed out, the evolution does not occur in the reverse direction.* This fact suggests that the word for *to have* develops in connection with the development of private property, while it is absent in societies with predominantly functional property, that is, possession for use. Further sociolinguistic studies should be able to show if and to what extent this hypothesis is valid.

If *having* seems to be a relatively simple concept, *being*, or the form "to be," is all the more complicated and difficult. "Being" is used in several different ways: (1) as a copula—such as "I am tall," "I am white," "I am poor," i.e., a grammatical denotation of identity (many languages do not have a word for "to be" in this sense; Spanish distinguishes between permanent qualities, *ser*, which belong to the essence of the subject, and contingent qualities, *estar*, which are not of the essence); (2) as the passive, suffering form of a verb—for example, "I am beaten" means I am the object of another's activity, not the subject of my activity, as in "I beat"; (3) as meaning to exist—wherein, as Benveniste has shown, the "to be" of existence is a different term from "to be" as a copula stating identity: "The two words have coexisted and can still coexist, although they are entirely different."

*The linguistic quotations are taken from Benveniste.

Benveniste's study throws new light on the meaning of "to be" as a verb in its own right rather than as a copula. "To be," in Indo-European languages, is expressed by the root *es*, the meaning of which is "to have existence, to be found in reality." Existence and reality are defined as "that which is authentic, consistent, true." (In Sanskrit, *sant*, "existent," "actual good," "true"; superlative *Sattama*, "the best.") "Being" in its etymological root is thus more than a statement of identity between subject and attribute; it is more than a *descriptive* term for a phenomenon. It denotes the reality of existence of who or what *is;* it states his/her/its authenticity and truth. Stating that somebody or something *is* refers to the person's or the thing's essence, not to his/her/its appearance.

This preliminary survey of the meaning of having and being leads to these conclusions:

1. By being or having I do not refer to certain separate qualities of a subject as illustrated in such statements as "I have a car" or "I am white" or "I am happy." I refer to two fundamental modes of existence, to two different kinds of orientation toward self and the world, to two different kinds of character structure the respective predominance of which determines the totality of a person's thinking, feeling, and acting.

2. In the having mode of existence my relationship to the world is one of possessing and owning, one in which I want to make everybody and everything, including myself, my property.

3. In the being mode of existence, we must identify two forms of being. One is in contrast to *having*, as exemplified in the Du Marais statement, and means aliveness and authentic relatedness to the world. The other form of being is in contrast to *appearing* and refers to the true nature, the true reality, of a person or a thing in contrast to deceptive appearances as exemplified in the etymology of being (Benveniste).

Philosophical Concepts of Being

The discussion of the concept of being is additionally complicated because being has been the subject matter of many thousands of philosophical books and "What is being?" has been one of the crucial questions of Western philosophy. While the concept of being will be treated here from anthropological and psychological points of view, the philosophical discussion is, of course, not unrelated to the anthropological problems. Since even a brief presentation of the development of the concept of being in the history of philosophy from the pre-Socratics to modern philosophy would go beyond the given limits of this book, I shall mention only one crucial point: the concept of *process, activity, and movement as an element in being.* As George Simmel has pointed out, the idea that being implies change, i.e., that being is *becoming,* has its two greatest and most uncompromising representatives at the beginning and at the zenith of Western philosophy: in Heraclitus and in Hegel.

The position that being is a permanent, timeless, and unchangeable substance and the opposite of becoming, as expressed by Parmenides, Plato, and the scholastic "realists," makes sense only on the basis of the idealistic notion that a thought (idea) is the ultimate reality. If the *idea* of love (in Plato's sense) is more real than the experience of loving, one can say that love as an idea is permanent and unchangeable. But when we start out with the reality of human beings existing, loving, hating, suffering, then there is no being that is not at the same time becoming and changing. Living structures can be only if they become; they can exist only if they change. Change and growth are inherent qualities of the life process.

Heraclitus' and Hegel's radical concept of life as a process and not as a substance is paralleled in the Eastern world by the philosophy of the Buddha. There is no room in Buddhist thought for the concept of any enduring permanent substance, neither things nor the self. Nothing is real but processes.* Contemporary scientific thought has brought about a renaissance of the philosophical concepts of "process thinking" by discovering and applying them to the natural sciences.

Having and Consuming

Before discussing some simple illustrations of the having and being modes of existence, another manifestation of having must be mentioned, that of *incorporating*. Incorporating a thing, for instance by eating or drinking, is an archaic form of possessing it. At a certain point in its development an infant tends to take things it wants into its mouth. This is the infant's form of taking possession, when its bodily development does not yet enable it to have other forms of controlling its possessions. We find the same connection between incorporation and possession in many forms of cannibalism. For example: by eating another human being, I acquire that person's powers (thus cannibalism can be the magic equivalent of acquiring slaves); by eating the heart of a brave man, I acquire his courage; by eating a totem animal, I acquire the divine substance the totem animal symbolizes.

Of course, most objects cannot be incorporated physically (and inasmuch as they could, they would be lost again in the process of elimination). But there is also *symbolic* and *magic* incorporation. If I believe I have incorporated a god's, a father's, or an animal's image, it can neither be taken away nor eliminated. I swallow the object symbolically and believe in its symbolic presence within myself. This is, for instance, how Freud explained the superego: the introjected sum total of the father's prohibitions and commands. An authority, an institution, an idea, an image can be introjected in the same way: I

*Z. Fišer, one of the most outstanding, though little-known, Czech philosophers, has related the Buddhist concept of process to authentic Marxian philosophy. Unfortunately, the work has been published only in the Czech language and hence has been inaccessible to most Western readers. (I know it from a private English translation.)

have them, eternally protected in my bowels, as it were. ("Introjection" and "identification" are often used synonymously, but it is difficult to decide whether they are really the same process. At any rate, "identification" should not be used loosely, when one should better talk of imitation or subordination.)

There are many other forms of incorporation that are not connected with physiological needs and, hence, are not limited. The attitude inherent in consumerism is that of swallowing the whole world. The consumer is the eternal suckling crying for the bottle. This is obvious in pathological phenomena, such as alcoholism and drug addiction. We apparently single out both these addictions because their effects interfere with the addicted person's social obligations. Compulsive smoking is not thus censured because, while not less of an addiction, it does not interfere with the smokers' social functions, but possibly "only" with their life spans.

Further attention is given to the many forms of everyday consumerism later on in this volume. I might only remark here that as far as leisure time is concerned, automobiles, television, travel, and sex are the main objects of present-day consumerism, and while we speak of them as leisure-time activities, we would do better to call them leisure-time *passivities.*

To sum up, to consume is one form of having, and perhaps the most important one for today's affluent industrial societies. Consuming has ambiguous qualities: It relieves anxiety, because what one has cannot be taken away; but it also requires one to consume ever more, because previous consumption soon loses its satisfactory character. Modern consumers may identify themselves by the formula: *I am = what I have and what I consume.*

II

Having and Being in Daily Experience

Because the society we live in is devoted to acquiring property and making a profit, we rarely see any evidence of the being mode of existence and most people see the having mode as the most natural mode of existence, even the only acceptable way of life. All of which makes it especially difficult for people to comprehend the nature of the being mode, and even to understand that having is only one possible orientation. Nevertheless, these two concepts are rooted in human experience. Neither one should be, or can be, examined in an abstract, purely cerebral way; both are reflected in our daily life and must be dealt with concretely. The following simple examples of how having and being are demonstrated in everyday life may help readers to understand these two alternative modes of existence

Learning

Students in the having mode of existence will listen to a lecture, hearing the words and understanding their logical structure and their meaning and, as best they can, will write down every word in their looseleaf notebooks—so that, later on, they can memorize their notes and thus pass an examination. But the content does not become part of their own individual system of thought, enriching and widening it. Instead, they transform the words they hear into fixed clusters of thought, or whole theories, which they store up. The students and the content of the lectures remain strangers to each other, except that each student has become the owner of a collection of statements made by somebody else (who had either created them or taken them over from another source).

Students in the having mode have but one aim: to hold onto what they "learned," either by entrusting it firmly to their memories or by carefully guarding their notes. They do not have to produce or create something new. In fact, the *having*-type individuals feel rather disturbed by new thoughts or ideas about a subject, because the new puts into question the fixed sum of information they have. Indeed, to one for whom having is the main form of relatedness to the world, ideas that cannot easily be pinned down (or penned down) are frightening—like everything else that grows and changes, and thus is not controllable.

The process of learning has an entirely different quality for students in the being mode of relatedness *to* the world. To begin with, they do not go to the course lectures, even to the first one in a course, as *tabulae rasae.* They have thought beforehand about the problems the lectures will be dealing with and have in mind certain questions and problems of their own. They have been occupied with the topic and it interests them. Instead of being passive receptacles of words and ideas, they listen, they *hear,* and most important, they *receive* and they *respond* in an active, productive way. What they listen to stimulates their own thinking processes. New questions, new ideas, new perspectives arise in their minds. Their listening is an alive process. They listen with interest, hear what the lecturer says, and spontaneously come to life in response to what they hear. They do not simply acquire knowledge that they can take home and memorize. Each student has been affected and has changed: each is different after the lecture than he or she was before it. Of course, this mode of learning can prevail only if the lecture offers stimulating material. Empty talk cannot be responded to in the being mode, and in such circumstances, students in the being mode find it best not to listen at all, but to concentrate on their own thought processes.

At least a passing reference should be made here to the word "interests," which in current usage has become a pallid, worn-out expression. Yet its essential meaning is contained in its root: Latin, *inter-esse,* "to be in [or] among" it. This active interest was expressed in Middle English by the term "to list" (adjective, listy; adverb, listily). In modern English, "to list" is only used in a spatial sense: "a ship lists"; the original meaning in a psychical sense we have only in the negative "listless." "To list" once meant "to be actively striving for," "to be genuinely interested in." The root is the same as that of "lust," but "to list" is not a lust one is *driven by,* but the *free and active interest in, or striving for.* "To list" is one of the key expressions of the anonymous author (mid-fourteenth century) of *The Cloud of Unknowing* (Evelyn Underhill, ed.). That the language has retained the word only in its negative sense is characteristic of the change of spirit in society from the thirteenth to the twentieth century.

Remembering

Remembering can occur in either the having or the being mode. What matters most for the difference between the two forms of remembering is the *kind* of connection that is made. In the having mode of remembering, the connection is entirely *mechanical,* as when the connection between one word and the next becomes firmly established by the frequency with which it is made. Or the connections may be purely *logical,* such as the connection between opposites, or between converging concepts, or with time, space, size, color, or within a given system of thought.

In the being mode, remembering is *actively* recalling words, ideas, sights, paintings, music; that is, connecting the single datum to be remembered and the many other data that it is connected with. The connections in the case of being are neither mechanical nor purely logical, but alive. One concept is connected with another by a productive act of thinking (or feeling) that is mobilized when one searches for the right word. A simple example: If I associate the word "pain" or "aspirin" with the word "headache," I deal with a logical, conventional association. But if I associate the word "stress" or "anger" with "headache," I connect the given datum with its possible consequences, an insight I have arrived at in studying the phenomenon. This latter type of remembering constitutes in itself an act of productive thinking. The most striking examples of this kind of alive remembering are the "free associations" devised by Freud.

Persons not mainly inclined toward storing up data will find that their memories, in order to function well, need a strong and immediate *interest.* For example, individuals have been known to remember words of a long-forgotten foreign language when it has been of vital importance to do so. And in my own experience, while I am not endowed with a particularly good memory, I have remembered the dream of a person I analyzed, be it two weeks or five years ago, when I again come face to face with and concentrate on the whole personality of that person. Yet not five minutes before, in the cold as it were, I was quite unable to remember that dream.

Remembering in the mode of being implies bringing to life something one saw or heard before. We can experience this productive remembering by trying to envision a person's face or scenery that we had once seen. We will not be able to remember instantly in either case; we must re-create the subject, bring it to life in our mind. This kind of remembering is not always easy; to be able to fully recall the face or the scenery one must once have seen it with sufficient concentration. When such remembering is fully achieved, the person whose face is recalled is as alive, the remembered scenery as vivid, as if that person or that view were actually physically before one.

The way those in the having mode remember a face or scenery is typified by the way most people look at a photograph. The photograph serves only as an aid to their memory in identifying a person or a scene, and the usual reaction it elicits is: "Yes, that's him"; or "Yes, I've been there." The photograph becomes, for most people, an *alienated* memory.

Memory entrusted to paper is another form of alienated remembering. By writing down what I want to remember I am sure to *have* that information, and I do not try to engrave it on my brain. I am sure of my possession—except that when I have lost my notes, I have lost my memory of the information, too. My capacity to remember has left me, for my memory bank had become an externalized part of me, in the form of my notes.

Considering the multitude of data that people in our contemporary society need to remember, a certain amount of notemaking and information deposited in books is unavoidable. But the tendency away from remembering is growing beyond all sensible proportions. One can easily and best observe in oneself that writing down things diminishes one's power of remembering, but some typical examples may prove helpful.

An everyday example occurs in stores. Today a salesclerk will rarely do a simple addition of two or three items in his or her head, but will immediately use a machine. The classroom provides another example. Teachers can observe that the students who carefully write down every sentence of the lecture will, in all likelihood, understand and remember less than the students who trusted their capacity to understand and, hence, remember at least the essentials. Further, musicians know that those who most easily sight-read a score have more difficulty in remembering the music without the score.* (Tos-

*This information was provided by Dr. Moshe Budmor.

canini, whose memory was known to be extraordinary, is a good example of a musician in the being mode.) For a final example, in Mexico I have observed that people who are illiterate or who write little have memories far superior to the fluently literate inhabitants of the industrialized countries. Among other facts, this suggests that literacy is by no means the blessing it is advertised to be, especially when people use it merely to read material that impoverishes their capacity to experience and to imagine.

Conversing

The difference between the having and being modes can be easily observed in two examples of conversations. Let us take a typical conversational debate between two men in which A *has* opinion X and B *has* opinion Y. Each identifies with his own opinion. What matters to each is to find better, i.e., more reasonable, arguments to defend his opinion. Neither expects to change his own opinion, or that his opponent's opinion will change. Each is afraid of changing his own opinion, precisely because it is one of his possessions, and hence its loss would mean an impoverishment.

The situation is somewhat different in a conversation that is not meant to be a debate. Who has not experienced meeting a person distinguished by prominence or fame or even by real qualities, or a person of whom one wants something: a good job, to be loved, to be admired? In any such circumstances many people tend to be at least mildly anxious, and often they "prepare" themselves for the important meeting. They think of topics that might interest the other; they think in advance how they might begin the conversation; some even map out the whole conversation, as far as their own part is concerned. Or they may bolster themselves up by thinking about what they *have:* their past successes, their charming personality (or their intimidating personality if this role is more effective), their social position, their connections, their appearance and dress. In a word, they mentally balance their worth, and based on this evaluation, they display their wares in the ensuing conversation. The person who is very good at this will indeed impress many people, although the created impression is only partly due to the individual's performance and largely due to the poverty of most people's judgment. If the performer is not so clever, however, the performance will appear wooden, contrived, boring and will not elicit much interest.

In contrast are those who approach a situation by preparing nothing in advance, not bolstering themselves up in any way. Instead, they respond spontaneously and productively; they forget about themselves, about the knowledge, the positions they have. Their egos do not stand in their own way, and it is precisely for this reason that they can fully respond to the other person and that person's ideas. They give birth to new ideas, because they are not holding onto anything and can thus produce and give. While the having persons rely on what they *have,* the being persons rely on the fact that they *are,* that they are alive and that something new will be born if only they have the courage to let go and to respond. They come fully alive in the conversation, because they do not stifle themselves by anxious concern with what they have. Their own aliveness is infectious and often helps the other person to transcend his or her egocentricity. Thus the conversation ceases to be an exchange of commodities (information, knowledge, status) and becomes a dialogue in which it does not matter any more who is right. The duelists begin to dance together, and they part not with triumph or sorrow—which are equally sterile—but with joy. (The essential factor in psychoanalytic therapy is this enlivening quality of the therapist. No amount of psychoanalytic interpretation will have an effect if the therapeutic atmosphere is heavy, unalive, and boring.)

Reading

What holds true for a conversation holds equally true for reading, which is—or should be—a conversation between the author and the reader. Of course, in reading (as well as in a personal conversation) *whom* I read from (or talk with) is important. Reading an artless, cheap novel is a form of day-dreaming. It does not permit productive response; the text is swallowed like a television show, or the potato chips one munches while watching TV. But a novel, say by Balzac, can be read with inner participation, productively—that is, in the mode of being. Yet probably most of the time it is also read in the mode of consuming—of having. Their curiosity having been aroused, the readers want to know the plot: whether the hero dies or lives, whether the heroine is seduced or resists; they want to know the answers. The novel serves as a kind of foreplay to excite them; the happy or unhappy end culminates their experience: when they know the end, they *have* the whole story, almost as real as if they rummaged in their own memories. But they have not enhanced their knowledge; they have not understood the person in the novel and thus have not deepened their insight into human nature, or gained knowledge about themselves.

The modes of reading are the same with regard to a book whose theme is philosophy or history. The way one reads a philosophy or history book is formed—or better, deformed—by education. The school aims to give each student a certain amount of "cultural property," and at the end of their schooling certifies the students as *having* at least the minimum amount. Students are taught to read a book so that they can repeat the author's main thoughts. This is how the students "know" Plato, Aristotle, Descartes, Spinoza, Leibniz, Kant, Heidegger, Sartre. The difference between various levels of education from high school to graduate school is mainly in the amount of cultural property that is acquired, which corresponds roughly to the amount of material property the students may be expected to own in later life. The so-called excellent students are the ones who can most accurately repeat what each of the various philosophers had to say. They are like a well-informed guide at a museum. What they do not learn is that which goes beyond this kind of property knowledge. They do not learn to question the philosophers, to talk to them; they do not learn to be aware of the philosophers' own contradictions, of their leaving out certain problems or evading issues; they do not learn to distinguish between what was new and what the authors could not help thinking because it was the "common sense" of their time; they do not learn to hear so that they are able to distinguish when the authors speak only from their brain and when their brain and heart speak together; they do not learn to discover whether the authors are authentic or fake; and many more things.

The mode of being readers will often come to the conclusion that even a highly praised book is entirely without value or is of very limited value. Or they may have fully understood a book, sometimes better than had the author, who may have considered everything he or she wrote as being equally important.

Exercising Authority

Another example of the difference between the modes of having and being is the exercise of authority. The crucial point is expressed in the difference between *having* authority and *being* an authority. Almost all of us exercise authority at least at some stage of our lives. Those who bring up children must exercise authority—whether they want to or not—in order to protect their children from dangers and give them at least minimal advice on how to act in various situations. In a patriarchal society women, too, are objects of authority, for most men. Most members of a bureaucratic, hierarchically organized society like ours exercise authority, except the people on the lowest social level, who are only objects of authority.

Our understanding of authority in the two modes depends on our recognizing that "authority" is a broad term with two entirely different meanings: it can be either "rational" or "irrational" authority. Rational authority is based on competence, and it helps the person who leans on it to grow. Irrational authority is based on power and serves to exploit the person subjected to it. (I have discussed this distinction in *Escape from Freedom.*)

Among the most primitive societies, i.e., the hunters and food gatherers, authority is exercised by the person who is generally recognized as being competent for the task. What qualities this competence rests on depends much on the specific circumstances, although the impression would be that they would include experience, wisdom, generosity, skill, "presence," courage. No permanent authority exists in many of these tribes, but an authority emerges in the case of need. Or there are different authorities for different occasions: war, religious practice, adjustment of quarrels. When the qualities on which the authority rests disappear or weaken, the authority itself ends. A very similar form of authority may be observed in many primitive societies, in which competence is often established not by physical strength but by such qualities as experience and "wisdom." In a very ingenious experiment with monkeys, J. M. R. Delgado (1967) has shown that if the dominant animal even momentarily loses the qualities that constitute its competence, its authority ends.

Being-authority is grounded not only in the individual's competence to fulfill certain social functions, but equally so in the very essence of a personality that has achieved a high degree of growth and integration. Such persons radiate authority and do not have to give orders, threaten, bribe. They are highly developed individuals who demonstrate by what they are—and not mainly by what they do or say—what human beings can be. The great Masters of Living were such authorities, and to a lesser degree of perfection, such individuals may be found on all educational levels and in the most diverse cultures. (The problem of education hinges on this point. If parents were more developed themselves and rested in their own center, the opposition between authoritarian and laissez-faire education would hardly exist. Needing this being-authority, the child reacts to it with great eagerness; on the other hand, the child rebels against pressure or neglect or "overfeeding" by people who show by their own behavior that they themselves have not made the effort they expect from the growing child.)

With the formation of societies based on a hierarchical order and much larger and more complex than those of the hunters and food gatherers, authority by competence yields to authority by social status. This does not mean that the existing authority is necessarily incompetent; it does mean that competence is not an essential element of authority. Whether we deal with monarchical authority—where the lottery of genes decides qualities of competence—or with an unscrupulous criminal who succeeds in becoming an authority by murder or treachery, or, as frequently in modern democracy, with authorities elected on the basis of their photogenic physiognomy or the amount of money they can spend on their election, in all these cases there may be almost no relation between competence and authority.

But there are even serious problems in the cases of authority established on the basis of some competence: a leader may have been competent in one field, incompetent in another—for instance, a statesman may be competent in conducting war and incompetent in the situation of peace; or a leader who is honest and courageous at the beginning of his or her career loses these qualities by the seduction of power; or age or physical troubles may lead to a certain deterioration. Finally, one must consider that it is much easier for the members of a small tribe to judge the behavior of an authority than it is for the millions of people in our system, who know their candidate only by the artificial image created by public relations specialists.

Whatever the reasons for the loss of the competence-form-ing qualities, in most larger and hierarchically organized societies the process of alienation of authority occurs. The real or alleged initial competence is transferred to the uniform or to the title of the authority. If the authority wears the proper uniform or has the proper title, this external sign of competence replaces the real competence and its qualities. The king —to use this title as a symbol for this type of authority—can be stupid, vicious, evil, i.e., utterly incompetent to *be* an authority, yet he *has* authority. As long as he has the title, he is supposed to have the qualities of competence. Even if the emperor is naked, everybody believes he wears beautiful clothes.

That people take uniforms and titles for the real qualities of competence is not something that happens quite of itself. Those who have these symbols of authority and those who benefit therefrom must dull their subject people's realistic, i.e., critical, thinking and make them believe the fiction. Anybody who will think about it knows the machinations of propaganda, the methods by which critical judgment is destroyed, how the mind is lulled into submission by clichés, how people are made dumb because they become dependent and lose their capacity to trust their eyes and judgment. They are blinded to reality by the fiction they believe.

Having Knowledge and Knowing

The difference between the mode of having and the mode of being in the sphere of *knowing* is expressed in two formulations: "I have knowledge" and "I know." *Having* knowledge is taking and keeping possession of available knowledge (information); *knowing* is functional and serves only as a means in the process of productive thinking.

Our understanding of the quality of knowing in the being mode of existence can be enhanced by the insights of such thinkers as the Buddha, the Hebrew prophets, Jesus, Master Eckhart, Sigmund Freud, and Karl Marx. In their view, knowing begins with the awareness of the deceptiveness of our common sense perceptions, in the sense that our picture of physical reality does not correspond to what is "really real" and, mainly, in the sense that most people are half-awake, half-dreaming, and are unaware that most of what they hold to be true and self-evident is illusion produced by the suggestive influence of the social world in which they live. Knowing, then, begins with the shattering of illusions, with *dis*illusionment *(Ent-täuschung)*. Knowing means to penetrate through the surface, in order to arrive at the roots, and hence the causes; knowing means to "see" reality in its nakedness. Knowing does not mean to be in possession of the truth; it means to penetrate the surface and to strive critically and actively in order to approach truth ever more closely.

This quality of creative penetration is expressed in the Hebrew *jadoa*, which means to know and to love, in the sense of male sexual penetration. The Buddha, the Awakened One, calls on people to wake up and liberate themselves from the illusion that craving for things leads to happiness. The Hebrew prophets appeal to the people to wake up and know that their idols are nothing but the work of their own hands, are illusions. Jesus says: "The truth shall make you free!" Master Eckhart expressed his concept of knowing many times; for instance, when speaking of God he says: "Knowledge is no particular thought but rather it peels off [all coverings] and is disinterested and runs naked to God, until it touches him and grasps him" (Blakney, p. 243). ("Nakedness" and "naked" are favorite expressions of Master Eckhart as well as of his contemporary, the anonymous author of *The Cloud of Unknowing.*) According to Marx, one needs to destroy illusions in order to create the conditions that make illusions unnecessary. Freud's concept of self-knowledge is based on the idea of destroying illusions ("rationalizations") in order to become aware of the unconscious reality. (The last of the Enlightenment thinkers, Freud can be called a revolutionary thinker in terms of the eighteenth-century Enlightenment philosophy, not in terms of the twentieth century.)

All these thinkers were concerned with human salvation; they were all critical of socially accepted thought patterns. To them the aim of knowing is not the certainty of "absolute truth," something one can feel secure with, but *the self-affirmation process of human reason*. Ignorance, for the one who *knows*, is as good as knowledge, since both are part of the process of knowing, even though ignorance of this kind is different from the ignorance of the unthinking. Optimum knowledge in the being mode is *to know more deeply*. In the having mode it is *to have more knowledge*.

Our education generally tries to train people to *have* knowledge as a possession, by and large commensurate with the amount of property or social prestige they are likely to have in later life. The minimum they receive is the amount they will need in order to function properly in their work. In addition they are each given a "luxury-knowledge package" to enhance their feeling of worth, with the size of each such package being in accord with the person's probable social prestige. The schools are the factories in which these overall knowledge packages are produced—although schools usually claim they mean to bring the students in touch with the highest achievements of the human mind. Many undergraduate colleges are particularly adroit in nurturing these illusions. From Indian thought and art to existentialism and surrealism, a vast smörgåsbord of knowledge is offered from which students pick a little here, a little there, and in the name of spontaneity and freedom are not urged to concentrate on one subject, not even ever to finish reading an entire book. (Ivan Illich's radical critique of the school system brings many of its failings into focus.)

Faith

In a religious, political, or personal sense the concept of faith can have two entirely different meanings, depending upon whether it is used in the having mode or in the being mode.

Faith, in the having mode, is the possession of an answer for which one has no rational proof. It consists of formulations created by others, which one accepts because one submits to those others—usually a bureaucracy. It carries the feeling of certainty because of the real (or only imagined) power of the bureaucracy. It is the entry ticket to join a large group of people. It relieves one of the hard task of thinking for oneself and making decisions. One becomes one of the *beati possidentes,* the happy owners of the right faith. Faith, in the having mode, gives certainty; it claims to pronounce ultimate, unshakable knowledge, which is believable because the power of those who promulgate and protect the faith seems unshakable. Indeed, who would not choose certainty, if all it requires is to surrender one's independence?

God, originally a symbol for the highest value that we can experience within us, becomes, in the having mode, an idol. In the prophetic concept, an idol is a *thing* that we ourselves make and project our own powers into, thus impoverishing ourselves. We then submit to our creation and by our submission are in touch with ourselves in an alienated form. While I can *have* the idol because it is a thing, by my submission to it, *it,* simultaneously, has *me.* Once He has become an idol, God's alleged qualities have as little to do with my personal experience as alienated political doctrines do. The idol may be praised as Lord of Mercy, yet any cruelty may be committed in its name, just as the alienated faith in human solidarity may not even raise doubts about committing the most inhuman acts. Faith, in the having mode, is a crutch for those who want to be certain, those who want an answer to life without daring to search for it themselves.

In the being mode, faith is an entirely different phenomenon. Can we live without faith? Must not the nursling have faith in its mother's breast? Must we all not have faith in other beings, in those whom we love, and in ourselves? Can we live without faith in the validity of norms for our life? Indeed, without faith we become sterile, hopeless, afraid to the very core of our being.

Faith, in the being mode, is not, in the first place, a belief in certain ideas (although it may be that, too) but an inner orientation, an *attitude*. It would be better to say that one *is in* faith than that one *has* faith. (The theological distinction between faith that *is* belief [*fides quae creditur*] and faith *as* belief [*fides qua creditur*] reflects a similar distinction between the *content* of faith and the *act* of faith.) One can be in faith toward oneself and toward others, and the religious person can be in faith toward God. The God of the Old Testament is, first of all, a negation of idols, of gods whom one can *have*. Though conceived in analogy to an Oriental king, the concept of God transcends itself from the very beginning. God must not have a name; no image must be made of God.

Later on, in Jewish and Christian development, the attempt is made to achieve the complete deidolization of God, or rather to fight the danger of idolization by postulating that not even God's qualities can be stated. Or most radically in Christian mysticism—from (Pseudo) Dionysius Areopagita to the unknown author of *The Cloud of Unknowing* and to Master Eckhart—the concept of God tends to be that of the One, the "Godhead" (the No-thing), thus joining views expressed in the Vedas and in Neoplatonic thinking. This faith in God is vouched for by inner experience of the divine qualities in oneself; it is a continuous, active process of self-creation—or, as Master Eckhart puts it, of Christ's eternally being born within ourselves.

My faith in myself, in another, in humankind, in our capacity to become fully human also implies certainty, but certainty based on my own experience and not on my submission to an authority that dictates a certain belief. It is certainty of a truth that cannot be proven by rationally compelling evidence, yet truth I am certain of because of my experiential, subjective evidence. (The Hebrew word for faith is *emunah*, "certainty"; *amen* means "certainly.")

If I am certain of a man's integrity, I could not prove his integrity up to his last day; strictly speaking, if his integrity remains inviolate to the time of his death, even that would not exclude a positivistic standpoint that he might have done violence to it had he lived longer. My certainty rests upon the knowledge in depth I have of the other and of my own experience of love and integrity. This kind of knowledge is possible only to the extent that I can drop my own ego and see the other man in *his* suchness, recognize the structure of forces in him, see him in his individuality and at the same time in his universal humanity. Then I know what the other can do, what he cannot do, and what he will not do. Of course, I do not mean by this that I could predict all his future behavior, but only the general lines of behavior that are rooted in basic character traits, such as integrity, responsibility, etc. (See the chapter on "Faith as a Character Trait" in *Man for Himself.*)

This faith is based on facts; hence it is rational. But the facts are not recognizable or "provable" by the method of conventional, positivistic psychology; I, the alive person, am the only instrument that can "register" them.

Loving

Loving also has two meanings, depending upon whether it is spoken of in the mode of having or in the mode of being.

Can one *have* love? If we could, love would need to be a thing, a substance that one can have, own, possess. The truth is, there is no such thing as "love." "Love" is abstraction, perhaps a goddess or an alien being, although nobody has ever seen this goddess. In reality, there exists only the *act of loving*. To love is a productive activity. It implies caring for, knowing, responding, affirming, enjoying: the person, the tree, the painting, the idea. It means bringing to life, increasing his/her/its aliveness. It is a process, self-renewing and self-increasing.

When love is experienced in the mode of having it implies confining, imprisoning, or controlling the object one "loves." It is strangling, deadening, suffocating, killing, not life-giving. What people *call* love is mostly a misuse of the word, in order to hide the reality of their not loving. How many parents love their children is still an entirely open question. Lloyd de Mause has brought out that for the past two millennia of Western history there have been reports of cruelty against children, ranging from physical to psychic torture, carelessness, sheer possessiveness, and sadism, so shocking that one must believe that loving parents are the exception rather than the rule.

The same may be said of marriages. Whether their marriage is based on love or, like traditional marriages of the past, on social convenience and custom, the couple who truly love each other seem to be the exception. What is social convenience, custom, mutual economic interest, shared interest in children, mutual dependency, or mutual hate or fear is consciously experienced as "love"—up to the moment when one or both partners recognize that they do not love each other, and that they never did. Today one can note some progress in this respect: people have become more realistic and sober, and many no longer feel that being sexually attracted means to love, or that a friendly, though distant, team relationship is a manifestation of loving. This new outlook has made for greater honesty—as well as more frequent change of partners. It has not necessarily led to a greater frequency of loving, and the new partners may love as little as did the old.

The change from "falling in love" to the illusion of "having" love can often be observed in concrete detail in the history of couples who have "fallen in love." (In *The Art of Loving* I pointed out that the word "falling" in the phrase "falling in love" is a contradiction in itself. Since loving is a productive activity, one can only *stand* in love or *walk* in love; one cannot "fall" in love, for falling denotes passivity.)

During courtship neither person is yet sure of the other, but each tries to win the other. Both are alive, attractive, interesting, even beautiful—inasmuch as aliveness always makes a face beautiful. Neither yet *has* the other; hence each one's energy is directed to *being*, i.e., to giving to and stimulating the other. With the act of marriage the situation frequently changes fundamentally. The marriage contract gives each partner the exclusive possession of the other's body, feelings, and care. Nobody has to be won over any more, because love has become something one *has,* a property. The two cease to make the effort to be lovable and to produce love, hence they become boring, and hence their beauty disappears. They are disappointed and puzzled. Are they not the same persons any more? Did they make a mistake in the first place? Each usually seeks the cause of the change in the other and feels defrauded. What they do not see is that they no longer are the same people they were when they were in love with each other; that the error that one can *have* love has led them to cease loving. Now, instead of loving each other, they settle for owning together what they have: money, social standing, a home, children. Thus, in some cases, the marriage initiated on the basis of love becomes transformed into a friendly ownership, a corporation in which the two egotisms are pooled into one: that of the "family."

When a couple cannot get over the yearning for the renewal of the previous feeling of loving, one or the other of the pair may have the illusion that a new partner (or partners) will satisfy their longing. They feel that all they want to have is love. But love to them is not an expression of their being; it is a goddess to whom they want to submit. They necessarily fail with their love because "love is a child of liberty" (as an old French song says), and the worshiper of the goddess of love eventually becomes so passive as to be boring and loses whatever is left of his or her former attractiveness.

This description is not intended to imply that marriage cannot be the best solution for two people who love each other. The difficulty does not lie in marriage, but in the possessive, existential structure of both partners and, in the last analysis, of their society. The advocates of such modern-day forms of living together as group marriage, changing partners, group sex, etc., try, as far as I can see, only to avoid the problem of their difficulties in loving by curing boredom with ever new stimuli and by wanting *to have* more "lovers," rather than to be able to love even one. (See the discussion of the distinction between "activating" and "passivating" stimuli in Chapter 10 of *The Anatomy of Human Destructiveness.*)

III

Having and Being in the Old and New Testaments and in the Writings of Master Eckhart

The Old Testament

One of the main themes of the Old Testament is: leave what you have; free yourself from all fetters; *be!*

The history of Hebrew tribes begins with the command to the first Hebrew hero, *Abraham*, to give up his country and his clan: "Go from your country and your kindred and your father's house to the land that I will show you" (Genesis 12:1). Abraham is to leave what he has—land and family—and go to the unknown. Yet his descendants settle on a new soil, and new clannishness develops. This process leads to more severe bondage. Precisely because they become rich and powerful in Egypt, they become slaves; they lose the vision of the one God, the God of their nomadic ancestors, and they worship idols, the gods of the rich turned later into their masters.

The second hero is *Moses.* He is charged by God to liberate his people, to lead them out of the country that has become their home (even though eventually a home for slaves), and to go into the desert "to celebrate." Reluctantly and with great misgiving, the Hebrews follow their leader Moses—into the desert.

The desert is the key symbol in this liberation. The desert

is no home: it has no cities; it has no riches; it is the place of nomads who own what they need, and what they need are the necessities of life, not possessions. Historically, nomadic traditions are interwoven in the report of the Exodus, and it may very well be that these nomadic traditions have determined the tendency against all nonfunctional property and the choice of life in the desert as preparation for the life of freedom. But these historical factors only strengthen the meaning of the desert as a symbol of the unfettered, nonpropertied life. Some of the main symbols of the Jewish festivals have their origin in the connection with the desert. The *unleavened bread* is the bread of those who are in a hurry to leave; it is the bread of the wanderers. The *suka* ("tabernacle") is the home of the wanderer: the equivalent of the tent, easily built and easily taken down. As defined in the Talmud it is "the transitory abode," to be lived in, instead of the "fixed abode" one owns.

The Hebrews yearn for the fleshpots of Egypt; for the fixed home, for the poor yet guaranteed food; for the visible idols. They fear the uncertainty of the propertyless desert life. They say: "Would that we had died by the hand of the Lord in the land of Egypt, when we sat by the fleshpots and ate bread to the full; for you have brought us out into this wilderness to kill this whole assembly with hunger" (Exodus: 16:3). God, as in the whole story of liberation, responds to the moral frailty of the people. He promises to feed them: in the morning with "bread," in the evening with quail. He adds two important injunctions: each should gather according to their needs: "And the people of Israel did so; they gathered, some more, some less. But when they measured it with an omer, he that gathered much had nothing over, and he that gathered little had no lack; each gathered according to what he could eat" (Exodus 16:17–18).

For the first time, a principle is formulated here that became famous through Marx: to each according to their needs. The right to be fed was established without qualification. God is here the nourishing mother who feeds her children, who do not have to achieve anything in order to establish their right to be fed. The second injunction is one against hoarding, greed, and possessiveness. The people of Israel were enjoined not to save anything till the next morning. "But they did not listen to Moses; some left part of it till the morning, and it bred worms and became foul; and Moses was angry with them. Morning by morning they gathered it, each as much as he could eat; but when the sun grew hot, it melted" (Exodus 16:20–21).

In connection with the collection of food the concept of the observation of the *Shabbat* ("Sabbath") is introduced. Moses tells the Hebrews to collect twice the usual amount of food on Friday: "Six days you shall gather it; but on the seventh day, which is a Sabbath, there will be none" (Genesis 16:26).

The Shabbat is the most important of the biblical concepts, and later of Judaism. It is the only strictly religious command in the Ten Commandments: its fulfillment is insisted upon by the otherwise antiritualistic prophets; it was a most strictly observed commandment throughout 2000 years of Diaspora life, wherein its observation often was hard and difficult. It can hardly be doubted that the Shabbat was the fountain of life for the Jews, who, scattered, powerless, and often despised and persecuted, renewed their pride and dignity when like kings they celebrated the Shabbat. Is the Shabbat nothing but a day of rest in the mundane sense of freeing people, at least on one day, from the burden of work? To be sure it is that, and this function gives it the dignity of one of the great innovations in human evolution. Yet if this were all that it was, the Shabbat would hardly have played the central role I have just described.

In order to understand this role we must penetrate to the core of the Shabbat institution. It is not rest *per se,* in the sense of not making an effort, physically or mentally. It is rest in the sense of the re-establishment of complete harmony between human beings and between them and nature. Nothing must be destroyed and nothing be built: the Shabbat is a day of truce in the human battle with the world. Neither must social change occur. Even tearing up a blade of grass is looked upon as a breach of this harmony, as is lighting a match. It is for this reason that carrying anything on the street is forbidden (even if it weighs as little as a handkerchief), while carrying a heavy load in one's garden is permitted. The point is that not the effort of carrying a load is forbidden, but the transfer of any object from one privately owned piece of land to another, because such transfer constituted, originally, a transfer of property. On the Shabbat one lives as if one *has* nothing, pursuing no aim except *being,* that is, expressing one's essential powers: praying, studying, eating, drinking, singing, making love.

The Shabbat is a day of joy because on that day one is fully oneself. This is the reason the Talmud calls a Shabbat the anticipation of the Messianic Time, and the Messianic Time the unending Shabbat: the day on which property and money as well as mourning and sadness are tabu; a day on which time is defeated and pure being rules. The historical predecessor, the Babylonian Shapatu, was a day of sadness and fear. The modern Sunday is a day of fun, consumption, and running away from oneself. One might ask if it is not time to re-establish the Shabbat as a universal day of harmony and peace, as the human day that anticipates the human future.

The vision of the Messianic Time is the other specifically Jewish contribution to world culture, and one essentially identical with that of the Shabbat. This vision, like the Shabbat, was the life-sustaining hope of the Jews, never given up in spite of the severe disappointments that came with the false messiahs, from Bar Kochba in the second century to our days. Like the Shabbat it was a vision of a historical period in which possession will have become meaningless, fear and war will have ended, and the expression of our essential powers will have become the aim of living.*

*I have analyzed the concept of Messianic Time in *You Shall Be as Gods.* The Shabbat, too, is discussed in that earlier book, as well as in the chapter on "The Sabbath Ritual" in *The Forgotten Language.*

The history of the Exodus moves to a tragic end. The Hebrews cannot bear to live without *having*. Although they can live without a fixed abode, and without food except that sent by God every day, they cannot live without a visible, present "leader."

Thus when Moses disappears on the mountain, the desperate Hebrews get Aaron to make them a visible manifestation of something they can worship: the Golden Calf. Here, one may say, they pay for God's error in having permitted them to take gold and jewelry out of Egypt. With the gold, they carried within themselves the craving for wealth; and when the hour of despair came, the possessive structure of their existence reasserted itself. Aaron makes them a calf from their gold, and the people say: "These are your Gods, O Israel, who brought you up out of the land of Egypt" (Exodus 32:4).

A whole generation had died and even Moses was not permitted to enter the new land. But the new generation was as little capable of being unfettered and of living on a land without being bound to it as were their fathers. They conquer new land, exterminate their enemies, settle on their soil, and worship their idols. They transform their democratic tribal life into that of Oriental despotism—small, indeed, but not less eager to imitate the great powers of the day. The revolution had failed; its only achievement was, if it was one, that the Hebrews were now masters and not slaves. They might not even be remembered today, except as a learned footnote in a history of the Near East, had the new message not found expression through revolutionary thinkers and visionaries who were not tainted, as was Moses, by the burden of leadership and specifically by the need to use dictatorial power methods (for instance the wholesale destruction of the rebels under Korach).

These revolutionary thinkers, the Hebrew prophets, renewed the vision of human freedom—of being unfettered of things—and the protest against submitting to idols—the work of the people's own hands. They were uncompromising and predicted that the people would have to be expelled from the land again if they became incestuously fixated to it and incapable of living in it as free people—that is, not able to love it without losing themselves in it. To the prophets the expulsion from the land was a tragedy, but the only way to final liberation; the new desert was to last not for one but for many generations. Even while predicting the new desert, the prophets were sustaining the faith of the Jews, and eventually of the whole human race, by the Messianic vision that promised peace and abundance without requiring the expulsion or extermination of a land's old inhabitants.

The real successors to the Hebrew prophets were the great scholars, the rabbis, and none more clearly so than the founder of the Diaspora: Rabbi Jochanan ben Sakai. When the leaders of the war against the Romans (A.D. 70) had decided that it was better for all to die than to be defeated and lose their state, Rabbi Sakai committed "treason." He secretly left Jerusalem, surrendered to the Roman general, and asked permission to found a Jewish university. This was the beginning of a rich Jewish tradition and, at the same time, of the loss of everything the Jews had *had:* their state, their temple, their priestly and military bureaucracy, their sacrificial animals, and their rituals. All were lost and they were left (as a group) with nothing except the ideal of being: knowing, learning, thinking, and hoping for the Messiah.

The New Testament

The New Testament continues the Old Testament's protest against the having structure of existence. Its protest is even more radical than the earlier Jewish protest had been. The Old Testament was not the product of a poor and downtrodden class, but sprang from nomadic sheepowners and independent peasants. A millennium later, the Pharisees, the learned men whose literary product was the Talmud, represented the middle class, ranging from some very poor to some very well-to-do members. Both groups were imbued with the spirit of social justice, the protection of the poor, and the assistance to all who were powerless, such as widows and national minorities *(gerim)*. But on the whole, they did not condemn wealth as evil or as incompatible with the principle of being. (See Louis Finkelstein's book on *The Pharisees.*)

Earliest Christians, on the contrary, were mainly a group of the poor and socially despised, of the downtrodden and outcasts, who—like some of the Old Testament prophets—castigated the rich and powerful, denouncing without compromise wealth and secular and priestly power, as unmitigated evils (see *The Dogma of Christ*). Indeed, as Max Weber said, the Sermon on the Mount was the speech of a great slave rebellion. The mood of the early Christians was one of full human solidarity, sometimes expressed in the idea of a spontaneous communal sharing of all material goods. (A. F. Utz discusses the early Christian communal ownership and earlier Greek examples of whom Luke probably knew.)

This revolutionary spirit of early Christianity appears with special clarity in the oldest parts of the gospels as they were known to the Christian communities that still had not separated from Judaism. (Those oldest parts of the gospels can be reconstructed from the common source of Matthew and Luke and are called "Q" [Q from German *Quelle,* "source"] by specialists in the history of the New Testament. The fundamental work in this field is by Siegried Schulz, who differentiates between an older and a younger tradition of "Q.")*

In these sayings we find as the central postulate that people must free themselves from all greed and cravings for possession and must totally liberate themselves from the structure of having, and conversely, that all positive ethical norms are rooted in an ethics of being, sharing, and solidarity. This basic

*I am indebted to Rainer Funk for his thorough information about this field and for his fruitful suggestions.

ethical position is applied both to one's relations to others and to one's relations to things. The radical renunciation of one's own rights (Matthew 5:39–42; Luke 6:29 f.) as well as the command to love one's enemy (Matthew 5:44–48; Luke 6:27 f., 32–36) stress, even more radically than the Old Testament's "love thy neighbor," full concern for other human beings and complete surrender of all selfishness. The norm not even to judge others (Matthew 7:1–5; Luke 6:37 f., 41 f.) is a further extension of the principle of forgetting one's ego and being totally devoted to the understanding and the well-being of the other.

Also with regard to things, total renunciation of the having structure is demanded. The oldest community insisted on the radical renunciation of property; it warns against collecting riches: "Do not lay up for yourselves treasures on earth, where moth and rust consume and where thieves break in and steal, but lay up for yourselves treasures in heaven, where neither moth nor rust consumes and where thieves do not break in and steal. For where your treasure is, there will your heart be also" (Matthew 6:19–21; Luke 12:33 f.). It is in the same spirit that Jesus says: "Blessed are you poor for yours is the kingdom of God" (Luke 6:20; Matthew 5:3). Indeed, early Christianity was a community of the poor and the suffering, filled with the apocalyptic conviction that the time had come for the final disappearance of the existing order, according to God's plan of salvation.

The apocalyptic concept of the "Last Judgment" was one version of the Messianic idea, current in Jewish circles of the time. Final salvation and judgment would be preceded by a period of chaos and destruction, a period so terrible that we find Talmudic rabbis asking God to spare them living in the pre-Messianic Time. What was new in Christianity was that Jesus and his followers believed that the Time was *now* (or in the near future), and that it had already begun with Jesus' appearance.

Indeed, one cannot help associating the situation of the

early Christians with what goes on in the world today. Not a few people, scientists rather than religionists (with the exception of the Jehovah's Witnesses), believe that we might be approaching the final catastrophe of the world. This is a rational and scientifically tenable vision. The situation of the early Christians was quite different. They lived in a small part of the Roman Empire at the height of its power and glory. There were no alarming signs of catastrophe. Yet this small group of poor Palestinian Jews carried the conviction that this powerful world would soon collapse. Realistically, to be sure, they were mistaken; as a result of the failure of Jesus' reappearance, Jesus' death and resurrection are interpreted in the gospels as constituting the beginning of the new eon, and after Constantine an attempt was made to shift the mediating role of Jesus to the papal church. Finally, for all practical purposes the church became the substitute—in fact, though not in theory—for the new eon.

One must take early Christianity more seriously than most people do, in order to be impressed by the almost unbelievable radicalism of this small group of people, who spoke the verdict over the existing world on *nothing but* their moral conviction. The majority of the Jews, on the other hand, not belonging exclusively to the poorest and most downtrodden part of the population, chose another way. They refused to believe that a new era had begun and continued to wait for the Messiah, who would come when humankind (and not only the Jews) had reached the point where the realm of justice, peace, and love could be established in a historical rather than in an eschatological sense.

The younger "Q" source has its origin in a further stage of development of early Christianity. Here, too, we find the same principle, and the story of Jesus' temptation by Satan expresses it in a very succinct form. In this story, the lust for having things and the craving for power and other manifestations of the having structure are condemned. To the first temptation—to transform stones into bread, symbolically expressing the craving for material things—Jesus answers: "Man shall not live by bread alone, but by every word that proceeds from the mouth of God" (Matthew 4:4; Luke 4:4). Satan tempts Jesus then with the promise of giving him complete power over nature (changing the law of gravity), and finally, with unrestricted power, dominion over all kingdoms of the earth, and Jesus declines (Matthew 4:5–10; Luke 4: 5–12). (Rainer Funk has called my attention to the fact that the temptation takes place in the desert, thus taking up the topic of the Exodus again.)

Jesus and Satan appear here as representatives of two opposite principles. Satan is the representative of material consumption and of power over nature and Man. Jesus is the representative of being, and of the idea that not-having is the premise for being. The world has followed Satan's principles, since the time of the gospels. Yet even the victory of these principles could not destroy the longing for the realization of full being, expressed by Jesus as well as by many other great Masters who lived before him and after him.

The ethical rigorism of rejection of the having orientation for the sake of the being orientation is to be found also in the Jewish communal orders, such as the Essenes and the order in which the Dead Sea scrolls originated. Throughout the history of Christianity it continues in the religious orders based on the vow of poverty and propertylessness.

Another manifestation of the radical concepts of early Christianity is to be found—in various degrees—in the writings of the church fathers, who in this respect are also influenced by Greek philosophical thought on the subject of private property versus common property. Space does not permit me to discuss these teachings in any detail, and even less the theological and sociological literature on the subject.* Although there are some differences in the degree of radicalism and a certain trend to a less radical view the more

*See the contributions of A. F. Utz, O. Schilling, H. Schumacher, and others.

the church became a powerful institution, it is undeniable that the early church thinkers shared a sharp condemnation of luxury and avarice and a contempt for wealth.

Justin writes, in the middle of the second century: "We who once loved riches [mobile goods] and possession [land] above everything else, now make that which we already have into common property and share it with the needy." In a "Letter of Diognetus" (also second century), there is a very interesting passage that reminds us of Old Testament thought about homelessness: "Any alien country is their [the Christians'] fatherland and every fatherland is alien to them." Tertullian (third century) considered all trade to be the result of cupidity, and he denies its necessity among people who are free from greed. He declares that trade always carries with it the danger of idolatry. Avarice he calls the root of all evil.*

For Basilius, as for the other church fathers, the purpose of all material goods is to serve people; characteristic of him is this question: "The one who takes away a garment from another is called a thief; but the one who does not clothe the poor, although he could—does he deserve another name?" (quoted by Utz). Basilius stressed the original community of goods and was understood by some authors to have represented communist tendencies. I conclude this brief sketch with Chrysostomus' warning (fourth century) that superfluous goods must not be produced or consumed. He says: "Do not say I use what is mine: you use what is alien to you; the indulgent, selfish use makes what is yours something alien; that is why I call it alien good, because you use it with a hardened heart and claim that it is right, that you alone live from what is yours."

I could go on for many pages quoting the views of the church fathers that private property and the egotistical use of any possession is immoral. Yet even the foregoing few state-

*The above passages are taken from Otto Schilling; see also his quotations from K. Farner and T. Sommerlad.

ments indicate the continuity of the rejection of the having orientation as we find it from Old Testament times, throughout early Christianity, and into the later centuries. Even Aquinas, battling against the openly communist sects, concludes that the institution of private property is justified only inasmuch as it best serves the purposes of satisfying the welfare of all.

Classic Buddhism emphasizes even more strongly than the Old and New Testaments the central importance of giving up craving for possessions of any kind, including one's own ego, the concept of a lasting substance, and even the craving for one's perfection.*

Master Eckhart (1260–c. 1327)

Eckhart has described and analyzed the difference between the having and being modes of existence with a penetration and clarity not surpassed by any teacher. A major figure of the Dominican Order in Germany, Eckhart was a scholarly theologian and the greatest representative and deepest and most radical thinker of German mysticism. His greatest influence radiated from his German sermons, which affected not only his contemporaries and disciples but also German mystics after him and, today, those seeking authentic guidance to a nontheistic, rational, yet religious, philosophy of life.

My sources for the Eckhart quotations that follow are Joseph L. Quint's great Eckhart work *Meister Eckhart, Die Deutschen Werke* (referred to here as "Quint D.W."), his *Meister Eckhart, Deutsche Predigten und Traktate* (referred to as "Quint D.P.T."), and the English translation by Raymond B. Blakney, *Meister Eckhart* (referred to here as "Blakney"). It should be noted that while Quint's editions contain only the passages he

---

*For a penetrating understanding of Buddhism, see the writings of Nyanaponika Mahatera, particularly *The Heart of Buddhist Meditation* and *Pathways of Buddhist Thought: Essays from the Wheel.*

considers have been proven authentic so far, the Blakney text (translated from the German, Pfeiffer, edition) includes writings whose authenticity Quint has not yet acknowledged. Quint himself has pointed out, however, that his recognition of authenticity is provisional, that very likely many of the other works that have been attributed to Master Eckhart will also be proven authentic. The italicized numbers that appear with the source notes refer to the Eckhart sermons as they are identified in the three sources.

Eckhart's Concept of Having

The classic source for Eckhart's views on the mode of having is his sermon on poverty, based on the text of Matthew 5:13: "Blessed are the poor in spirit, for theirs is the kingdom of heaven." In this sermon Eckhart discusses the question: What is spiritual poverty? He begins by saying that he does not speak of *external* poverty, a poverty of things, although that kind of poverty is good and commendable. He wants to speak of *inner* poverty, the poverty referred to in the gospel verse, which he defines by saying: "He is a poor man who *wants* nothing, *knows* nothing and *has* nothing" (Blakney, *28;* Quint D.W., *52;* Quint D.P.T., *32*).

Who is the person who *wants* nothing? A man or woman who has chosen an ascetic life would be our common response. But this is not Eckhart's meaning, and he scolds those who understand not wanting anything as an exercise of repentance and an external religious practice. He sees the subscribers to that concept as people who hold onto their selfish egos. "These people have the name of being saintly on the basis of the external appearances, but inside they are asses, because they don't grasp the true meaning of divine truth" (my translation of Quint's text).

For Eckhart is concerned with the kind of "wanting" that is also fundamental in Buddhist thought; that is, greed, craving for things and for one's own ego. The Buddha considers this wanting to be the cause of human suffering, not enjoy-ment. When Eckhart goes on to speak of having no will, he does not mean that one should be weak. The will he speaks of is identical with craving, a will that one is *driven* by—that is, in a true sense, *not* will. Eckhart goes as far as to postulate that one should not even want to do God's will—since this, too, is a form of craving. *The person who wants nothing is the person who is not greedy for anything:* this is the essence of Eckhart's concept of nonattachment.

Who is the person who *knows* nothing? Does Eckhart estab-lish that it is one who is an ignorant dumb being, an unedu-cated, uncultured creature? How could he, when his main effort was to educate the uneducated and when he himself was a man of great erudition and knowledge that he never at-tempts to hide or minimize?

Eckhart's concept of *not knowing anything* is concerned with the difference between *having* knowledge and the *act* of *know-ing,* i.e., penetrating to the roots and, hence, to the causes of a thing. Eckhart distinguishes very clearly between a particu-lar thought and the *process* of thinking. Stressing that it is better to know God than to love God, he writes: "Love has to do with desire and purpose, whereas knowledge is no particu-lar thought, but rather it peels off all [coverings] and is disin-terested and runs naked to God, until it touches him and grasps him" (Blakney, Fragment 27; not authenticated by Quint).

But on another level (and Eckhart speaks throughout on several levels) Eckhart goes much further. He writes:

Again, he is poor who knows nothing. We have sometimes said that man ought to live as if he did not live, neither for self, nor for the truth, nor for God. But to that point, we shall say something else and go further. The man who is to achieve this poverty shall live as a man who does not even know that he lives, neither for himself, nor for the truth, nor for god. More; he shall be quit and empty of all knowledge, so that no knowledge of god exists in him; for when a man's existence is of God's external species, there is no other life in him: his life is himself. Therefore we say that a man ought to be empty of his own knowledge, as he was when he did not exist, and let God achieve what he will and man be unfettered (Blakney, *28;* Quint D.W., *52;* Quint D.P.T., *32;* a small portion is my translation of Quint's German text).*

To understand Eckhart's position, it is necessary to grasp the true meaning of these words. When he says that "a man ought to be empty of his own knowledge," he does not mean that one should forget *what* one knows, but rather one should forget *that* one knows. This is to say that we should not look at our knowledge as a possession, in which we find security and which gives us a sense of identity; we should not be "filled" with our knowledge, or hang onto it, or crave it. Knowledge should not assume the quality of a dogma, which enslaves us. All this belongs to the mode of having. In the mode of being, knowledge is nothing but the penetrating activity of thought—without ever becoming an invitation to stand still in order to find certainty. Eckhart continues:

> What does it mean that a man should *have* nothing?
> Now pay earnest attention to this: I have often said, and great authorities agree, that to be a proper abode for God and fit for God to act in, a man should also be free from all [his own] things and [his own] actions, both inwardly and outwardly. Now we shall say something else. If it is the case that a man is emptied of things, creatures, himself and god, and if still God could find a place in him to act, then we say: As long as that [place] exists, this man is not poor with the most intimate poverty. For God does not intend that man shall have a place reserved for God to work in, since true

---

*Blakney uses a capital "G" for God when Eckhart refers to the Godhead and a lower-case "g" when Eckhart refers to the biblical god of creation.

poverty of spirit requires that man shall be emptied of God and all his works, so that if God wants to act in the soul, he himself must be the place in which he acts—and that he would like to do. . . . Thus we say that a man should be so poor that he is not and has not a place for God to act in. To reserve a place would be to maintain distinctions. *Therefore I pray God that he may quit me of god"* (Blakney, pp. 230–231).

Eckhart could not have expressed his concept of not having more radically. First of all, we should be free from our own things and our own actions. This does not mean that we should neither possess anything nor do anything; it means we should not be bound, tied, chained to what we own and what we have, not even to God.

Eckhart approaches the problems of having on another level when he discusses the relation between possession and freedom. Human freedom is restricted to the extent to which we are bound to possession, works, and lastly, to our own egos. By being bound to our egos (Quint translates the original middle-German *Eigenschaft* as *Ich-bindung* or *Ichsucht,* "egoboundness" or "egomania"), we stand in our own way and are blocked from bearing fruit, from realizing ourselves fully (Quint D.P.T., Introduction, p. 29). D. Mieth, in my opinion, is entirely right when he maintains that freedom as a condition of true productivity is nothing but giving up one's ego, as love in the Paulinian sense is free from all egoboundness. Freedom in the sense of being unfettered, free from the craving for holding onto things and one's ego, is the condition for love and for productive being. Our human aim, according to Eckhart, is to get rid of the fetters of egoboundness, egocentricity, that is to say the *having mode* of existence, in order to arrive at full being. I have not found any author whose thoughts about the nature of the having orientation in Eckhart are as similar to my own thinking as those expressed by Mieth (1971). He speaks of the *Besitzstruktur des Menschen* ("the property structure of the people") in the same way, as far as I can see, that I speak of the "having mode," or the "having structure of existence." He refers to the Marxian concept of "expropriation," when he speaks of the break-through of one's own inner property structure, adding that it is the most radical form of expropriation.

In the having mode of existence what matters is not the various *objects* of having, but our whole human attitude. Everything and anything can become an object of craving: things we use in daily life, property, rituals, good deeds, knowledge, and thoughts. While they are not in themselves "bad," they become bad; that is, when we hold onto them, when they become chains that interfere with our freedom, they block our self-realization.

Eckhart's Concept of Being

Eckhart uses being in two different, though related, meanings. In a narrower, psychological sense, being denotes the *real* and often unconscious motivations that impel human beings, in contrast to deeds and opinions as such and separated from the acting and thinking person. Quint justly calls Eckhart an extraordinary analyst of the soul *(genialer Seelenanalytiker)*: "Eckhart never tires of uncovering the most secret ties of human behavior, the most hidden stirring of selfishness, of intentions and opinions, of denouncing the passionate longing for gratitude and rewards" (Quint D.P.T., Introduction, p. 29; my translation). This insight into the hidden motives makes Eckhart most appealing to the post-Freudian reader, who has overcome the naïveté of pre-Freudian and still current behavioristic views, which claim that behavior and opinion are two final data that can be as little broken down as the atom was supposed to be at the beginning of this century. Eckhart expressed this view in numerous statements, of which the following is characteristic: "People should not consider so much what they are to *do* as what they *are*. . . . Thus take care that your emphasis is laid on *being* good and not on the number or kind of things to be done. Emphasize rather the fundamentals on which your work rests." Our being is the reality, the spirit that moves us, the character that impels our behavior; in contrast, the deeds or opinions that are separated from our dynamic core have no reality.

The second meaning is wider and more fundamental: being is life, activity, birth, renewal, outpouring, flowing out, productivity. In this sense, being is the opposite of having, of egoboundness and egotism. Being, to Eckhart, means to be active in the classic sense of the productive expression of one's human powers, not in the modern sense of being busy. Activity to him means "to go out of oneself" (Quint D.P.T., *6;* my translation), which he expresses in many word pictures: he calls being a process of "boiling," of "giving birth," something that "flows and flows in itself and beyond itself" (E. Benz et al., quoted in Quint D.P.T., p. 35; my translation). Sometimes he uses the symbol of running in order to indicate the active character: "Run into peace! The man who is in the state of running, of continuous running into peace is a heavenly man. He continually runs and moves and seeks peace in running" (Quint D.P.T., *8;* my translation). Another definition of activity is: The active, alive man is like a "vessel that grows as it is filled and will never be full" (Blakney, p. 233; not authenticated by Quint).

Breaking through the mode of having is the condition for all genuine activity. In Eckhart's ethical system the supreme virtue is the state of productive inner activity, for which the premise is the overcoming of all forms of egoboundness and craving.

PART TWO

ANALYZING THE FUNDAMENTAL DIFFERENCES BETWEEN THE TWO MODES OF EXISTENCE

IV

What Is the Having Mode?

The Acquisitive Society—Basis for the Having Mode

Our judgments are extremely biased because we live in a society that rests on private property, profit, and power as the pillars of its existence. To acquire, to own, and to make a profit are the sacred and unalienable rights of the individual in the industrial society.* What the sources of property are does not matter; nor does possession impose any obligations on the property owners. The principle is: "Where and how my property was acquired or what I do with it is nobody's business but my own; as long as I do not violate the law, my right is unrestricted and absolute."

This kind of property may be called *private* property (from Latin *privare*, "to deprive of "), because the person or persons who own it are its sole masters, with full power to deprive others of its use or enjoyment. While private ownership is supposed to be a natural and universal category, it is in fact an exception rather than the rule if we consider the whole of human history (including prehistory), and particularly the cultures outside Europe in which economy was not life's main concern. Aside from private property, there are: *self-created*

---

*R. H. Tawney's 1920 work, *The Acquisitive Society*, is still unsurpassed in its understanding of modern capitalism and options for social and human change. The contributions by Max Weber, Brentano, Schapiro, Pascal, Sombart, and Kraus contain fundamental insights for understanding industrial society's influence on human beings.

property, which is exclusively the result of one's own work; *restricted property,* which is *restricted* by the obligation to help one's fellow beings; *functional,* or *personal,* property, which consists either of tools for work or of objects for enjoyment; *common* property, which a group shares in the spirit of a common bond, such as the Israeli kibbutzim.

The norms by which society functions also mold the character of its members (social character). In an industrial society these are: the wish to acquire property, to keep it, and to increase it, i.e., to make a profit, and those who own property are admired and envied as superior beings. But the vast majority of people own no property in a real sense of capital and capital goods, and the puzzling question arises: How can such people fulfill or even cope with their passion for acquiring and keeping property, or how can they feel like owners of property when they haven't any property to speak of?

Of course, the obvious answer is that even people who are property poor own *something*—and they cherish their little possessions as much as the owners of capital cherish their property. And like the big property owners, the poor are obsessed by the wish to preserve what they do have and to increase it, even though by an infinitesimal amount (for instance by saving a penny here, two cents there).

Perhaps the greatest enjoyment is not so much in owning material things but in owning living beings. In a patriarchal society even the most miserable of men in the poorest of classes can be an owner of property—in his relationship to his wife, his children, his animals, over whom he can feel he is absolute master. At least for the man in a patriarchal society, having many children is the only way to own persons without needing to work to attain ownership, and without capital investment. Considering that the whole burden of childbearing is the woman's, it can hardly be denied that the production of children in a patriarchal society is a matter of crude exploitation of women. In turn, however, the mothers have their own form of ownership, that of the children when they are small. The circle is endless and vicious: the husband exploits the wife, she exploits the small children, and the adolescent males soon join the elder men in exploiting the women, and so on.

The male hegemony in a patriarchal order has lasted roughly six or seven millennia and still prevails in the poorest countries or among the poorest classes of society. It is, however, slowly diminishing in the more affluent countries or societies—emancipation of women, children, and adolescents seems to take place when and to the degree that a society's standard of living rises. With the slow collapse of the old-fashioned, patriarchal type of ownership of persons, wherein will the average and the poorer citizens of the fully developed industrial societies now find fulfillment of their passion for acquiring, keeping, and increasing property? The answer lies in extending the area of ownership to include friends, lovers, health, travel, art objects, God, one's own ego. A brilliant picture of the bourgeois obsession with property is given by Max Stirner. Persons are transformed into things; their relations to each other assume the character of ownership. "Individualism," which in its positive sense means liberation from social chains, means, in the negative sense, "self-ownership," the right—and the duty—to invest one's energy in the success of one's own person.

Our ego is the most important object of our property feeling, for it comprises many things: our body, our name, our social status, our possessions (including our knowledge), the image we have of ourselves and the image we want others to have of us. Our ego is a mixture of real qualities, such as knowledge and skills, and of certain fictitious qualities that we build around a core of reality. But the essential point is not so much what the ego's content is, but that the ego is felt as a thing we each possess, and that this "thing" is the basis of our sense of identity.

This discussion of property must take into account that an important form of property attachment that flourished in the nineteenth century has been diminishing in the decades since the end of the First World War and is little evident today. In the older period, everything one owned was cherished, taken care of, and used to the very limits of its utility. Buying was "keep-it" buying, and a motto for the nineteenth century might well have been: "Old is beautiful!" Today, consumption is emphasized, not preservation, and buying has become "throw-away" buying. Whether the object one buys is a car, a dress, a gadget, after using it for some time, one gets tired of it and is eager to dispose of the "old" and buy the latest model. Acquisition → transitory having and using → throwing away (or if possible, profitable exchange for a better model) → new acquisition, constitutes the vicious circle of consumer-buying and today's motto could indeed be: "New is beautiful!"

Perhaps the most striking example of today's consumer-buying phenomenon is the private automobile. Our age deserves to be dubbed "the age of the automobile," for our whole economy has been built around automobile production, and our whole life is greatly determined by the rise and fall of the consumer market for cars.

To those who have one, their car seems like a vital necessity; to those who do not yet own one, especially people in the so-called socialist states, a car is a symbol of joy. Apparently, however, affection for one's car is not deep and abiding, but a love affair of somewhat short duration, for owners change their cars frequently; after two years, even after just one, an auto owner tires of the "old car" and starts shopping around for a "good deal" on a new vehicle. From shopping around to purchase, the whole transaction seems to be a game in which even trickery is sometimes a prime element, and the "good deal" is enjoyed as much as, if not more than, the ultimate prize: that brand-new model in the driveway.

Several factors must be taken into account in order to solve the puzzle of the seemingly flagrant contradiction between the owners' property relationship to their automobiles and their so-short-lived interest in them. First, there is the element of depersonalization in the owner's relationship to the car; the car is not a concrete object that its owner is fond of, but a status symbol, an extension of power—an ego builder; having acquired a car, the owner has actually acquired a new piece of ego. A second factor is that buying a new car every two years instead of, say, every six increases the buyer's thrill of acquisition; the act of making the new car one's own is a kind of defloration—it enhances one's sense of control, and the more often it happens, the more thrilled one is. The third factor is that frequent car buying means frequent opportunities to "make a deal"—to make a profit by the exchange—a satisfaction deeply rooted in men and women today. The fourth factor is one of great importance: the need to experience *new* stimuli, because the old stimuli are flat and exhausted after but a short while. In an earlier discussion of stimuli *(The Anatomy of Human Destructiveness)* I differentiated between "activating" and "passivating" stimuli and suggested the following formulation: "The more 'passivating' a stimulus is, the more frequently it must be changed in intensity and/or in kind; the more 'activating' it is, the longer it retains its stimulating quality and the less necessary is change in intensity and content." The fifth and most important factor lies in the change in social character that has occurred during the past century and a half, i.e., from the "hoarding" to the "marketing" character. While the change does not do away with the having orientation, it does modify it considerably. (This development of the marketing character is discussed in Chapter VII.)

The proprietary feeling also shows up in other relationships, for example toward doctors, dentists, lawyers, bosses, workers. People express it in speaking of *"my* doctor," *"my* dentist," *"my* workers," and so on. But aside from their property attitude toward other human beings, people experience an unending number of objects, even feelings, as property. Take health and illness, for example. People who discuss their health do so with a proprietary feeling, referring to *their* sicknesses, *their* operations, *their* treatments—*their* diets, *their* medicines. They clearly consider that health and sickness are property; their property relationship to their bad health is analogous, say, to that of a stockholder whose shares are losing part of their original value in a badly falling market.

Ideas and beliefs can also become property, as can even habits. For instance, anyone who eats an identical breakfast at the same time each morning can be disturbed by even a slight change in that routine, because his habit has become a property whose loss endangers his security.

The picture of the universality of the having mode of existence may strike many readers as too negative and one-sided; and indeed it is. I wanted to portray the socially prevalent attitude first in order to give as clear a picture as possible. But there is another element that can give this picture a degree of balance, and that is a growing attitude among the young generation that is quite different from the majority. Among these young people we find patterns of consumption that are not hidden forms of acquisition and having, but expressions of genuine joy in doing what one likes to do without expecting anything "lasting" in return. These young people travel long distances, often with hardships, to hear music they like, to see a place they want to see, to meet people they want to meet. Whether their aims are as valuable as they think they are is not the question here; even if they are without sufficient seriousness, preparation, or concentration, these young people dare to *be,* and they are not interested in what they get in return or what they can keep. They also seem much more sincere than the older generation, although often philosophically and politically naive. They do not polish their egos all the time in order to be a desirable "object" on the market. They do not protect their image by constantly lying, with or without knowing it; they do not expend their energy in repressing truth, as the majority does. And frequently, they impress their elders by their honesty—for their elders secretly admire people who can see or tell the truth. Among them are politically and religiously oriented groups of all shadings, but also many without any particular ideology or doctrine who may say of themselves that they are just "searching." While they may not have found themselves, or a goal that gives guidance to the practice of life, they are searching to be themselves instead of having and consuming.

This positive element in the picture needs to be qualified, however. Many of these same young people (and their number has been markedly decreasing since the late sixties) had not progressed from freedom *from* to freedom *to;* they simply rebelled without attempting to find a goal toward which to move, except that of freedom from restrictions and dependence. Like that of their bourgeois parents, their motto was "New is beautiful!" and they developed an almost phobic disinterest in all tradition, including the thoughts that the greatest minds have produced. In a kind of naïve narcissism they believed that they could discover by themselves all that is worth discovering. Basically, their ideal was to become small children again, and such authors as Marcuse produced the convenient ideology that return to childhood—not development to maturity—is the ultimate goal of socialism and revolution. They were happy as long as they were young enough for this euphoria to last; but many of them have passed this period with severe disappointment, without having acquired well-founded convictions, without a center within themselves. They often end up as disappointed, apathetic persons—or as unhappy fanatics of destruction.

Not all who had started with great hopes ended up with disappointment, however, but it is unfortunately impossible to know what their number is. To my knowledge, no valid statistical data or sound estimates are available, and even if they were available, it is almost impossible to be sure how to qualify the individuals. Today, millions of people in America and Europe try to find contact with tradition and with teachers who can show them the way. But in large part the doctrines and teachers are either fraudulent, or vitiated by the spirit of public relations ballyhoo, or mixed up with the financial and prestige interests of the respective gurus. Some people may genuinely benefit from such methods in spite of the sham; others will apply them without any serious intention of inner change. But only a detailed quantitative and qualitative analysis of the new believers could show how many belong to each group.

My personal estimate is that the young people (and some older ones) who are seriously concerned with changing from the having to the being mode number more than a few dispersed individuals. I believe that quite a large number of groups and individuals are moving in the direction of being, that they represent a new trend transcending the having orientation of the majority, and that they are of historical significance. It will not be the first time in history that a minority indicates the course that historical development will take. The existence of this minority gives hope for the general change in attitude from having to being. This hope is all the more real since some of the factors that made it possible for these new attitudes to emerge are historical changes that can hardly be reversed: the breakdown of patriarchal supremacy over women and of parents' domination of the young. While the political revolution of the twentieth century, the Russian revolution, has failed (it is too early to judge the final outcome of the Chinese revolution), the victorious revolutions of our century, even though they are only in their first stages, are the women's, the children's, and the sexual revolutions. Their principles have already been accepted by the consciousness of a great many individuals, and every day the old ideologies become more ridiculous.

The Nature of Having

The nature of the having mode of existence follows from the nature of private property. In this mode of existence all that matters is my acquisition of property and my unlimited right to keep what I have acquired. The having mode excludes others; it does not require any further effort on my part to keep my property or to make productive use of it. The Buddha has described this mode of behavior as craving, the Jewish and Christian religions as coveting; it transforms everybody and everything into something dead and subject to another's power.

The sentence "I have something" expresses the relation between the subject, *I* (or he, we, you, they), and the object, *O*. It implies that the subject is permanent and the object is permanent. But is there permanence in the subject? Or in the object? I shall die; I may lose the social position that guarantees my having something. The object is similarly not permanent: it can be destroyed, or it can be lost, or it can lose its value. Speaking of having something permanently rests upon the illusion of a permanent and indestructible substance. If I seem to have everything, I have—in reality—nothing, since my having, possessing, controlling an object is only a transitory moment in the process of living.

In the last analysis, the statement *"I* [subject] have *O* [object]"* expresses a definition of *I* through my possession of *O*. The subject is not *myself* but *I am what I have.* My property constitutes myself and my identity. The underlying thought in the statement "I am I" is *"I am I because I have X"*—X equaling all natural objects and persons to whom I relate myself through my power to control them, to make them permanently mine.

In the having mode, there is no alive relationship between me and what I have. It and I have become things, and I have *it,* because I have the force to make it mine. But there is also a reverse relationship: *it has me,* because my sense of identity, i.e., of sanity, rests upon my having *it* (and as many things as possible). The having mode of existence is not established by an alive, productive process between subject and object; it makes *things* of both object and subject. The relationship is one of deadness, not aliveness.

Having—Force—Rebellion

The tendency to grow in terms of their own nature is common to all living beings. Hence we resist any attempt to prevent our growing in the ways determined by our structure. In order to break this resistance, whether it is conscious or not, physical or mental force is necessary. Inanimate objects resist control of their physical composition in various degrees through the energy inherent in their atomic and molecular structures. But they do not fight against being used. The use of heteronomous force with living beings (i.e., the force that tends to bend us in directions contrary to our given structure and that is detrimental to our growth) arouses resistance. This resistance can take all forms, from overt, effective, direct, active resistance to indirect, ineffectual, and, very often, unconscious resistance.

What is restricted is the free, spontaneous expression of the infant's, the child's, the adolescent's, and eventually the adult's will, their thirst for knowledge and truth, their wish for affection. The growing person is forced to give up most of his or her autonomous, genuine desires and interests, and his or her own will, and to adopt a will and desires and feelings that are not autonomous but superimposed by the social patterns of thought and feeling. Society, and the family as its psychosocial agent, has to solve a difficult problem: *How to break a person's will without his being aware of it?* Yet by a complicated process of indoctrination, rewards, punishments, and fitting ideology, it solves this task by and large so well that most people believe they are following their own will and are unaware that their will itself is conditioned and manipulated.

The greatest difficulty in this suppression of the will exists with regard to sexuality, because we deal here with a strong tendency of the natural order that is less easy to manipulate than many other desires. For this reason people try harder to fight their sexual desires than almost any other human desire. No need to cite the various forms of the vilification of sex from moral grounds (its evilness) to health grounds (masturbation does physical harm). The church had to forbid birth control and extramarital sex, and it still sticks to these principles even today when prudence would recommend a more tolerant course.

The effort made to suppress sex would be beyond our understanding if it were for the sake of sex as such. Not sex, however, but the breaking of human will is the reason for vilifying sex. A great number of the so-called primitive societies have no sex tabu whatever. Since they function without exploitation and domination, they do not have to break the individual's will. They can afford not to stigmatize sex and to enjoy the pleasure of sexual relations without guilt feelings. Most remarkable in these societies is that this sexual freedom does not lead to sexual greed; that after a period of relatively transient sexual relations couples find each other; that they then have no desire to swap partners, but are also free to separate when love has gone. For these not-property-oriented groups sexual enjoyment is an expression of being, not the result of sexual possessiveness. In saying this I do not imply that we should return to living as these primitive societies do—not that we could, even if we wanted to, for the simple reason that the process of individuation and individual differentiation and distance that civilization has brought about gives individual love a different quality from that in primitive society. We cannot regress; we can only move forward. What matters is that new forms of propertylessness will do away with the sexual greed that is characteristic of all having societies.

Sexual desire is one expression of independence that is expressed very early in life (masturbation). Its denunciation serves to break the will of the child and make it feel guilty, and thus more submissive. To a large extent the impulse to break sexual tabus is essentially an attempt at rebellion aimed at restoring one's freedom. But the breaking of sexual tabus as such does not lead to greater freedom; the rebellion is drowned, as it were, in the sexual satisfaction . . . and in the person's subsequent guilt. Only the achievement of inner independence is conducive to freedom and ends the need for fruitless rebellion. The same holds true for all other behavior that aims at doing the forbidden as an attempt to restore one's freedom. *Indeed, tabus create sexual obsessiveness and perversions, but sexual obsessiveness and perversions do not create freedom.*

The rebellion of the child manifests itself in many other ways: by the child's not accepting the rules of cleanliness training; by not eating, or by overeating; by aggression and sadism, and by many kinds of self-destructive acts. Often the rebellion manifests itself in a kind of general "slow-down strike"—a withdrawal of interest in the world, laziness, passivity, up to the most pathological forms of slow self-destruction. The effects of this power struggle between children and parents is the subject of David E. Schecter's paper on "Infant Development." All data indicate that *heteronomous interference with the child's and the later person's growth process is the deepest root of mental pathology, especially of destructiveness.*

It must be clearly understood, though, that freedom is not laissez-faire and arbitrariness. Human beings have a specific structure—like any other species—and can grow only in terms of this structure. Freedom does not mean freedom *from* all guiding principles. It means the freedom *to grow* according to the laws of the structure of human existence (autonomous restrictions). It means obedience to the laws that govern optimal human development. Any authority that furthers this goal is "rational authority" when this furtherance is achieved by way of helping to mobilize the child's activity, critical thinking, and faith in life. It is "irrational authority" when it imposes on the child heteronomous norms that serve the purposes of the authority, but not the purposes of the child's specific structure.

The having mode of existence, the attitude centered on property and profit, necessarily produces the desire—indeed the need—for power. To control other living human beings we need to use power to break their resistance. To maintain control over private property we need to use power to protect it from those who would take it from us because they, like us, can never have enough; the desire to have private property produces the desire to use violence in order to rob others in overt or covert ways. In the having mode, one's happiness lies in one's superiority over others, in one's power, and in the last analysis, in one's capacity to conquer, rob, kill. In the being mode it lies in loving, sharing, giving.

Other Factors Supporting the Having Mode

Language is an important factor in fortifying the having orientation. The name of a person—and we all have names (and maybe numbers if the present-day trend toward depersonalization continues)—creates the illusion that he or she is a final, immortal being. The person and the name become equivalent; the name demonstrates that the person is a lasting, indestructible substance—and not a process. Common nouns have the same function: i.e., love, pride, hate, joy give the appearance of fixed substances, but such nouns have no reality and only obscure the insight that we are dealing with processes going on in a human being. But even nouns that are names of *things,* such as "table" or "lamp," are misleading. The words indicate that we are speaking of fixed substances, although things are nothing but a process of energy that causes certain sensations in our bodily system. But these sensations are not *perceptions* of specific things like table or lamp; these perceptions are the result of a cultural process of learning, a process that makes certain sensations assume the form of specific percepts. We naively believe that things like tables and lamps exist as such, and we fail to see that society teaches us to transform sensations into perceptions that permit us to manipulate the world around us in order to enable us to survive in a given culture. Once we have given such percepts a name, the name seems to guarantee the final and unchangeable reality of the percept.

The need to have has still another foundation, the *biologically given desire to live*. Whether we are happy or unhappy, our body impels us to strive for *immortality*. But since we know by experience that we shall die, we seek for solutions that make us believe that, in spite of the empirical evidence, we are immortal. This wish has taken many forms: the belief of the Pharaohs that their bodies enshrined in the pyramids would be immortal; many religious fantasies of life after death, in the happy hunting grounds of early hunter societies; the Christian and Islam paradise. In contemporary society since the eighteenth century, "history" and "the future" have become the substitutes for the Christian heaven: fame, celebrity, even notoriety—anything that seems to guarantee a footnote in the record of history—constitutes a bit of immortality. The craving for fame is not just secular vanity—it has a religious quality for those who do not believe in the traditional hereafter any more. (This is particularly noticeable among political leaders.) Publicity paves the way to immortality, and the public relations agents become the new priests.

But perhaps more than anything else, possession of property constitutes the fulfillment of the craving for immortality, and it is for this reason that the having orientation has such strength. If my *self* is constituted by what I *have*, then I am immortal if the things I have are indestructible. From Ancient Egypt to today—from physical immortality, via mummification of the body, to mental immortality, via the last will—people have remained alive beyond their physical/mental lifetimes. Via the legal power of the last will the disposal of our property is determined for generations to come; through the laws of inheritance, I—inasmuch as I am an owner of capital —become immortal.

The Having Mode and the Anal Character

A helpful approach to understanding the mode of having is to recall one of Freud's most significant findings, that after going through their infant phase of mere passive receptivity followed by a phase of aggressive exploitative receptivity, all children, before they reach maturity, go through a phase Freud designated the *anal-erotic.* Freud discovered that this phase often remains dominant during a person's development, and that when it does it leads to the development of the *anal character,* i.e., the character of a person whose main energy in life is directed toward having, saving, and hoarding money and material things as well as feelings, gestures, words, energy. It is the character of the stingy individual and is usually connected with such other traits as orderliness, punctuality, stubbornness, each to a more than ordinary degree. An important aspect of Freud's concept is the symbolic connection between money and feces—gold and dirt—of which he quotes a number of examples. His concept of the anal character as one that has not reached maturity is in fact a sharp criticism of bourgeois society of the nineteenth century, in which the qualities of the anal character constituted the norm for moral behavior and were looked upon as the expression of "human nature." Freud's equation: money = feces, is an implicit, although not intended, criticism of the functioning of bourgeois society and its possessiveness and may be compared with Marx's discussion of money in the *Economic and Philosophical Manuscripts.*

It is of little importance in this context that Freud believed that a special phase of the libido development was primary and that the character formation was secondary (while in my opinion it is the product of the interpersonal constellation in one's early life and, most of all, the social conditions conducive to its formation). What matters is Freud's view that *the predominant orientation in possession occurs in the period before the achievement of full maturity and is pathological if it remains perma-*

nent. For Freud, in other words, the person exclusively concerned with having and possession is a neurotic, mentally sick person; hence it would follow that the society in which most of the members are anal characters is a sick society.

Asceticism and Equality

Much of the moral and political discussion has centered on the question: To have or not to have? On the moral-religious level this meant the alternative between the ascetic life and the nonascetic life, the latter including both productive enjoyment and unlimited pleasure. This alternative loses most of its meaning if one's emphasis is not *on* the single act of behavior but on the attitude underlying it. Ascetic behavior, with its constant preoccupation with nonenjoyment, may be only the negation of strong desires for having and consuming. In the ascetic these desires can be repressed, yet in the very attempt to suppress having and consuming, the person may be equally preoccupied with having and consuming. This denial by overcompensation is, as psychoanalytic data show, very frequent. It occurs in such cases as fanatical vegetarians repressing destructive impulses, fanatical antiabortionists repressing their murderous impulses, fanatics of "virtue" repressing their own "sinful" impulses. What matters here is not a certain conviction as such, but the fanaticism that supports it. This, like all fanaticism, suggests the suspicion that it serves to cover other, and usually the opposite, impulses.

In the economic and political field a similar erroneous alternative is between unrestricted inequality and absolute equality of income. If everybody's possessions are functional and personal, then whether someone has somewhat more than another person does not constitute a social problem, for since possession is not essential, envy does not grow. On the other hand, those who are concerned with equality in the sense that each one's share must be exactly equal to anyone else's show that their own having orientation is as strong as ever, except that it is denied by their preoccupation with exact equality. Behind this concern their real motivation is visible: envy. Those demanding that nobody should have more than themselves are thus protecting themselves from the envy they would feel if anyone had even an ounce more of anything. What matters is that both luxury and poverty shall be eradicated; equality must not mean the quantitative equality of each morsel of material goods, but that income is not differentiated to a point that creates different experiences of life for different groups. In the *Economic and Philosophical Manuscripts* Marx pointed this out in what he calls "crude communism," which "negates the personality of man in every sphere"; this type of communism "is only the culmination of such envy and leveling-down on the basis of a preconceived minimum."

Existential Having

In order to fully appreciate the mode of having that we are dealing with here, yet another qualification seems necessary, that of the function of *existential having;* for human existence requires that we have, keep, take care of, and use certain things in order to survive. This holds true for our bodies, for food, shelter, clothing, and for the tools necessary to produce our needs. This form of having may be called existential having because it is rooted in human existence. It is a rationally directed impulse in the pursuit of staying alive—in contrast to the *characterological having* we have been dealing with so far, which is a passionate drive to retain and keep that is not innate, but that has developed as the result of the impact of social conditions on the human species as it is biologically given.

Existential having is not in conflict with being; characterological having necessarily is. Even the "just" and the "saintly," inasmuch as they are human, must want to have in the existential sense—while the average person wants to have in the existential *and* in the characterological sense. (See the earlier discussion of existential and characterological dichotomies in *Man for Himself.*)

V

What Is the Being Mode?

Most of us know more about the mode of having than we do about the mode of being, because having is by far the more frequently experienced mode in our culture. But something more important than that makes defining the mode of being so much more difficult than defining the mode of having, namely the very nature of the difference between these two modes of existence.

Having refers to *things* and things are fixed and *describable.* Being refers to *experience,* and human experience is in principle not describable. What is fully describable is our *persona*—the mask we each wear, the ego we present—for this persona is in itself a thing. In contrast, the living human being is not a dead image and cannot be described like a thing. In fact, the living human being cannot be described at all. Indeed, much can be said about me, about my character, about my total orientation to life. This insightful knowledge can go very far in understanding and describing my own or another's psychical structure. But the total me, my whole individuality, my suchness that is as unique as my fingerprints are, can never be fully understood, not even by empathy, for no two human beings are entirely alike.* Only in the process of mutual alive relatedness can the other and I overcome the barrier of sepa-

*This is the limitation of even the best psychology, a point I have discussed in detail, comparing "negative psychology" and "negative theology" in an essay, "On the Limitations and Dangers of Psychology" (1959).

rateness, inasmuch as we both participate in the dance of life. Yet our full identification of each other can never be achieved.

Even a single act of behavior cannot be fully described. One could write pages of description of the Mona Lisa's smile, and still the pictured smile would not have been caught in words —but not because her smile is so "mysterious." Everybody's smile is mysterious (unless it is the learned, synthetic smile of the marketplace). No one can fully describe the expression of interest, enthusiasm, biophilia, or of hate or narcissism that one may see in the eyes of another person, or the variety of facial expressions, of gaits, of postures, of intonations that exists among people.

Being Active

The mode of being has as its prerequisites independence, freedom, and the presence of critical reason. Its fundamental characteristic is that of being active, not in the sense of outward activity, of busyness, but of inner activity, the productive use of our human powers. To be active means to give expression to one's faculties, talents, to the wealth of human gifts with which—though in varying degrees—every human being is endowed. It means to renew oneself, to grow, to flow out, to love, to transcend the prison of one's isolated ego, to be interested, to "list," to give. Yet none of these experiences can be fully expressed in words. The words are vessels that are filled with experience that overflows the vessels. The words point to an experience; they are not the experience. The moment that I express what I experience exclusively in thought and words, the experience has gone: it has dried up, is dead, a mere thought. Hence being is indescribable in words and is communicable only by sharing my experience. In the structure of having, the dead word rules; in the structure of being, the alive and inexpressible experience rules. (Of course, in the being mode there is also thinking that is alive and productive.)

Perhaps the being mode may best be described in a symbol suggested to me by Max Hunziger: A blue glass appears to be blue when light shines through it because it absorbs all other colors and thus does not let them pass. This is to say, we call a glass "blue" precisely because it does not retain the blue waves. It is named not for what it possesses but for what it gives out.

Only to the extent that we decrease the mode of having, that is of nonbeing—i.e., stop finding security and identity by clinging to what we have, by "sitting on it," by holding onto our ego and our possessions—can the mode of being emerge. "To be" requires giving up one's egocentricity and selfishness, or in words often used by the mystics, by making oneself "empty" and "poor."

But most people find giving up their having orientation too difficult; any attempt to do so arouses their intense anxiety and feels like giving up all security, like being thrown into the ocean when one does not know how to swim. They do not know that when they have given up the crutch of property, they can begin to use their own proper forces and walk by themselves. What holds them back is the illusion that they could not walk by themselves, that they would collapse if they were not supported by the things they have. They are like the child who is afraid that it will never be able to walk, after it has fallen the first time. But nature and human help prevent human beings from becoming cripples. Those who believe that they would collapse without using the crutches of having also need some human help.

Activity and Passivity

Being, in the sense we have described it, implies the faculty of being active; passivity excludes being. However, "active" and "passive" are among the most misunderstood words, because their meaning is completely different today from what it was from classic antiquity and the Middle Ages to the period beginning with the Renaissance. In order to understand the concept of being, the concept of activity and passivity must be clarified.

In modern usage activity is usually defined as a quality of behavior that brings about a visible effect by expenditure of energy. Thus, for instance, farmers who cultivate their lands are called active; so are workers on assembly lines, salespeople who persuade their customers to buy, investors who invest their own or other people's money, physicians who treat their patients, clerks who sell postage stamps, bureaucrats who file papers. While some of these activities may require more interest and concentration than others, this does not matter with regard to "activity." Activity, by and large, is *socially recognized purposeful behavior that results in corresponding socially useful changes.*

Activity in the modern sense refers only to *behavior,* not to the person behind the behavior. It makes no difference whether people are active because they are driven by external force, like a slave, or by internal compulsion, like a person driven by anxiety. It does not matter whether they are interested in their work, like a carpenter or a creative writer, or a scientist or a gardener; or whether they have no inner relation to and satisfaction in what they are doing, like the worker on the assembly line or the postal clerk.

The modern sense of activity makes no distinction between *activity* and mere *busyness.* But there is a fundamental difference between the two that corresponds to the terms "alienated" and "nonalienated" in respect to activities. In alienated activity I do not experience myself as the acting subject of my activity; rather, I experience the *outcome* of my activity—and that as something "over there," separated from me and standing above and against me. In alienated activity *I* do not really act; I am *acted upon* by external or internal forces. I have become separated from the result of my activity. The best observable case of alienated activity in the field of psychopathology is that of compulsive-obsessional persons. Forced by an inner urge to do something against their own wills—such as counting steps, repeating certain phrases, performing certain private rituals—they can be extremely active in the pursuit of this aim; but as psychoanalytic investigation has amply shown, they are driven by an inner force that they are unaware of. An equally clear example of alienated activity is posthypnotic behavior. Persons under hypnotic suggestion to do this or that upon awakening from the hypnotic trance will do these things without any awareness that they are not doing what they *want* to do, but are following their respective hypnotists' previously given orders.

In nonalienated activity, I experience *myself* as the *subject* of my activity. Nonalienated activity is a process of giving birth to something, of producing something and remaining related to what I produce. This also implies that my activity is a manifestation of my powers, that I and my activity and the result of my activity are one. I call this nonalienated activity *productive activity.* *

"Productive" as used here does not refer to the capacity to create something new or original, as an artist or scientist may be creative. Neither does it refer to the product of my activity, but to its *quality.* A painting or a scientific treatise may be quite unproductive, i.e., sterile; on the other hand, the process going on in persons who are aware of themselves in depth, or who truly "see" a tree rather than just look at it, or who read a poem and experience in themselves the movement of feelings the poet has expressed in words—that process may be very productive, although nothing is "produced." Productive activity denotes the state of inner activity; it does not necessarily have a connection with the creation of a work of art, of science, or of something "useful." Productiveness is a character orientation all human beings are capable of, to the extent that they are not emotionally crippled. Productive persons

---

*I used the terms "spontaneous activity" in *Escape from Freedom* and "productive activity" in my later writings.

animate whatever they touch. They give birth to their own faculties and bring life to other persons and to things.

"Activity" and "passivity" can each have two entirely different meanings. Alienated activity, in the sense of mere busyness, is actually "passivity," in the sense of productivity; while passivity, in terms of nonbusyness, may be nonalienated activity. This is so difficult to understand today because most activity is alienated "passivity," while productive passivity is rarely experienced.

Activity—Passivity, According to the Masters of Thought

"Activity" and "passivity" were not used in the current sense in the philosophical tradition of preindustrial society. They hardly could have been, since the alienation of work had not reached a point comparable to the one existing now. For this reason such philosophers as *Aristotle* do not even make a clear-cut distinction between "activity" and mere "busyness." In Athens, alienated work was done only by slaves; work which involved bodily labor seems to have been excluded from the concept of *praxis* ("practice"), a term that refers only to almost any kind of activity a *free* person is likely to perform, and essentially the term Aristotle used for a person's free activity. (See Nicholas Lobkowicz, *Theory and Practice.*) Considering this background, the problem of subjectively meaningless, alienated, purely routinized work could hardly arise for free Athenians. Their freedom implied precisely that because they were not slaves, their activity was productive and meaningful to them.

That Aristotle did not share our present concepts of activity and passivity becomes unmistakably clear if we will consider that for him the highest form of praxis, i.e., of activity—even above political activity—is the *contemplative life,* devoted to the search for truth. The idea that contemplation was a form of inactivity was unthinkable for him. Aristotle considers contemplative life the *activity* of the best part in us, the *nous.* The slave can enjoy sensuous pleasure, even as the free do. But *eudaimonia*, "well-being," consists not in pleasures but in *activities in accordance with virtue* (*Nichomachean Ethics*, 1177a, 2 ff.).

Like Aristotle's, *Thomas Aquinas*' position is also in contrast to the modern concept of activity. For Aquinas, too, the life devoted to inner stillness and spiritual knowledge, the *vita contemplativa*, is the highest form of human activity. He concedes that the daily life, the *vita activa*, of the average person, is also valuable, and it leads to well-being (*beatitudo*), provided —and this qualification is crucial—that the aim toward which all one's activities are directed is well-being and that one is able to control one's passions and one's body (Thomas Aquinas, *Summa*, 2–2:182, 183; 1–2:4,6).

But the problem of the *vita contemplativa* and the *vita activa* goes far beyond this point. For while Aquinas' attitude is one of a certain compromise, the author of *The Cloud of Unknowing*, a contemporary of *Master Eckhart*, argues sharply against the value of the active life, while Eckhart, on the other hand, speaks out very much in favor of it. The contradiction is not as sharp as it may appear, however, because all agree that activity is "wholesome" only when it is rooted in and expresses the ultimate ethical and spiritual demands. For this reason, for all these teachers, busyness, i.e., activity separated from people's spiritual ground, is to be rejected.*

As a person and as a thinker *Spinoza* embodied the spirit and the values that were alive in Eckhart's time, roughly four centuries earlier; yet he also keenly observed the changes that had occurred in society and in the average person. He was the founder of modern scientific psychology; one of the discoverers of the dimension of the unconscious, and with this enriched insight he gave a more systematic and precise analysis of the difference between activity and passivity than had any of his predecessors.

In his *Ethics*, Spinoza distinguishes between activity and

---

*The writings of W. Lange, N. Lobkowicz, and D. Mieth (1971) can provide further insights into this problem of contemplative life and active life.

passivity (to act and to suffer) as the two fundamental aspects of the mind's operation. The first criterion for *acting* is that an action follows from human nature: "I say that we act when anything is done, either within us or without us, of which we are the adequate cause, that is to say, when from our nature anything follows, either within or without us, which by that nature alone can be clearly and distinctly understood. On the other hand I say that we suffer [i.e., in Spinoza's sense, are passive] when anything is done within us, or when anything follows from our nature of which we are not the cause except partially" (*Ethics*, 3, def. 2).

These sentences are difficult for the modern reader, who is accustomed to think that the term "human nature" does not correspond to any demonstrable empirical data. But for Spinoza, as for Aristotle, this is not so; nor is it for some contemporary neurophysiologists, biologists, and psychologists. Spinoza believes that human nature is as characteristic for human beings as horse nature is for the horse; furthermore, that goodness or badness, success or failure, well-being or suffering, activity or passivity depend on the degree to which persons succeed in realizing the optimal development of their own natures. Optimal realization of one's species nature (in the case of people, human nature) is the goal of life; the closer we arrive at the model of human nature, the greater are our freedom and our well-being.

In Spinoza's model of human beings the attribute of activity is inseparable from another: reason. Inasmuch as we act in accordance with the conditions of our existence, and are aware of these conditions as real and necessary ones, we know the truth about ourselves. "Our mind acts at times and at times suffers: in so far as it has adequate ideas, it necessarily acts: and in so far as it has inadequate ideas, it necessarily suffers" (*Ethics*, 3, prop. 1).

Desires are divided into active and passive ones *(actiones* and *passiones).* The former are rooted in the conditions of our existence (the natural and not the pathological distortions), and the latter are not thus rooted but are caused by inner or outer distorting conditions. The former exist to the extent that we are free; the latter are caused by inner or outer force. All "active affects" are necessarily good: "passions" can be good or evil. According to Spinoza, activity, reason, freedom, well-being, joy, and self-perfection are inseparably connected —in the same way as passivity, irrationality, bondage, sadness, powerlessness, and strivings contrary to the demands of human nature are (*Ethics,* 4, app. 2, 3, 5; props. 40, 42).

One understands Spinoza's ideas about passions and passivity fully only if one proceeds to the last—and most modern —step of his thinking: that to be driven by irrational passions is to be mentally sick. To the degree that we achieve optimal growth, we are not only (relatively) free, strong, rational, and joyous but also mentally healthy; to the degree that we fail to reach this aim, we are unfree, weak, lacking rationality, and depressed. Spinoza, to my knowledge, was the first modern thinker to postulate that mental health and sickness are outcomes of right and wrong living respectively.

For Spinoza mental health is, in the last analysis, a manifestation of right living; mental illness, a symptom of the failure to live according to the requirements of human nature. "But if the *greedy* person thinks only of money and possessions, the ambitious one only of fame, one does not think of them as being insane, but only as annoying; generally one has contempt for them. But *factually,* greediness, ambition, and so forth are forms of insanity, although usually one does not think of them as 'illness' " (*Ethics,* 4, prop. 44). In this statement, so foreign to the thinking of our time, Spinoza considers passions that do not correspond to the needs of human nature as pathological; in fact, he goes so far as to call them a form of insanity.

Spinoza's concepts of activity and passivity are a most radical critique of industrial society. In contrast to today's belief that persons driven mainly by greed for money, possession, or fame are normal and well adjusted, they are considered by

Spinoza utterly passive and basically sick. The active persons in Spinoza's sense, which he personified in his own life, have become exceptions, and are somewhat suspected of being "neurotic" because they are so little adapted to so-called normal activity.

Marx wrote (in the *Economic and Philosophical Manuscripts*) that "free conscious activity" (i.e., human activity) is "the species character of man." Labor, for him, represents human activity, and human activity is life. Capital, on the other hand, represents for Marx the amassed, the past, and in the last analysis, the dead *(Grundrisse)*. One cannot fully understand the affective charge which the struggle between capital and labor had for Marx unless one considers that for him it was the fight between aliveness and deadness, the present versus the past, people versus things, being versus having. For Marx the question was: Who should rule whom—should life rule the dead, or the dead rule life? Socialism, for him, represented a society in which life had won over the dead.

Marx's whole critique of capitalism and his vision of socialism are rooted in the concept that human self-activity is paralyzed in the capitalist system and that the goal is to restore full humanity by restoring activity in all spheres of life.

Despite the formulations influenced by the classic economists, the cliché that Marx was a determinist, making human beings the passive objects of history and depriving them of their activity, is the very opposite of his thinking, as any who themselves read Marx, rather than a few isolated sentences taken out of context, will be easily convinced. Marx's views could not be more clearly expressed than they are in his own statement: "History does nothing; it possesses no colossal riches, it 'fights no fight.' It is rather man—real, living man— who acts, possesses and fights everything. It is by no means 'History' which uses man as a means to carry out its ends as if it were a person apart; rather History is nothing but the activity of man in pursuit of his ends" (Marx and Engels, *The Holy Family*).

Of near contemporaries none has perceived the passive character of modern activity as penetratingly as has *Albert Schweitzer,* who, in his study of the decay and restoration of civilization, saw modern Man as unfree, incomplete, unconcentrated, pathologically dependent, and "absolutely passive."

Being as Reality

Thus far I have described the meaning of being by contrasting it to having. But a second, equally important meaning of being is revealed by contrasting it to *appearing.* If I appear to be kind while my kindness is only a mask to cover my exploitativeness—if I appear to be courageous while I am extremely vain or perhaps suicidal—if I appear to love my country while I am furthering my selfish interests, the appearance, i.e., my overt behavior, is in drastic contradiction to the reality of forces that motivate me. My behavior is different from my character. My character structure, the true motivation of my behavior, constitutes my real being. My behavior may partly reflect my being, but it is usually a mask that I have and that I wear for my own purposes. Behaviorism deals with this mask as if it were a reliable scientific datum; true insight is focused on the inner reality, which is usually neither conscious nor directly observable. This concept of being as "unmasking," as is expressed by Eckhart, is central in Spinoza's and Marx's thought and is the fundamental discovery of Freud.

To understand the discrepancy between behavior and character, between my mask and the reality it hides, is the main achievement of Freud's psychoanalysis. He devised a method (free association, analysis of dreams, transference, and resistance) that aimed at uncovering the instinctual (essentially sexual) desires that had been repressed in early childhood. Even when later developments in psychoanalytic theory and therapy proceeded to emphasize traumatic events in the field of early interpersonal relations rather than of instinctual life,

the principle remained the same: What is repressed are early
and—as I believe—later traumatic desires and fears; the way
to recovery from symptoms or from a more general malaise
lies in uncovering this repressed material. In other words,
what is repressed are the irrational, infantile, and individual
elements of experience.

On the other hand, the common-sense views of a normal,
i.e., socially adapted, citizen were supposed to be rational and
not in need of depth analysis. But this is not true at all. Our
conscious motivations, ideas, and beliefs are a blend of false
information, biases, irrational passions, rationalizations,
prejudices, in which morsels of truth swim around and give
the reassurance, albeit false, that the whole mixture is real and
true. The thinking process attempts to organize this whole
cesspool of illusions according to the laws of logic and plausi-
bility. This level of consciousness is supposed to reflect reality; it is the map we use for organizing our life. This false map
is not repressed. *What is repressed is the knowledge of reality, the
knowledge of what is true.* If we ask, then: *What is unconscious?* the
answer must be: Aside from irrational passions, almost the
whole of knowledge of reality. The unconscious is basically
determined by society, which produces irrational passions
and provides its members with various kinds of fiction and
thus forces the truth to become the prisoner of the alleged
rationality.

. Stating that the truth is repressed is based, of course, on the
premise that we know the truth and repress this knowledge;
in other words, that there is "unconscious knowledge." My
experience in psychoanalysis—of others and of myself—is
that this is indeed true. We perceive reality, and we cannot
help perceiving it. Just as our senses are organized to see,
hear, smell, touch when we are brought together with reality,
our reason is organized to recognize reality, i.e., to see things
as they are, to perceive the truth. I am not of course referring
to the part of reality that requires scientific tools or methods
in order to be perceived. I am referring to what is recognizable by concentrated "seeing," especially the reality in our-

selves and in others. We know when we meet a dangerous person, when we meet somebody we can fully trust; we know when we are lied to, or exploited, or fooled, when we have sold ourselves a bill of goods. We know almost everything that is important to know about human behavior, just as our ancestors had a remarkable knowledge about the movements of the stars. But while they were *aware* of their knowledge and used it, we repress our knowledge immediately, because if it were conscious it would make life too difficult and, as we persuade ourselves, too "dangerous."

The proof of this statement is easy to find. It exists in many dreams in which we exhibit a deep insight into the essence of other people, and of ourselves, which we completely lack in the daytime. (I included examples of "insight dreams" in *The Forgotten Language.*) It is evidenced in those frequent reactions in which we suddenly see somebody in an entirely different light, and then feel as if we had had this knowledge all the time before. It can be found in the phenomenon of resistance when the painful truth threatens to come to the surface: in slips of the tongue, in awkward expressions, in a state of trance, or in instances when a person says something, as in an aside, that is the very opposite of what he or she always claimed to believe, and then seems to forget this aside a minute later. Indeed, a great deal of our energy is used to hide from ourselves what we know, and the degree of such repressed knowledge can hardly be overestimated. A Talmudic legend has expressed this concept of the repression of the truth, in a poetic form: when a child is born, an angel touches its head, so that it forgets the knowledge of the truth that it has at the moment of birth. If the child did not forget, its life would become unbearable.

Returning to our main thesis: Being refers to the real, in contrast to the falsified, illusionary picture. In this sense, any attempt to increase the sector of being means increased insight into the reality of one's self, of others, of the world around us. The main ethical goals of Judaism and Christianity —overcoming greed and hate—cannot be realized without

another factor that is central in Buddhism and also plays a
role in Judaism and in Christianity: The way to being is penetration through the surface and insight into reality.

The Will to Give, to Share, to Sacrifice

In contemporary society the having mode of existing is
assumed to be rooted in human nature and, hence, virtually
unchangeable. The same idea is expressed in the dogma that
people are basically lazy, passive by nature, and that they do
not want to work or to do anything else, unless they are driven
by the incentive of material gain . . . or hunger . . . or the fear
of punishment. This dogma is doubted by hardly anybody,
and it determines our methods of education and of work. But
it is little more than an expression of the wish to prove the
value of our social arrangements by imputing to them that
they follow the needs of human nature. To the members of
many different societies of both past and present, the concept
of innate human selfishness and laziness would appear as
fantastic as the reverse sounds to us.

The truth is that both the having and the being modes of
existence are potentialities of human nature, that our biological urge for survival tends to further the having mode, but
that selfishness and laziness are not the only propensities
inherent in human beings.

We human beings have an inherent and deeply rooted desire to be: to express our faculties, to be active, to be related
to others, to escape the prison cell of selfishness. The truth
of this statement is proven by so much evidence that a whole
volume could easily be filled with it. D. O. Hebb has formulated the gist of the problem in the most general form by
stating that *the only behavioral problem is to account for inactivity,
not for activity.* The following data are evidence for this general
thesis:*

1. The data on animal behavior. Experiments and direct

---

*I have dealt with some of this evidence in *The Anatomy of Human Destructiveness.*

observation show that many species undertake difficult tasks with pleasure, even when no material rewards are offered.

2. Neurophysiological experiments demonstrate the activity inherent in the nerve cells.

3. Infantile behavior. Recent studies show the capacity and need of small infants to respond actively to complicated stimuli—findings in contrast to Freud's assumption that the infant experiences the outside stimulus as a threat and that it mobilizes its aggressiveness in order to remove the threat.

4. Learning behavior. Many studies show that the child and adolescent are lazy because learning material is presented to them in a dry and dead way that is incapable of arousing their genuine interest; if the pressure and the boredom are removed and the material is presented in an alive way, remarkable activity and initiative are mobilized.

5. Work behavior. E. Mayo's classic experiment has shown that even work which in itself is boring becomes interesting if the workers know that they are participating in an experiment conducted by an alive and gifted person who has the capacity to arouse their curiosity and their participation. The same has been shown in a number of factories in Europe and in the United States. The managers' stereotype of the workers is: workers are not really interested in active participation; all they want are higher wages, hence profit sharing might be an incentive for higher work productivity, but not the workers' participation. While the managers are right as far as the work methods they offer are concerned, experience has shown— and has convinced not a few managers—that if the workers can be truly active, responsible, and knowledgeable in their work role, the formerly uninterested ones change considerably and show a remarkable degree of inventiveness, activity, imagination, and satisfaction.*

*In his forthcoming book *The Gamesmen: The New Corporate Leaders* (which I was privileged to read in manuscript), Michael Maccoby mentions some recent democratic participatory projects, especially his own research in The Bolivar Project. Bolivar is dealt with in the working papers on that project and will be the subject, along with another project, of a larger work that Maccoby is presently planning.

6. The wealth of data to be found in social and political life. The belief that people do not want to make sacrifices is notoriously wrong. When Churchill announced at the beginning of the Second World War that what he had to demand from the British was blood, sweat, and tears, he did not deter them, but on the contrary, he appealed to their deep-seated human desire to make sacrifices, to give of themselves. The reaction of the British—and of the Germans and the Russians as well—toward the indiscriminate bombing of population centers by the belligerents proves that common suffering did not weaken their spirit; it strengthened their resistance and proved wrong those who believed terror bombing could break the morale of the enemy and help finish the war.

It is a sad commentary on our civilization, however, that war and suffering rather than peacetime living can mobilize human readiness to make sacrifices, and that the times of peace seem mainly to encourage selfishness. Fortunately, there are situations in peacetime in which human strivings for giving and solidarity manifest themselves in individual behavior. The workers' strikes, especially up to the period of the First World War, are an example of such essentially nonviolent behavior. The workers sought higher wages, but at the same time, they risked and accepted severe hardships in order to fight for their own dignity and the satisfaction of experiencing human solidarity. The strike was as much a "religious" as an economic phenomenon. While such strikes still do occur even today, most present-day strikes are for economic reasons— although strikes for better working conditions have increased recently.

The need to give and to share and the willingness to make sacrifices for others are still to be found among the members of certain professions, such as nurses, physicians, monks, and nuns. The goal of helping and sacrificing is given only lip service by many, if not most, of these professionals; yet the character of a goodly number corresponds to the values they profess. We find the same needs affirmed and expressed in many communes throughout the centuries, whether religious, socialist, or humanist. We find the wish to give in the people who volunteer their blood (without payment), in the many situations in which people risk their lives to save another's. We find the manifestation of the will to give in people who genuinely love. "False love," i.e., shared mutual selfishness, makes people more selfish (and this is the case often enough). Genuine love increases the capacity to love and to give to others. The true lover loves the whole world, in his or her love for a specific person.*

Conversely, we find that not a few people, especially younger ones, cannot stand the luxury and selfishness that surround them in their affluent families. Quite against the expectations of their elders, who think that their children "have everything they wish," they rebel against the deadness and isolation of their lives. For the fact is, they do not have everything they wish and they wish for what they do not have.

Outstanding examples of such people from past history are the sons and daughters of the rich in the Roman Empire, who embraced the religion of poverty and love; another is the Buddha, who was a prince and had every pleasure and luxury that he could possibly want, but discovered that having and consuming cause unhappiness and suffering. A more recent example (second half of the nineteenth century) is the sons and daughters of the Russian upper class, the *Narodniki*. Finding themselves no longer able to stand the life of idleness and injustice they had been born into, these young people left their families and joined the poor peasants, lived with them, and helped to lay one of the foundations of the revolutionary struggle in Russia.

*One of the most important sources for understanding the natural human impulse to give and to share is P. A. Kropotkin's classic, *Mutual Aid: A Factor of Evolution* (1902). Two other important works are *The Gift Relationship: From Human Blood to Social Policy* by Richard Titmuss (in which he points to the manifestations of the people's wish to give, and stresses that our economic system prevents people from freely exercising their right to give), and Edmund S. Phelps, ed., *Altruism, Morality and Economic Theory.*

We can witness a similar phenomenon among the sons and daughters of the well-to-do in the United States and Germany, who see their life in their affluent home environment as boring and meaningless. But more than that, they find the world's callousness toward the poor and the drift toward nuclear war for the sake of individual egotism unbearable. Thus, they move away from their home environment, looking for a new lifestyle—and remain unsatisfied because no constructive effort seems to have a chance. Many among them were originally the most idealistic and sensitive of the young generation; but at this point, lacking in tradition, maturity, experience, and political wisdom, they become desperate, narcissistically overestimate their own capacities and possibilities, and try to achieve the impossible by the use of force. They form so-called revolutionary groups and expect to save the world by acts of terror and destruction, not seeing that they are only contributing to the general tendency to violence and inhumanity. They have lost their capacity to love and have replaced it with the wish to sacrifice their lives. (Self-sacrifice is frequently the solution for individuals who ardently desire to love, but who have lost the capacity to love and see in the sacrifice of their own lives an experience of love in the highest degree.) But these self-sacrificing young people are very different from the *loving martyrs,* who want to live because they love life and who accept death only when they are forced to die in order not to betray themselves. Our present-day self-sacrificing young people are the accused, but they are also the accusers, in demonstrating that in our social system some of the very best young people become so isolated and hopeless that nothing but destruction and fanaticism are left as a way out of their despair.

The human desire to experience union with others is rooted in the specific conditions of existence that characterize the human species and is one of the strongest motivators of human behavior. By the combination of minimal instinctive determination and maximal development of the capacity for reason, we human beings have lost our original oneness with nature. In order not to feel utterly isolated—which would, in fact, condemn us to insanity—we need to find a new unity: with our fellow beings and with nature. This human need for unity with others is experienced in many ways: in the symbiotic tie to mother, an idol, one's tribe, one's nation, one's class, one's religion, one's fraternity, one's professional organization. Often, of course, these ties overlap, and often they assume an ecstatic form, as among members of certain religious sects or of a lynch mob, or in the outbursts of national hysteria in the case of war. The outbreak of the First World War, for example, occasioned one of the most drastic of these ecstatic forms of "union." Suddenly, from one day to the next, people gave up their lifelong convictions of pacifism, antimilitarism, socialism; scientists threw away their lifelong training in objectivity, critical thinking, and impartiality in order to join the big *We.*

The desire to experience union with others manifests itself in the lowest kind of behavior, i.e., in acts of sadism and destruction, as well as in the highest: solidarity on the basis of an ideal or conviction. It is also the main cause of the need to adapt; human beings are more afraid of being outcasts than even of dying. Crucial to every society is the kind of union and solidarity it fosters and the kind it *can* further, under the given conditions of its socioeconomic structure.

These considerations seem to indicate that both tendencies are present in human beings: the one, to *have*—to possess—that owes its strength in the last analysis to the biological factor of the desire for survival; the other, to *be*—to share, to give, to sacrifice—that owes its strength to the specific conditions of human existence and the inherent need to overcome one's isolation by oneness with others. From these two contradictory strivings in every human being it follows that the social structure, its values and norms, decides which of the two becomes dominant. Cultures that foster the greed for possession, and thus the having mode of existence, are rooted in one human potential; cultures that foster being and sharing are rooted in the other potential. We must decide which of these two potentials we want to cultivate, realizing, however, that our decision is largely determined by the socioeconomic structure of our given society that inclines us toward one or the other solution.

From my observations in the field of group behavior my best guess is that the two extreme groups, respectively manifesting deeply ingrained and almost unalterable types of having and of being, form a small minority; that in the vast majority both possibilities are real, and which of the two becomes dominant and which is repressed depends on environmental factors.

This assumption contradicts a widely held psychoanalytic dogma that environment produces essential changes in personality development in infancy and early childhood, but that after this period the character is fixed and hardly changed by external events. This psychoanalytic dogma has been able to gain acceptance because the basic conditions of their childhood continue into most people's later life, since in general, the same social conditions continue to exist. But numerous instances exist in which a drastic change in environment leads to a fundamental change in behavior, i.e., when the negative forces cease to be fed and the positive forces are nurtured and encouraged.

To sum up, the frequency and intensity of the desire to share, to give, and to sacrifice are not surprising if we consider the conditions of existence of the human species. What is surprising is that this need could be so repressed as to make acts of selfishness the rule in industrial (and many other) societies and acts of solidarity the exception. But, paradoxically, this very phenomenon is caused by the need for union. A society whose principles are acquisition, profit, and property produces a social character oriented around having, and once the dominant pattern is established, nobody wants to be an outsider, or indeed an outcast; in order to avoid this risk everybody adapts to the majority, who have in common only their mutual antagonism.

As a consequence of the dominant attitude of selfishness, the leaders of our society believe that people can be motivated only by the expectation of material advantages, i.e., by rewards, and that they will not react to appeals for solidarity and sacrifice. Hence, except in times of war, these appeals are rarely made, and the chances to observe the possible results of such appeals are lost.

Only a radically different socioeconomic structure and a radically different picture of human nature could show that bribery is not the only way (or the best way) to influence people.

VI

Further Aspects of Having and Being

Security—Insecurity

Not to move forward, to stay where we are, to regress, in other words to rely on what we have, is very tempting, for what we *have,* we know; we can hold onto it, feel secure in it. We fear, and consequently avoid, taking a step into the unknown, the uncertain; for, indeed, while the *step* may not appear risky to us *after* we have taken it, *before* we take that step the new aspects beyond it appear very risky, and hence frightening. Only the old, the tried, is safe; or so it seems. Every new step contains the danger of failure, and that is one of the reasons people are so afraid of freedom.*

Naturally, at every state of life the old and accustomed is different. As infants we *have* only our body and our mother's breasts (originally still undifferentiated). Then we start to orient ourselves to the world, beginning the process of making a place for ourselves in it. We begin wanting to *have* things: we *have* our mother, father, siblings, toys; later on we *acquire* knowledge, a job, a social position, a spouse, children, and then we *have* a kind of afterlife already, when we acquire a burial plot and life insurance and make our "last will."

Yet in spite of the security of having, people admire those with a vision of the new, those who break a new path, who have the courage to move forward. In mythology this mode

*This is the main topic in *Escape from Freedom.*

of existence is represented symbolically by the *hero*. Heroes are those with the courage to leave what they have—their land, their family, their property—and move out, not without fear, but without succumbing to their fear. In the Buddhist tradition the Buddha is the hero who leaves all possessions, all certainty contained in Hindu theology—his rank, his family —and moves on to a life of nonattachment. Abraham and Moses are heroes in the Jewish tradition. The Christian hero is Jesus, who had nothing and—in the eyes of the world—is nothing, yet who acts out of the fullness of his love for all human beings. The Greeks have secular heroes, whose aim is victory, satisfaction of their pride, conquest. Yet, like the spiritual heroes, Hercules and Odysseus move forward, undeterred by the risks and dangers that await them. The fairy tale heroes meet the same criteria: leaving, moving forward, and tolerating uncertainty.

We admire these heroes because we deeply feel their way is the way we would want to be—if we could. But being afraid, we believe that we cannot be that way, that only the heroes can. The heroes become idols; we transfer to them our own capacity to move, and then stay where we are—"because we are not heroes."

This discussion might seem to imply that while being a hero is desirable, it is foolish and against one's self-interest. Not so, by any means. The cautious, the having persons enjoy security, yet by necessity they are very insecure. They depend on what they have: money, prestige, their ego—that is to say, on something outside themselves. But what becomes of them if they lose what they have? For, indeed, whatever one has can be lost. Most obviously, one's property can be lost—and with it usually one's position, one's friends—and at any moment one can, and sooner or later one is bound to, lose one's life. *If I am what I have and if what I have is lost, who then am I?* Nobody but a defeated, deflated, pathetic testimony to a wrong way of living. Because I *can* lose what I have, I am necessarily constantly worried that I *shall* lose what I have. I am afraid of thieves, of economic changes, of revolutions, of sickness, of death, and I am afraid of love, of freedom, of growth, of change, of the unknown. Thus I am continuously worried, suffering from a chronic hypochondriasis, with regard not only to loss of health but to any other loss of what I have; I become defensive, hard, suspicious, lonely, driven by the need to have more in order to be better protected. Ibsen has given a beautiful description of this self-centered person in his *Peer Gynt.* The hero is filled only with himself; in his extreme egoism he believes that he is *himself,* because *he* is a "bundle of desires." At the end of his life he recognizes that because of his property-structured existence, he has failed to be himself, that he is like an onion without a kernel, an unfinished man, who never was himself.

The anxiety and insecurity engendered by the danger of losing what one has are absent in the being mode. If *I am who I am* and not what I have, nobody can deprive me of or threaten my security and my sense of identity. My center is within myself; my capacity for being and for expressing my essential powers is part of my character structure and depends on me. This holds true for the normal process of living, not, of course, for such circumstances as incapacitating illness, torture, or other cases of powerful external restrictions.

While having is based on some thing that is diminished by use, being grows by practice. (The "burning bush" that is not consumed is the biblical symbol for this paradox.) The powers of reason, of love, of artistic and intellectual creation, all essential powers grow through the process of being expressed. What is spent is not lost, but on the contrary, what is kept is lost. The only threat to my security in being lies in myself: in lack of faith in life and in my productive powers; in regressive tendencies; in inner laziness and in the willingness to have others take over my life. But these dangers are not *inherent* in being, as the danger of losing is inherent in having.

Solidarity—Antagonism

The experience of loving, liking, enjoying something without wanting to *have* it is the one Suzuki referred to in contrasting the Japanese and the English poems (see Chapter I). It is indeed not easy for modern Western Man to experience enjoyment separate from having. However, neither is it entirely foreign to us. Suzuki's example of the flower would not apply if instead of looking at the flower the wanderer looked at a mountain, a meadow, or anything that cannot be physically taken away. To be sure, many, or most, people would not really *see* the mountain, except as a cliché; instead of *seeing* it they would want to know its name and its height—or they might want to climb it, which can be another form of taking possession of it. But some can genuinely see the mountain and enjoy it. The same may be said in respect to appreciating works of music: that is, buying a recording of music one loves can be an act of possessing the work, and perhaps the majority of people who enjoy art really do "consume" it; but a minority probably still responds to music and art with genuine joy and without any impulse to "have."

Sometimes one can read people's responses in their facial expressions. I recently saw a television film of the extraordinary acrobats and jugglers of the Chinese circus during which the camera repeatedly surveyed the audience, to register the response of individuals in the crowd. Most of the faces were lit up, brought to life, became beautified in response to the graceful, alive performance. Only a minority seemed cold and unmoved.

Another example of enjoying without wanting to possess may be readily seen in our response to small children. Here, too, I suspect a great deal of self-deceptive behavior takes place, for we like to see ourselves in the role of lovers of children. But even though there may be reason for suspicion, I believe that genuine, alive response to infants is not at all rare. This may be partly so because, in contrast to their feel-

ings about adolescents and adults, most people are not afraid
of children and so feel free to respond to them lovingly, which
we cannot do if fear stands in our way.

The most relevant example for enjoyment without the craving to have what one enjoys may be found in interpersonal
relations. A man and a woman may enjoy each other on many
grounds; each may like the other's attitudes, tastes, ideas,
temperament, or whole personality. Yet only in those who
must *have* what they like will this mutual enjoyment habitually
result in the desire for sexual possession. For those in a dominant mode of being, the other person is enjoyable, and even
erotically attractive, but she or he does not have to be
"plucked," to speak in terms of Tennyson's poem, in order
to be enjoyed.

Having-centered persons want to *have* the person they like
or admire. This can be seen in relations between parents and
their children, between teachers and students, and between
friends. Neither partner is satisfied simply to enjoy the other
person; each wishes to have the other person for him- or
herself. Hence, each is jealous of those who also want to
"have" the other. Each partner seeks the other like a ship-
wrecked sailor seeks a plank—for survival. Predominantly
"having" relationships are heavy, burdened, filled with conflicts and jealousies.

Speaking more generally, the fundamental elements in the
relation between individuals in the having mode of existence
are competition, antagonism, and fear. The antagonistic element in the having relationship stems from its nature. If having is the basis of my sense of identity because "I am what I
have," the wish to have must lead to the desire to have much,
to have more, to have most. In other words, *greed* is the natural outcome of the having orientation. It can be the greed of
the miser or the greed of the profit hunter or the greed of the
womanizer or the man chaser. Whatever constitutes their
greed, the greedy can never have enough, can never be "satisfied." In contrast to physiological needs, such as hunger,

that have definite satiation points due to the physiology of the body, *mental* greed—and all greed is mental, even if it is satisfied via the body—has no satiation point, since its consummation does not fill the inner emptiness, boredom, loneliness, and depression it is meant to overcome. In addition, since what one has can be taken away in one form or another, one must have more, in order to fortify one's existence against such danger. If everyone wants to have more, everyone must fear one's neighbor's aggressive intention to take away what one has. To prevent such attack one must become more powerful and preventively aggressive oneself. Besides, since production, great as it may be, can never keep pace with *unlimited* desires, there must be competition and antagonism among individuals in the struggle for getting the most. And the strife would continue even if a state of absolute abundance could be reached; those who have less in physical health and in attractiveness, in gifts, in talents would bitterly envy those who have "more."

That the having mode and the resulting greed necessarily lead to interpersonal antagonism and strife holds true for nations as it does for individuals. For as long as nations are composed of people whose main motivation is having and greed, they cannot help waging war. They necessarily covet what another nation has, and attempt to get what they want by war, economic pressure, or threats. They will use these procedures against weaker nations, first of all, and form alliances that are stronger than the nation that is to be attacked. Even if it has only a reasonable chance to win, a nation will wage war, not because it suffers economically, but because the desire to have more and to conquer is deeply ingrained in the social character.

Of course there are times of peace. But one must distinguish between lasting peace and peace that is a transitory phenomenon, a period of gathering strength, rebuilding one's industry and army—in other words, between peace that is a permanent state of harmony and peace that is essentially only a truce. While the nineteenth and twentieth centuries had periods of truce, they are characterized by a state of chronic war among the main actors on the historical stage. Peace as a state of lasting harmonious relations between nations is only possible when the having structure is replaced by the being structure. The idea that one can build peace while encouraging the striving for possession and profit is an illusion, and a dangerous one, because it deprives people of recognizing that they are confronted with a clear alternative: either a radical change of their character or the perpetuity of war. This is indeed an old alternative; the leaders have chosen war and the people followed them. Today and tomorrow, with the incredible increase in the destructiveness of the new weapons, the alternative is no longer war—but mutual suicide.

What holds true of international wars is equally true for class war. The war between classes, essentially the exploiting and the exploited, has always existed in societies that were based on the principle of greed. There was no class war where there was neither a need for or a possibility of exploitation nor a greedy social character. But there are bound to be classes in any society, even the richest, in which the having mode is dominant. As already noted, given unlimited desires, even the greatest production cannot keep pace with everybody's fantasy of having more than their neighbors. Necessarily, those who are stronger, more clever, or more favored by other circumstances will try to establish a favored position for themselves and try to take advantage of those who are less powerful, either by force and violence or by suggestion. Oppressed classes will overthrow their rulers, and so on; the class struggle might perhaps become less violent, but it cannot disappear as long as greed dominates the human heart. The idea of a classless society in a so-called socialist world filled with the spirit of greed is as illusory—and dangerous— as the idea of permanent peace among greedy nations.

In the being mode, private having (private property) has

little affective importance, because I do not need to own something in order to enjoy it, or even in order to use it. In the being mode, more than one person—in fact millions of people—can share in the enjoyment of the same object, since none need—or want—to *have* it, as a condition of enjoying it. This not only avoids strife; it creates one of the deepest forms of human happiness: shared enjoyment. Nothing unites people more (without restricting their individuality) than sharing their admiration and love for a person; sharing an idea, a piece of music, a painting, a symbol; sharing in a ritual—and sharing sorrow. The experience of sharing makes and keeps the relation between two individuals alive; it is the basis of all great religious, political, and philosophical movements. Of course, this holds true only as long as and to the extent that the individuals genuinely love or admire. When religious and political movements ossify, when bureaucracy manages the people by means of suggestions and threats, the sharing stops.

While nature has devised, as it were, the prototype—or perhaps the symbol—of shared enjoyment in the sexual act, empirically the sexual act is not necessarily an enjoyment that is shared; the partners are frequently so narcissistic, self-involved, and possessive that one can speak only of simultaneous, but not of shared pleasure.

In another respect, however, nature offers a less ambiguous symbol for the distinction between having and being. The erection of the penis is entirely functional. The male does not *have* an erection, like a property or a permanent quality (although how many men wish to *have* one is anybody's guess). The penis *is* in a state of erection, as long as the man is in a state of excitement, as long as he desires the person who has aroused his excitement. If for one reason or another something interferes with this excitement, the man *has* nothing. And in contrast to practically all other kinds of behavior, the erection cannot be faked. George Groddek, one of the most outstanding, although relatively little known, psychoanalysts, used to comment that a man, after all, is a man for only a few minutes; most of the time he is a little boy. Of course, Groddek did not mean that a man becomes a little boy in his total being, but precisely in that aspect which for many a man is the proof that he is a man. (See the paper I wrote [1943] on "Sex and Character.")

Joy—Pleasure

Master Eckhart taught that aliveness is conducive to *joy.* The modern reader is apt not to pay close attention to the word "joy" and to read it as if Eckhart had written "pleasure." Yet the distinction between joy and pleasure is crucial, particularly so in reference to the distinction between the being and the having modes. It is not easy to appreciate the difference, since we live in a world of "joyless pleasures."

What is pleasure? Even though the word is used in different ways, considering its use in popular thought, it seems best defined as the satisfaction of a desire that does not require activity (in the sense of aliveness) to be satisfied. Such pleasure can be of high intensity: the pleasure in having social success, earning more money, winning a lottery; the conventional sexual pleasure; eating to one's "heart's content"; winning a race; the state of elation brought about by drinking, trance, drugs; the pleasure in satisfying one's sadism, or one's passion to kill or dismember what is alive.

Of course, in order to become rich or famous, individuals must be very active in the sense of busyness, but not in the sense of the "birth within." When they have achieved their goal they may be "thrilled," "intensely satisfied," feel they have reached a "peak." But what peak? Maybe a peak of excitement, of satisfaction, of a trancelike or an orgiastic state. But they may have reached this state driven by passions that, though human, are nevertheless pathological, inasmuch as they do not lead to an intrinsically adequate solution of the human condition. Such passions do not lead to greater human growth and strength but, on the contrary, to human crippling. The pleasures of the radical hedonists, the satisfaction of ever new cupidities, the pleasures of contemporary society produce different degrees of *excitements*. But they are not conducive to *joy*. In fact, the lack of joy makes it necessary to seek ever new, ever more exciting pleasures.

In this respect, modern society is in the same position the Hebrews were in three thousand years ago. Speaking to the people of Israel about one of the worst of their sins, Moses said: "You did not serve the Lord your God with *joy* and *gladness* of heart, in the midst of the fullness of all things" (Deuteronomy 28:47). Joy is the concomitant of productive activity. It is not a "peak experience," which culminates and ends suddenly, but rather a plateau, a feeling state that accompanies the productive expression of one's essential human faculties. Joy is not the ecstatic fire of the moment. Joy is the glow that accompanies being.

Pleasure and thrill are conducive to sadness after the so-called peak has been reached; for the thrill has been experienced, but the vessel has not grown. One's inner powers have not increased. One has made the attempt to break through the boredom of unproductive activity and for a moment has unified all one's energies—except reason and love. One has attempted to become superhuman, without being human. One seems to have succeeded to the moment of triumph, but the triumph is followed by deep sadness: because nothing has changed within oneself. The saying "After intercourse the animal is sad" (*"Post coitum animal triste est"*) expresses the same phenomenon with regard to loveless sex, which is a "peak experience" of intense excitation, hence thrilling and pleasureful, and necessarily followed by the disappointment of its ending. Joy in sex is experienced only when physical intimacy is at the same time the intimacy of loving.

As is to be expected, joy must play a central role in those religious and philosophical systems that proclaim *being* as the goal of life. Buddhism, while rejecting pleasure, conceives a state of Nirvana to be a state of joy, which is manifested in the reports and pictures of the Buddha's death. (I am indebted to the late D. T. Suzuki for pointing this out to me in a famous picture of the Buddha's death.)

The Old Testament and the later Jewish tradition, while warning against the pleasures that spring from the satisfaction of cupidity, see in joy the mood that accompanies being. The Book of Psalms ends with the group of fifteen psalms that are one great hymn of joy, and the dynamic psalms begin in fear and sadness and end in joy and gladness.* The Sabbath is the day of joy, and in the Messianic Time joy will be the prevailing mood. The prophetic literature abounds with the expression of joy in such passages as: "Then there will the virgins rejoice in the dance, both young men and old together: for I will turn their mourning into joy" (Jeremiah 31:13) and "With joy you will draw water" (Isaiah 12:3). God calls Jerusalem "the city of my joy" (Jeremiah 49:25).

We find the same emphasis in the Talmud: "The joy of a mitzvah [the fulfillment of a religious duty] is the only way to get the holy spirit" (Berakoth 31,a). Joy is considered so fundamental that, according to Talmudic law, the mourning for a close relative, whose death occurred less than a week earlier, must be interrupted by the joy of Sabbath.

The Hasidic movement, whose motto, "Serve God with joy," was a verse from the psalms, created a form of living in which joy was one of the outstanding elements. Sadness and depression were considered signs of spiritual error, if not outright sin.

In the Christian development even the name of the gospels —Glad Tidings—shows the central place of gladness and joy. In the New Testament, joy is the fruit of giving up having, while sadness is the mood of the one who hangs onto possessions. (See, for instance, Matthew 13:44 and 19:22.) In many

*I have analyzed these psalms in *You Shall Be as God.*

of Jesus' utterances joy is conceived as a concomitant of living in the mode of being. In his last speech to the Apostles, Jesus tells of joy in the final form: "These things I have spoken to you, that my joy be in you, and that your joy may be full" (John 15:11).

As indicated earlier, joy also plays a supreme role in Master Eckhart's thinking. Here in his words is one of the most beautiful and poetic expressions of the idea of the creative power of laughter and joy: "When God laughs at the soul and the soul laughs back at God, the persons of the Trinity are begotten. To speak in hyperbole, when the Father laughs to the son and the son laughs back to the Father, that laughter gives pleasure, that pleasure gives joy, that joy gives love and love gives the persons [of the Trinity] of which the Holy Spirit is one" (Blakney, p. 245).

Spinoza gives joy a supreme place in his anthropological-ethical system. "Joy," he says, "is man's passage from a lesser to a greater perfection. *Sorrow* is man's passage from a greater to a less perfection" (*Ethics*, 3, defs. 2, 3).

Spinoza's statements will be fully understood only if we put them in the context of his whole system of thought. In order not to decay, we must strive to approach the "model of human nature," that is, we must be optimally free, rational, active. We must become what we can be. This is to be understood as the good that is potentially inherent in our nature. Spinoza understands "good" as "everything which we are certain is a means by which we may approach nearer and nearer to the model of human nature we have set before us"; he understands "evil" as "on the contrary . . . everything which we are certain hinders us from reaching that model" (*Ethics,* 4, Preface). Joy is good; sorrow (*tristitia,* better translated as "sadness," "gloom") is bad. Joy is virtue; sadness is sin.

Joy, then, is what we experience in the process of growing nearer to the goal of becoming ourself.

Sin and Forgiveness

In its classic concept in Jewish and Christian theological thought, sin is essentially identical with *disobedience* toward the will of God. This is quite apparent in the commonly held source of the first sin, Adam's disobedience. In the Jewish tradition this act was not understood as "original" sin that all of Adam's descendants inherited, as in the Christian tradition, but only as the *first* sin—not necessarily present in Adam's descendants.

Yet the common element is the view that disobedience of God's commands *is* sin, whatever the commands are. This is not surprising if we consider that the image of God in that part of the biblical story is of a strict authority, patterned on the role of an Oriental King of Kings. It is furthermore not surprising if we consider that the church, almost from its start, adjusted itself to a social order that, then in feudalism as now in capitalism, required for its functioning strict obedience of the individuals to the laws, those that serve their true interests as well as those that do not. How oppressive or how liberal the laws and what the means for their enforcement are make little difference with regard to the central issue: the people must learn to fear authority, and not only in the person of the "law enforcement" officers because they carry weapons. This fear is not enough of a safeguard for the proper functioning of the state; the citizen must internalize this fear and transform obedience into a moral and religious category: sin.

People respect the laws not only because they are afraid but also because they feel guilty for their disobedience. This feeling of guilt can be overcome by the forgiveness that only the authority itself can grant. The conditions for such forgiveness are: the sinner repents, is punished, and by accepting punishment submits again. The sequence: sin (disobedience) → feeling of guilt → new submission (punishment) → forgiveness, is a vicious circle, inasmuch as each act of disobedience leads to increased obedience. Only a few are not thus cowed. Prometheus is their hero. In spite of the most cruel punishment Zeus afflicts him with, Prometheus does not submit, nor does he feel guilty. He knew that taking the fire away from the gods and giving it to human beings was an act of compassion; he had been disobedient, but he had not sinned. He had, like many other loving heroes (martyrs) of the human race, broken through the equation between disobedience and sin.

Society, though, is not made up of heroes. As long as the tables were set for only a minority, and the majority had to serve the minority's purposes and be satisfied with what was left over, the sense that disobedience is sin had to be cultivated. Both state and church cultivated it, and both worked together, because both had to protect their own hierarchies. The state needed religion to have an ideology that fused disobedience and sin; the church needed believers whom the state had trained in the virtues of obedience. Both used the institution of the family, whose function it was to train the child in obedience from the first moment it showed a will of its own (usually, at the latest, with the beginning of toilet training). The self-will of the child had to be broken in order to prepare it for its proper functioning later on as a citizen.

Sin in the conventional theological and secular sense is a concept within the authoritarian structure, and this structure belongs to the having mode of existence. Our human center does not lie in ourselves, but in the authority to which we submit. We do not arrive at well-being by our own productive activity, but by passive obedience and the ensuing approval by the authority. We *have* a leader (secular or spiritual, king, queen or God) in whom we *have* faith; we *have* security . . . as long as we *are*—nobody. That the submission is not necessarily conscious as such, that it can be mild or severe, that the psychic and social structure need not be totally authoritarian, but may be only partially so, must not blind us to the fact that *we live in the mode of having to the degree that we internalize the authoritarian structure of our society.*

As Alfons Auer has emphasized very succinctly, Thomas

Aquinas' concept of authority, disobedience, and sin is a humanistic one: i.e., sin is not disobedience of irrational authority, but the violation of human *well-being*. */ Thus Aquinas can state: "God can never be insulted by us, except we act against our own well-being" (S.c. gent. 3, 122). To appreciate this position, we must consider that, for Thomas, the human good *(bonum humanum)* is determined neither arbitrarily by purely subjective desires, nor by instinctively given desires ("natural," in the Stoic sense), nor by God's arbitrary will. It is determined by our rational understanding of human nature and of the norms that, based on this nature, are conducive to our optimum growth and well-being. (It should be noted that as an obedient son of the church and a supporter of the existing social order against the revolutionary sects, Thomas Aquinas could not be a pure representative of nonauthoritarian ethic; his use of the word "disobedience" for both kinds of disobedience served to obscure the intrinsic contradiction in his position.)

While sin as disobedience is part of the authoritarian and, that is, the *having* structure, it has an entirely different meaning in the nonauthoritarian structure, which is rooted in the *being* mode. This other meaning, too, is implied in the biblical story of the Fall and can be understood by a different interpretation of that story. God had put Man into the Garden of Eden and warned him not to eat either from the Tree of Life or from the Tree of Knowledge of Good and Evil. Seeing that "it was not good that Man should be alone," God created Woman. Man and Woman should become one. Both were naked, and "they were not ashamed." This statement is usually interpreted in terms of conventional sexual mores, which assume that, naturally, a man and a woman would be ashamed if their genitals were uncovered. But this seems hardly all the

---

*Professor Auer's yet unpublished paper on the autonomy of ethics according to Thomas Aquinas (which I am indebted to him for letting me read in manuscript) is very helpful to an understanding of Aquinas' ethical concept. So also is his article on the question "Is sin an insult to God?" (See Bibliography.)

text has to say. On a deeper level, this statement could imply that although Man and Woman faced each other totally, they did not, and they even could not, feel ashamed, for they did not experience each other as strangers, as separated individuals, but as "one."

This prehuman situation changes radically after the Fall, when Man and Woman become fully human, i.e., endowed with reason, with awareness of good and evil, with awareness of each other as separate beings, with awareness that their original oneness is broken and that they have become strangers to one another. They are close to each other, and yet they feel separate and distant. They feel the deepest shame there is: the shame of facing a fellow being "nakedly" and simultaneously experiencing the mutual estrangement, the unspeakable abyss that separates each from the other. "They made themselves aprons," thus trying to avoid the full human encounter, the nakedness in which they see each other. But the shame, as well as the guilt, cannot be removed by concealment. They did not reach out to each other in love; perhaps they desired each other physically, but physical union does not heal human estrangement. That they do not love each other is indicated in their attitude toward each other: Eve does not try to protect Adam, and Adam avoids punishment by denouncing Eve as the culprit rather than defending her.

What is the sin they have committed? To face each other as separated, isolated, selfish human beings who cannot overcome their separation in the act of loving union. This sin is rooted in our very human existence. Being deprived of the original harmony with nature, characteristic of the animal whose life is determined by built-in instincts, being endowed with reason and self-awareness, we cannot help experiencing our utter separateness from every other human being. In Catholic theology this state of existence, complete separateness and estrangement from each other, not bridged by love, is the definition of "Hell." It is unbearable for us. We must overcome the torture of absolute separateness in some way:

by submission or by domination or by trying to silence reason and awareness. Yet all these ways succeed only for the moment, and block the road to a true solution. There is but one way to save ourselves from this hell: to leave the prison of our egocentricity, to reach out and to *one* ourselves with the world. If egocentric separateness is the cardinal sin, then the sin is atoned in the act of loving. The very word "atonement" expresses this concept, for it etymologically derives from "at-*one*ment," the Middle-English expression for union. Since the sin of separateness is not an act of disobedience, it does not need to be *forgiven*. But it does need to be *healed;* and love, not acceptance of punishment, is the healing factor.

Rainer Funk has pointed out to me that the concept of sin as disunion has been expressed by some of the church fathers, who followed Jesus' nonauthoritarian concept of sin, and suggests the following examples (taken from Henri de Lubac): Origines says, "Where there are sins there is diversity. But where virtue rules there is uniqueness, there is oneness." Maximus Confessor says that through Adam's sin the human race, "which should be a harmonious whole without conflict between mine and thine, was transformed into a dust cloud of individuals." Similar thoughts concerning the destruction of the original unity in Adam can also be found in the ideas of St. Augustine and, as Professor Auer points out, in the teaching of Thomas Aquinas. De Lubac says, summing up: "As work of 'restitution' *(Wiederherstellung),* the fact of salvation appears necessary as the regaining of the lost oneness, as the restitution of the supernatural oneness with God and at the same time the oneness of men among each other" (my translation; see also "The Concept of Sin and Repentance" in *You Shall Be as Gods* for an examination of the whole problem of sin).

To sum up, in the having mode, and thus the authoritarian structure, sin is disobedience and is overcome by repentance →punishment→renewed submission. In the being mode, the nonauthoritarian structure, sin is unresolved estrangement, and it is overcome by the full unfolding of reason and love, by at-onement.

One can indeed interpret the story of the Fall in both ways, because the story itself is a blending of authoritarian and liberating elements. But in themselves the concepts of sin as, respectively, disobedience and alienation are diametrically opposed.

The Old Testament story of the Tower of Babel seems to contain the same idea. The human race has reached here a state of union, symbolized by the fact that all humanity has one language. By their own ambition for power, by their craving to *have* the great tower, the people destroy their unity and are disunited. In a sense, the story of the Tower is the second "Fall," the sin of historical humanity. The story is complicated by God's being afraid of the people's unity and the power following from it. "Behold, they are one people, and they have all one language; and this is only the beginning of what they will do, and nothing that they propose to do will now be impossible for them. Come, let us go down and there confuse their language, that they may not understand one another's speech" (Genesis 11:6-7). Of course, the same difficulty already exists in the story of the Fall; there God is afraid of the power that man and woman would exercise if they ate of the fruit of both trees.

Fear of Dying—Affirmation of Living

As stated earlier, the fear that one may lose one's possessions is an unavoidable consequence of a sense of security that is based on what one has. I want to carry this thought a step further.

It may be possible for us not to attach ourselves to *property* and, hence, not fear losing it. But what about the fear of losing life itself—the fear of dying? Is this a fear only of older people or of the sick? Or is everybody afraid of dying? Does the fact that we are bound to die permeate our whole life? Does the fear of dying grow only more intense and more conscious the closer we come to the limits of life by age or sickness?

We have need of large systematic studies by psychoanalysts investigating this phenomenon from childhood to old age and dealing with the unconscious as well as the conscious manifestations of the fear of dying. These studies need not be restricted to individual cases; they could examine large groups, using existing methods of sociopsychoanalysis. Since such studies do not now exist, we must draw tentative conclusions from many scattered data.

Perhaps the most significant datum is the deeply engraved desire for immortality that manifests itself in the many rituals and beliefs that aim at preserving the human body. On the other hand, the modern, specifically American denial of death by the "beautification" of the body speaks equally for the repression of the fear of dying by merely camouflaging death.

There is only one way—taught by the Buddha, by Jesus, by the Stoics, by Master Eckhart—to truly overcome the fear of dying, and that way is by *not hanging onto life, not experiencing life as a possession*. The fear of dying is not truly what it seems to be: the fear of stopping living. Death does not concern us, Epicurus said, "since while we are, death is not yet here; but when death is here we are no more" (Diogenes Laertius). To be sure, there can be fear of suffering and pain that may precede dying, but this fear is different from that of dying. While the fear of dying may thus seem irrational, this is not so if life is experienced as possession. The fear, then, is not of dying, but of *losing what I have:* the fear of losing my body, my ego, my possessions, and my identity; the fear of facing the abyss of nonidentity, of "being lost."

To the extent that we live in the having mode, we must fear dying. No rational explanation will take away this fear. But it may be diminished, even at the hour of death, by our reassertion of our bond to life, by a response to the love of others that may kindle our own love. Losing our fear of dying should not begin as a preparation for death, but as the continuous effort to *reduce the mode of having and to increase the mode of being.* As Spinoza says, the wise think about life, not about death. The instruction on how to die is indeed the same as the instruction on how to live. The more we rid ourselves of the craving for possession in all its forms, particularly our ego-boundness, the less strong is the fear of dying, since there is nothing to lose.*

Here, Now—Past, Future

The mode of being exists only in the here and now *(hic et nunc)*. The mode of having exists only in time: past, present, and future.

In the having mode we are bound to what we have amassed in the *past:* money, land, fame, social status, knowledge, children, memories. We think about the past, and we feel by *remembering* feelings (or what appear to be feelings) of the past. (This is the essence of sentimentality.) We *are* the past; we can say: "I am what I was."

The *future* is the anticipation of what will become the past. It is experienced in the mode of having as is the past and is expressed when one says: "This person *has* a future," indicating that the individual will *have* many things even though he or she does not now have them. The Ford company's advertising slogan, "There's a Ford in your future," stressed *having* in the future, just as in certain business transactions one buys or sells "commodity futures." The fundamental experience of having is the same, whether we deal with past or future.

The *present* is the point where past and future join, a frontier station in time, but not different in quality from the two realms it connects.

*I restrict this discussion to the fear of dying as such and shall not enter into discussion of an insoluble problem, the pain of suffering that our death can inflict upon those who love us.

Being is not necessarily outside of time, but time is not the dimension that governs being. The painter has to wrestle with color, canvas, and brushes, the sculptor with stone and chisel. Yet the creative act, their "vision" of what they are going to create, transcends time. It occurs in a flash, or in many flashes, but time is not experienced in the vision. The same holds true for the thinkers. Writing down their ideas occurs in time, but conceiving them is a creative event outside of time. It is the same for every manifestation of being. The experience of loving, of joy, of grasping truth does not occur in time, but in the here and now. The *here and now is eternity,* i.e., timelessness. But eternity is not, as popularly misunderstood, indefinitely prolonged time.

One important qualification must be made, though, regarding relationship to the past. Our references here have been to remembering the past, thinking, ruminating about it; in this mode of "having" the past, the past is dead. But one can also bring the past to life. One can experience a situation of the past with the same freshness as if it occurred in the here and now; that is, one can re-create the past, bring it to life (resurrect the dead, symbolically speaking). To the extent that one does so, the past ceases to be the past; it *is* the here and now.

One can also experience the future as if it were the here and now. This occurs when a future state is so fully anticipated in one's own experience that it is only the future "objectively," i.e., in external fact, but not in the subjective experience. This is the nature of genuine utopian thinking (in contrast to utopian daydreaming); it is the basis of genuine faith, which does not need the external realization "in the future" in order to make the experience of it real.

The whole concept of past, present, and future, i.e., of time, enters into our lives due to our bodily existence: the limited duration of our life, the constant demand of our body to be taken care of, the nature of the physical world that we have to use in order to sustain ourselves. Indeed, we cannot live in eternity; being mortal, we cannot ignore or escape time. The rhythm of night and day, of sleep and wakefulness, of growing and aging, the need to sustain ourselves by work and to defend ourselves, all these factors force us to *respect* time if we want to live, and our bodies make us want to live. But that we *respect* time is one thing; that we *submit* to it is another. In the mode of being, we respect time, but we do not submit to it. But this respect for time *becomes submission* when the having mode predominates. In this mode not only things are things, but all that is alive becomes a thing. In the mode of having, time becomes our ruler. In the being mode, time is dethroned; it is no longer the idol that rules our life.

In industrial society time rules supreme. The current mode of production demands that every action be exactly "timed," that not only the endless assembly line conveyor belt but, in a less crude sense, most of our activities be ruled by time. In addition, time not only is time, "time is money." The machine must be used maximally; therefore the machine forces its own rhythm upon the worker.

Via the machine, time has become our ruler. Only in our free hours do we seem to have a certain choice. Yet we usually organize our leisure as we organize our work. Or we rebel against tyrant time by being absolutely lazy. By not doing anything except disobeying time's demands, we have the illusion that we are free, when we are, in fact, only paroled from our time-prison.

PART THREE

THE NEW MAN AND THE NEW SOCIETY

VII

Religion, Character, and Society

This chapter deals with the thesis that social change interacts with a change in the social character; that "religious" impulses contribute the energy necessary to move men and women to accomplish drastic social change, and hence, that a new society can be brought about only if a profound change occurs in the human heart—if a new object of devotion takes the place of the present one.*

The Foundations of Social Character

The starting point for these reflections is the statement that the character structure of the average individual and the socioeconomic structure of the society of which he or she is a part are interdependent. I call the blending of the individual psychical sphere and the socioeconomic structure *social character*. (Much earlier, 1932, I had used "libidinous structure of society" to express this phenomenon.) The socioeconomic structure of a society molds the social character of its members so that they *wish* to do what they *have* to do. Simultaneously, the social character influences the socioeconomic structure of society, acting either as cement to give further stability to the social structure or, under special circum-

---

*This chapter rests heavily upon my previous work, particularly *Escape from Freedom* (1941) and *Psychoanalysis and Religion* (1950), in both of which are quoted the most important books in the rich literature on this subject.

stances, as dynamite that tends to break up the social structure.

Social Character vis-à-vis Social Structure

The relation between social character and social structure is never static, since both elements in this relationship are never-ending processes. A change in either factor means a change in both. Many political revolutionaries believe that one must first change the political and economic structure radically, and that then, as a second and almost necessary step, the human mind will also change: that the new society, once established, will quasiautomatically produce the new human being. They do not see that the new elite, being motivated by the same character as the old one, will tend to re-create the conditions of the old society in the new sociopolitical institutions the revolution has created; that the victory of the revolution will be its defeat as a revolution—although not as a historical phase that paved the way for the socioeconomic development that was hobbled in its full development. The French and Russian revolutions are textbook examples. It is noteworthy that Lenin, who had not believed that quality of character was important for a person's revolutionary function, changed his view drastically in the last year of his life when he sharply saw Stalin's defects of character and demanded, in his last will, that because of these defects Stalin should not become his successor.

On the other side are those who claim that first the nature of human beings must change—their consciousness, their values, their character—and that only then can a truly human society be built. The history of the human race proves them wrong. Purely psychical change has always remained in the private sphere and been restricted to small oases, or has been completely ineffective when the preaching of spiritual values was combined with the practice of the opposite values.

Social Character and "Religious" Needs

The social character has a further and significant function beyond that of serving the needs of society for a certain type of character and satisfying the individual's character-conditioned behavioral needs. Social character must fulfill any human being's inherent religious needs. To clarify, "religion" as I use it here does not refer to a system that has necessarily to do with a concept of God or with idols or even to a system perceived as religion, but to *any group-shared system of thought and action that offers the individual a frame of orientation and an object of devotion.* Indeed, in this broad sense of the word no culture of the past or present, and it seems no culture in the future, can be considered as not having religion.

This definition of "religion" does not tell us anything about its specific content. People may worship animals, trees, idols of gold or stone, an invisible god, a saintly person, or a diabolic leader; they may worship their ancestors, their nation, their class or party, money or success. Their religion may be conducive to the development of destructiveness or of love, of domination or of solidarity; it may further their power of reason or paralyze it. They may be aware of their system as being a religious one, different from those of the secular realm, or they may think that they have no religion, and interpret their devotion to certain allegedly secular aims, such as power, money, or success, as nothing but their concern for the practical and the expedient. The question is not one of *religion or not?* but of *which kind of religion?*—whether it is one that furthers human development, the unfolding of specifically human powers, or one that paralyzes human growth.

A specific religion, provided it is effective in motivating conduct, is not a sum total of doctrines and beliefs; it is rooted in a specific character structure of the individual and, inasmuch as it is the religion of a group, in the social character. Thus, our religious attitude may be considered an aspect of our character structure, for *we are what we are devoted to, and*

what we are devoted to is what motivates our conduct. Often, however, individuals are not even aware of the real objects of their
personal devotion and mistake their "official" beliefs for their
real, though *secret* religion. If, for instance, a man worships
power while professing a religion of love, the religion of
power is his secret religion, while his so-called official religion, for example Christianity, is only an ideology.

The religious need is rooted in the basic conditions of
existence of the human *species.* Ours is a species by itself, just
as is the species chimpanzee or horse or swallow. Each species
can be and is defined by its specific physiological and anatomical characteristics. There is general agreement on the human
species in biological terms. I have proposed that the human
species—i.e., human nature—can also be defined *psychically.*
In the biological evolution of the animal kingdom the human
species emerges when two trends in the animal evolution
meet. One trend is *the ever-decreasing determination of behavior by
instincts* ("instincts" is used here not in the dated sense of
instinct as excluding learning but in the sense of organic
drives). Even taking into account the many controversial
views about the nature of instincts, it is generally accepted
that the higher an animal has risen in the stages of evolution,
the less is its behavior determined by phylogenetically pro-
grammed instincts.

The process of ever-decreasing determination of behavior
by instincts can be plotted as a continuum, at the zero end of
which we will find the lowest forms of animal evolution with
the highest degree of instinctive determination; this decreases
along with animal evolution and reaches a certain level with
the mammals; it decreases further in the development going
up to the primates, and even here we find a great gulf between
monkeys and apes (as R. M. Yerkes and A. V. Yerkes have
shown in their classic investigation, 1929). In the species
Homo, instinctive determination has reached its minimum.

The other trend to be found in animal evolution is *the growth
of the brain, particularly of the neocortex.* Here, too, we can plot

the evolution as a continuum: at one end, the lowest animals, with the most primitive nervous structure and a relatively small number of neurons; at the other, *Homo sapiens,* with a larger and more complex brain structure, especially a neocortex three times the size of that of our primate ancestors, and a truly fantastic number of interneuronal connections.

Considering these data, the human species can be defined as the primate who emerged at the point of evolution where instinctive determination had reached a minimum and the development of the brain a maximum. This combination of minimal instinctive determination and maximal brain development had never occurred before in animal evolution and constitutes, biologically speaking, a completely new phenomenon.

Lacking the capacity to act by the command of instincts while possessing the capacity for self-awareness, reason, and imagination—new qualities that go beyond the capacity for instrumental thinking of even the cleverest primates—the human species needed a *frame of orientation* and an *object of devotion* in order to survive.

Without a map of our natural and social world—a picture of the world and of one's place in it that is structured and has inner cohesion—human beings would be confused and unable to act purposefully and consistently, for there would be no way of orienting oneself, of finding a fixed point that permits one to organize all the impressions that impinge upon each individual. Our world makes sense to us, and we feel certain about our ideas, through the consensus with those around us. Even if the map is wrong, it fulfills its psychological function. But the map has never been entirely wrong—nor has it ever been entirely right. It has always been enough of an approximation to the explanation of phenomena to serve the purpose of living. Only to the degree that the *practice* of life is freed from its contradictions and its irrationality can the map correspond to reality.

The impressive fact is that no culture has been found in which such a frame of orientation does not exist. Neither has any individual. Often individuals may disclaim having any such overall picture and believe that they respond to the various phenomena and incidents of life from case to case, as their judgment guides them. But it can be easily demonstrated that they simply take their own philosophy for granted because to them it is only common sense, and they are unaware that all their concepts rest upon a commonly accepted frame of reference. When such persons are confronted with a fundamentally different total view of life, they judge it as "crazy" or "irrational" or "childish," while they consider themselves as being only "logical." The deep need for a frame of reference is particularly evident in children. At a certain age, children will often make up their own frame of orientation in an ingenious way, using the few data available to them.

But a map is not enough as a guide for action; we also need a goal that tells us where to go. Animals have no such problems. Their instincts provide them with a map as well as with goals. But lacking instinctive determination and having a brain that permits us to think of many directions in which we can go, we need an object of total devotion, a focal point for all our strivings and the basis for all our effective—not only our proclaimed—values. We need such an object of devotion in order to integrate our energies in one direction, to transcend our isolated existence, with all its doubts and insecurities, and to answer our need for a meaning to life.

Socioeconomic structure, character structure, and religious structure are inseparable from each other. If the religious system does not correspond to the prevalent social character, if it conflicts with the social practice of life, it is only an ideology. We have to look behind it for the *real* religious structure, even though we may not be conscious of it as such —unless the human energies inherent in the religious structure of character act as dynamite and tend to undermine the given socioeconomic conditions. However, as there are always individual exceptions to the dominant social character, there are also individual exceptions to the dominant religious character. They are often the leaders of religious revolutions and the founders of new religions.

The "religious" orientation, as the experiential core of all "high" religions, has been mostly perverted in the development of these religions. The way individuals consciously conceive of their personal orientation does not matter; they may be "religious" without considering themselves to be so —or they may be nonreligious, although considering themselves Christian. We have no word to denote the *experiential* content of religion, aside from its conceptual and institutional aspect. Hence, I use quotation marks to denote "religious" in the *experiential,* subjective orientation, regardless of the conceptual structure in which the person's "religiosity" is expressed.*

Is the Western World Christian?

According to the history books and the opinion of most people, Europe's conversion to Christianity took place first within the Roman Empire under Constantine, followed by the conversion of the heathen in Northern Europe by Bonifacius, the "Apostle of the Germans," and others in the eighth century. *But was Europe ever truly Christianized?*

In spite of the affirmative answer generally given to this question, a closer analysis shows that Europe's conversion to Christianity was largely a sham; that at most one could speak of a limited conversion to Christianity from the twelfth to the sixteenth centuries and that for the centuries before and after this period the conversion was, for the most part, one to an ideology and a more or less serious submission to the church; it did not mean a change of heart, i.e., of the character struc-

---

*Nobody has dealt with the theme of atheistic religious experience more profoundly and more boldly than has Ernst Bloch (1972).

ture, except for numerous genuinely Christian movements.

In these four hundred years Europe had begun to be Christianized. The church tried to enforce the application of Christian principles on the handling of property, prices, and support of the poor. Many partly heretic leaders and sects arose, largely under the influence of mysticism that demanded the return to the principles of Christ, including the condemnation of property. Mysticism, culminating in Master Eckhart, played a decisive role in this antiauthoritarian humanistic movement and, not accidentally, women became prominent as mystical teachers and as students. Ideas of a world religion or of a simple undogmatic Christianity were voiced by many Christian thinkers; even the idea of the God of the Bible became questionable. The theological and nontheological humanists of the Renaissance, in their philosophy and in their Utopias, continued the line of the thirteenth century, and indeed, between the Late Middle Ages (the "Medieval Renaissance") and the Renaissance proper no sharp dividing line exists. To show the spirit of the High and the Late Renaissance, I quote Frederick B. Artz's summary picture:

> In society, the great mediaeval thinkers held that all men are equal in the sight of God and that even the humblest has an infinite worth. In economics, they taught that work is a source of dignity not of degradation, that no man should be used for an end independent of his welfare, and that justice should determine wages and prices. In politics, they taught that the function of the state is moral, that law and its administration should be imbued with Christian ideas of justice, and that the relations of ruler and ruled should always be founded on reciprocal obligation. The state, property, and the family are all trusts from God to those who control them, and they must be used to further divine purposes. Finally, the mediaeval ideal included the strong belief that all nations and peoples are part of one great community. As Goethe said, "Above the nations is

humanity," or as Edith Cavell wrote in 1915 in the margin of her *Imitation of Christ* the night before she was executed, "Patriotism is not enough."

Indeed, had European history continued in the spirit of the thirteenth century, had it developed the spirit of scientific knowledge and individualism slowly and in an evolutionary way, we might now have been in a fortunate position. But reason began to deteriorate into manipulative intelligence and individualism into selfishness. The short period of Christianization ended and Europe returned to its original paganism.

However the concepts may differ, one belief defines any branch of Christianity: the belief in Jesus Christ as the Savior who gave his life out of love for his fellow creatures. He was the hero of love, a hero without power, who did not use force, who did not want to rule, who did not want to *have* anything. He was a hero of being, of giving, of sharing. These qualities deeply appealed to the Roman poor as well as to some of the rich, who choked on their selfishness. Jesus appealed to the hearts of the people, even though from an intellectual standpoint he was at best considered to be naïve. This belief in the hero of love won hundreds of thousands of adherents, many of whom changed their practice of life, or became martyrs themselves.

The Christian hero was the martyr, for as in the Jewish tradition, the highest achievement was to give one's life for God or for one's fellow beings. The martyr is the exact opposite of the pagan hero personified in the Greek and Germanic heroes. The heroes' aim was to conquer, to be victorious, to destroy, to rob; their fulfillment of life was pride, power, fame, and superior skill in killing (St. Augustine compared Roman history with that of a band of robbers). For the pagan hero a man's worth lay in his prowess in attaining and holding onto power, and he gladly died on the battlefield in the moment of victory. Homer's *Iliad* is the poetically magnificent descrip-

tion of glorified conquerors and robbers. The martyr's characteristics are *being*, giving, sharing; the hero's, *having*, exploiting, forcing. (It should be added that the formation of the
pagan hero is connected with the patriarchal victory over
mother-centered society. Men's dominance of women is the
first act of conquest and the first exploitative use of force; in
all patriarchal societies after the men's victory, these principles have become the basis of men's character.)

Which of the two irreconcilably opposed models for our
own development still prevails in Europe? If we look into
ourselves, into the behavior of almost all people, into our
political leaders, it is undeniable that our model of what is
good and valuable is the pagan hero. European–North American history, in spite of the conversion to the church, is a
history of conquest, pride, greed; our highest values are: to
be stronger than others, to be victorious, to conquer others
and exploit them. These values coincide with our ideal of
"manliness": only the one who can fight and conquer is a
man; anyone who is not strong in the use of force is weak, i.e.,
"unmanly."

It is not necessary to prove that the history of Europe is a
history of conquest, exploitation, force, subjugation. Hardly
any period is not characterized by these factors, no race or
class exempted, often including genocide, as with the American Indians, and even such religious enterprises as the Cru-
sades are no exception. Was this behavior only outwardly
economically or politically motivated, and were the slave trad-
ers, the rulers of India, the killers of Indians, the British who
forced the Chinese to open their land to the import of opium,
the instigators of two World Wars and those who prepare the
next war, were all these Christians in their hearts? Or were
perhaps only the leaders rapacious pagans while the great
mass of the population remained Christians? If this were so,
we might feel more cheerful. Unfortunately, it is not so. To
be sure, the leaders were often more rapacious than their
followers because they had more to gain, but they could not

have realized their plans were it not that the wish to conquer and to be victorious was and still is part of the social character.

One has only to recall the wild, crazy enthusiasm with which people participated in the various wars of the past two centuries—the readiness of millions to risk national suicide in order to protect the image of "the strongest power," or of "honor," or of profits. And for another example, consider the frenzied nationalism of people watching the contemporary Olympic Games, which allegedly serve the cause of peace. Indeed, the popularity of the Olympic Games is in itself a symbolic expression of Western paganism. They celebrate the pagan hero: the winner, the strongest, the most self-assertive, while overlooking the dirty mixture of business and publicity that characterizes the contemporary imitation of the Greek Olympic Games. In a Christian culture the Passion Play would take the place of Olympic Games; yet the one famous Passion Play we have is the tourist sensation in Oberammergau.

If all this is correct, why do not Europeans and Americans frankly abandon Christianity as not fitting our times? There are several reasons: for example, religious ideology is needed in order to keep people from losing discipline and thus threatening social coherence. But there is a still more important reason: people who are firm believers in Christ as the great lover, the self-sacrificing God, can turn this belief, in an alienated way, into the experience that it is Jesus who loves *for them.* Jesus thus becomes an idol; the belief in him becomes the substitute for one's own act of loving. In a simple, unconscious formula: "Christ does all the loving for us; we can go on in the pattern of the Greek hero, yet we are saved because the alienated 'faith' in Christ is a substitute for the *imitation* of Christ." That Christian belief is also a cheap cover for one's own rapacious attitude goes without saying. Finally, I believe that human beings are so deeply endowed with a need to love that acting as wolves causes us necessarily to have a guilty conscience. Our professed belief in love anesthetizes us to some degree against the pain of the unconscious feeling of guilt for being entirely without love.

"Industrial Religion"

The religious and philosophical development after the end of the Middle Ages is too complex to be treated within the present volume. It can be characterized by the struggle between two principles: the Christian, spiritual tradition in theological or philosophical forms and the pagan tradition of idolatry and inhumanity that assumed many forms in the development of what might be called the "religion of industrialism and the cybernetic era."

Following the tradition of the Late Middle Ages, the humanism of the Renaissance was the first great flowering of the "religious" spirit after the end of the Middle Ages. The ideas of human dignity, of the unity of the human race, of universal political and religious unity found in it an unencumbered expression. The seventeenth- and eighteenth-century Enlightenment expressed another great flowering of humanism. Carl Becker (1932) has shown to what extent the Enlightenment philosophy expressed the "religious attitude" that we find in the theologians of the thirteenth century: "If we examine the foundation of this faith, we find that at every turn the *Philosophers* betrayed their debt to medieval thought without being aware of it." The French Revolution, to which Enlightenment philosophy had given birth, was more than a political revolution. As Tocqueville noted (quoted by Becker), it was a "political revolution which functioned in the manner and which took on in some sense the aspect of a *religious revolution* [emphasis added]. Like Islamism and the Protestant revolt it overflowed the frontiers of countries and nations and was extended by preaching and propaganda."

Radical humanism in the nineteenth and twentieth centuries is described later on, in my discussion of the humanist protest against the paganism of the industrial age. But to provide a base for that discussion we must now look at the new paganism that has developed side by side with humanism, threatening at the present moment of history to destroy us.

The change that prepared the first basis for the development of the "industrial religion" was the elimination, by Luther, of the motherly element in the church. Although it may appear an unnecessary detour, I must dwell on this problem for a while, because it is important to our understanding of the development of the new religion and the new social character.

Societies have been organized according to two principles: patricentric (or patriarchal) and matricentric (or matriarchal). The matricentric principle, as J. J. Bachofen and L. H. Morgan have shown for the first time, is centered in the figure of the loving mother. The motherly principle is that of *unconditional love;* the mother loves her children not because they please her, but because they are her (or another woman's) children. For this reason the mother's love cannot be acquired by good behavior, nor can it be lost by sinning. Motherly love is *mercy* and *compassion* (in Hebrew *rachamim,* the root of which is *rechem,* the "womb").

Fatherly love, on the contrary, is *conditional;* it depends on the achievements and good behavior of the child; father loves that child most who is most like him, i.e., whom he wishes to inherit his property. Father's love can be lost, but it can also be regained by repentance and renewed submission. Father's love is *justice.*

The two principles, the feminine-motherly and the masculine-fatherly, correspond not only to the presence of a masculine and feminine side in any human being but specifically to the need for mercy *and* justice in every man and woman. The deepest yearning of human beings seems to be a constellation in which the two poles (motherliness and fatherliness, female and male, mercy and justice, feeling and thought, nature and intellect) are united in a synthesis, in which both sides of the polarity lose their antagonism and, instead, color each other. While such a synthesis cannot be fully reached in a patriarchal society, it existed to some extent in the Roman Church. The Virgin, the church as the all-loving mother, the pope and the priest as motherly figures represented motherly, unconditional, all-forgiving love, side by side with the fatherly elements of a strict, patriarchal bureaucracy with the pope at the top ruling by power.

Corresponding to these motherly elements in the religious system was the relationship toward nature in the process of production: the work of the peasant as well as of the artisan was not a hostile exploitative attack against nature. It was cooperation with nature: not raping but transforming nature according to its own laws.

Luther established a purely patriarchal form of Christianity in Northern Europe that was based on the urban middle class and the secular princes. The essence of this new social character is submission under patriarchal authority, with *work* as the only way to obtain love and approval.

Behind the Christian façade arose a new *secret* religion, "industrial religion," that is rooted in the character structure of modern society, but is not recognized as "religion." The industrial religion is completely incompatible with genuine Christianity. It reduces people to servants of the economy and of the machinery that their own hands build.

The industrial religion had its basis in a new social character. Its center was fear of and submission to powerful male authorities, cultivation of the sense of guilt for disobedience, dissolution of the bonds of human solidarity by the supremacy of self-interest and mutual antagonism. The "sacred" in industrial religion was work, property, profit, power, even though it furthered individualism and freedom within the limits of its general principles. By transforming Christianity into a strictly patriarchal religion it was still possible to express the industrial religion in Christian terminology.

The "Marketing Character" and "Cybernetic Religion"

The most important fact for understanding both the character and the secret religion of contemporary human society is the change in the social character from the earlier era of capitalism to the second part of the twentieth century. The authoritarian-obsessive-hoarding character that had begun to develop in the sixteenth century, and continued to be the dominant character structure at least in the middle classes until the end of the nineteenth century, was slowly blended with or replaced by the *marketing character*. (I described the blends of various character orientations in *Man for Himself*.)

I have called this phenomenon the marketing character because it is based on experiencing oneself as a commodity, and one's value not as "use value" but as "exchange value." The living being becomes a commodity on the "personality market." The principle of evaluation is the same on both the personality and the commodity markets: on the one, personalities are offered for sale; on the other, commodities. Value in both cases is their exchange value, for which "use value" is a necessary but not a sufficient condition.

Although the proportion of skill and human qualities on the one hand and personality on the other hand as prerequisites for success varies, the "personality factor" always plays a decisive role. Success depends largely on how well persons sell themselves on the market, how well they get their personalities across, how nice a "package" they are; whether they are "cheerful," "sound," "aggressive," "reliable," "ambitious"; furthermore, what their family backgrounds are, what clubs they belong to, and whether they know the "right" people. The type of personality required depends to some degree on the special field in which a person may choose to work. A stockbroker, a salesperson, a secretary, a railroad executive, a college professor, or a hotel manager must each offer a different kind of personality that, regardless of their differences, must fulfill one condition: to be in demand.

What shapes one's attitude toward oneself is the fact that skill and equipment for performing a given task are not sufficient; one must be able to "put one's personality across" in competition with many others in order to have success. If it were enough for the purpose of making a living to rely on what one knows and what one can do, one's self-esteem would be in proportion to one's capacities, that is, to one's use value. But since success depends largely on how one sells one's personality, one experiences oneself as a commodity or, rather, simultaneously as the seller *and* the commodity to be sold. A person is not concerned with his or her life and happiness, but with becoming salable.

The aim of the marketing character is complete adaptation, so as to be desirable under all conditions of the personality market. The marketing character personalities do not even *have* egos (as people in the nineteenth century did) to hold onto, that belong to them, that do not change. For they constantly change their egos, according to the principle: "I am as you desire me."

Those with the marketing character structure are without goals, except moving, doing things with the greatest efficiency; if asked *why* they must move so fast, why things have to be done with the greatest efficiency, they have no genuine answer, but offer rationalizations, such as, "in order to create more jobs," or "in order to keep the company growing." They have little interest (at least consciously) in philosophical or religious questions, such as *why* one lives, and *why* one is going in this direction rather than in another. They have their big, ever-changing egos, but none has a self, a core, a sense of identity. The "identity crisis" of modern society is actually the crisis produced by the fact that its members have become selfless instruments, whose identity rests upon their participation in the corporations (or other giant bureaucracies), as a primitive individual's identity rested upon membership in the clan.

The marketing character neither loves nor hates. These

"old-fashioned" emotions do not fit into a character structure that functions almost entirely on the cerebral level and avoids feelings, whether good or evil ones, because they interfere with the marketing characters' main purpose: selling and exchanging—or to put it even more precisely, *functioning* according to the logic of the "megamachine" of which they are a part, without asking any questions except how well they function, as indicated by their advancement in the bureaucracy.

Since the marketing characters have no deep attachment to themselves or to others, they do not care, in any deep sense of the word, not because they are so selfish but because their relations to others and to themselves are so thin. This may also explain why they are not concerned with the dangers of nuclear and ecological catastrophes, even though they know all the data that point to these dangers. That they are not concerned with the danger to their personal lives might still be explained by the assumption that they have great courage and unselfishness; but the lack of concern even for their children and grandchildren excludes such explanation. The lack of concern on all these levels is the result of the loss of any emotional ties, even to those "nearest" to them. The fact is, nobody is close to the marketing characters; neither are they close to themselves.

The puzzling question why contemporary human beings love to buy and to consume, and yet are so little attached to what they buy, finds its most significant answer in the marketing character phenomenon. The marketing characters' lack of attachment also makes them indifferent to things. What matters is perhaps the prestige or the comfort that things give, but things per se have no substance. They are utterly expendable, along with friends or lovers, who are expendable, too, since no deeper tie exists to any of them.

The marketing character goal, *"proper functioning"* under the given circumstances, makes them respond to the world mainly cerebrally. Reason in the sense of *understanding* is an exclusive quality of *Homo sapiens; manipulative intelligence* as a tool for the achievement of practical purposes is common to animals and humans. Manipulative intelligence without reason is dangerous because it makes people move in directions that may be self-destructive from the standpoint of reason. In fact, the more brilliant the uncontrolled manipulative intelligence is, the more dangerous it is.

It was no less a scientist than Charles Darwin who demonstrated the consequences and the human tragedy of a purely scientific, alienated intellect. He writes in his autobiography that until his thirtieth year he had intensely enjoyed music and poetry and pictures, but that for many years afterward he lost all his taste for these interests: "My mind seems to have become a kind of machine for grinding general laws out of large collections of fact. . . . The loss of these tastes is a loss of happiness, and may possibly be injurious to the intellect, and more probably to the moral character, by enfeebling the emotional part of our nature."(Quoted by E. F. Schumacher; q.v.)

The process Darwin describes here has continued since his time at a rapid pace; the separation from reason and heart is almost complete. It is of special interest that this deterioration of reason had not taken place in the majority of the leading investigators in the most exacting and revolutionary sciences (in theoretical physics, for example) and that they were people who were deeply concerned with philosophical and spiritual questions. I refer to such individuals as A. Einstein, N. Bohr, L. Szillard, W. Heisenberg, E. Schrödinger.

The supremacy of cerebral, manipulative thinking goes together with an atrophy of emotional life. Since it is not cultivated or needed, but rather an impediment to optimal functioning, emotional life has remained stunted and never matured beyond the level of a child's. As a result the marketing characters are peculiarly naive as far as emotional problems are concerned. They may be attracted by "emotional people," but because of their own naiveté, they often cannot judge whether such people are genuine or fakers. This may explain why so many fakers can be successful in the spiritual and religious fields; it may also explain why politicians who portray strong emotions have a strong appeal for the marketing character—and why the marketing character cannot discriminate between a genuinely religious person and the public relations product who fakes strong religious emotions.

The term "marketing character" is by no means the only one to describe this type. It can also be described by using a Marxian term, the *alienated character;* persons of this character are alienated from their work, from themselves, from other human beings, and from nature. In psychiatric terms the marketing person could be called a schizoid character; but the term may be slightly misleading, because a schizoid person living with other schizoid persons and performing well and being successful, because of his schizoid character entirely lacks the feeling of uneasiness that the schizoid character has in a more "normal" environment.

During the final revision of the manuscript of this book I had the opportunity to read Michael Maccoby's forthcoming work *The Gamesmen: The New Corporate Leaders* in manuscript. In this penetrating study Maccoby analyzes the character structure of two hundred and fifty executives, managers, and engineers in two of the best-run large companies in the United States. Many of his findings confirm what I have described as features of the cybernetic person, particularly the predominance of the cerebral along with the underdevelopment of the emotional sphere. Considering that the executives and managers described by Maccoby are and will be among the leaders of American society, the social importance of Maccoby's findings is substantial.

The following data, drawn by Maccoby from his three to twenty personal interviews with each member of the group studied, give us a clear picture of this character type.*

---

*Reprinted by permission. Cf. a parallel study by Ignacio Millan, *The Character of Mexican Executives,* to be published soon.

Deep scientific interest in understanding, dynamic sense of the work, animated	0%
Centered, enlivening, craftsmanlike, but lacks deeper scientific interest in the nature of things	22%
The work itself stimulates interest, which is not self-sustained	58%
Moderate productive, not centered. Interest in work is essentially instrumental, to ensure security, income	18%
Passive unproductive, diffused	2%
Rejecting of work, rejects the real world	0%
	100%

Two features are striking: (1) deep interest in understanding ("reason") is absent, and (2) for the vast majority either the stimulation of their work is not self-sustaining or the work is essentially a means for ensuring economic security.

In complete contrast is the picture of what Maccoby calls "the love scale":

Loving, affirmative, creatively stimulating	0%
Responsible, warm, affectionate, but not deeply loving	5%
Moderate interest in another person, with more loving possibilities	40%
Conventional concern, decent, role oriented	41%
Passive, unloving, uninterested	13%
Rejecting of life, hardened heart	1%
	100%

No one in the study could be characterized as deeply loving, although 5 percent show up as being "warm and affectionate." All the rest are listed as having moderate interest, or conventional concern, or as unloving, or outright rejecting of life—indeed a striking picture of emotional underdevelopment in contrast to the prominence of cerebralism.

The "cybernetic religion" of the marketing character corresponds to that total character structure. Hidden behind the façade of agnosticism or Christianity is a thoroughly pagan religion, although people are not conscious of it as such. This pagan religion is difficult to describe, since it can only be inferred from what people do (and do *not* do) and not from their conscious thoughts about religion or dogmas of a religious organization. Most striking, at first glance, is that Man has made himself into a god because he has acquired the technical capacity for a "second creation" of the world, replacing the first creation by the God of traditional religion. We can also formulate: We have made the machine into a god and have become godlike by serving the machine. It matters little the formulation we choose; what matters is that human beings, in the state of their greatest real *impotence, imagine* themselves in connection with science and technique to be *omnipotent.*

This aspect of cybernetic religion corresponds to a more hopeful period of development. But the more we are caught in our isolation, in our lack of emotional response to the world, and at the same time the more unavoidable a catastrophic end seems to be, the more malignant becomes the new religion. We cease to be the masters of technique and become instead its slaves—and technique, once a vital element of creation, shows its other face as the goddess of destruction (like the Indian goddess Kali), to which men and women are willing to sacrifice themselves and their children. While consciously still hanging onto the hope for a better future, cybernetic humanity represses the fact that they have become worshipers of the goddess of destruction.

This thesis has many kinds of proof, but none more compelling than these two: that the great (and even some smaller) powers continue to build nuclear weapons of ever-increasing capacity for destruction and do not arrive at the one sane solution—destruction of all nuclear weapons and the atomic energy plants that deliver the material for nuclear weapons—and that virtually nothing is done to end the danger of ecological catastrophe. In short, nothing serious is being done to plan for the survival of the human race.

The Humanist Protest

The dehumanization of the social character and the rise of the industrial and cybernetic religions led to a protest movement, to the emergence of a new humanism, that has its roots in Christian and philosophical humanism from the Late Middle Ages to the Age of Enlightenment. This protest found expression in theistic Christian as well as in pantheistic or nontheistic philosophical formulations. It came from two opposite sides: from the romantics, who were politically conservatives, and from the Marxian and other socialists (and some anarchists). The right and the left were unanimous in their critique of the industrial system and the damage it did to human beings. Catholic thinkers, such as Franz von Baader, and conservative political leaders, such as Benjamin Disraeli, formulated the problem, sometimes in identical ways to those of Marx.

The two sides differed in the ways they thought human beings could be saved from the danger of being transformed into things. The romantics on the right believed that the only way was to stop the unhindered "progress" of the industrial system and to return to previous forms of the social order, though with some modifications.

The protest from the left may be called *radical humanism,* even though it was sometimes expressed in theistic and sometimes in nontheistic terms. The socialists believed that the economic development could not be halted, that one could not return to a previous form of social order, and that the only way to salvation lay in going forward and creating a new society that would free people from alienation, from submission to the machine, from the fate of being dehumanized. Socialism was the synthesis of medieval religious tradition and the post-Renaissance spirit of scientific thinking and political action. It was, like Buddhism, a "religious" mass movement that, even though speaking in secular and atheistic terms, aimed at the liberation of human beings from selfishness and greed.

At least a brief commentary is necessary to explain my characterization of Marxian thought, in view of its complete perversion by Soviet communism and reformist Western socialism to a materialism aimed at achieving wealth for everybody. As Hermann Cohen, Ernst Bloch, and a number of other scholars have stated during the past decades, socialism was the secular expression of prophetic Messianism. Perhaps the best way to demonstrate this is to quote from the Code of Maimonides his characterization of the Messianic Time:

> The Sages and Prophets did not long for the days of the Messiah that Israel might exercise dominion over the world, or rule over the heathens, or be exalted by the nations, or that it might eat and drink and rejoice. Their aspiration was that Israel be free to devote itself to the Law and its wisdom, with no one to oppress or disturb it, and thus be worthy of life in the world to come.
>
> In that era there will be neither famine nor war, neither jealousy nor strife. Earthly goods* will be abundant, comforts within the reach of all. The one preoccupation of the whole world will be to know the Lord. Hence Israelites will be very wise, they will know the things that are now concealed and will attain an understanding of their creator to the utmost capacity of the human mind, as it is written: For

*My translation from the Hebrew text, instead of "blessings" in the Hershman translation, published by Yale University Press.

the earth shall be full of the knowledge of the Lord, as the waters cover the sea (Isaiah 11:9).

In this description the goal of history is to enable human beings to devote themselves entirely to the study of wisdom and the knowledge of God; not power or luxury. The Messianic Time is one of universal peace, absence of envy, and material abundance. This picture is very close to the concept of the goal of life as Marx expressed it toward the end of the third volume of his *Capital:*

> The realm of freedom does not commence until the point is passed where labor under the compulsion of necessity and of external utility is required. In the very nature of things it lies beyond the sphere of material production in the strict meaning of the term. Just as the savage must wrestle with nature, in order to satisfy his wants, in order to maintain his life and reproduce it, so civilized man has to do it, and he must do it in all forms of society and under all possible modes of production. With his development the realm of natural necessity expands, because his wants increase; but at the same time the forces of production increase, by which these wants are satisfied. The freedom in this field cannot consist of anything else but of the fact that socialized man, the associated producers, regulate their interchange with nature rationally, bring it under their common control, instead of being ruled by it as by some blind power; that they accomplish their task with the least expenditure of energy and under conditions most adequate to their human nature and *most worthy of it.* But it always remains a realm of necessity. Beyond it begins that *development of human power which is its own end,* the true realm of freedom, which, however, can flourish only upon that realm of necessity as its basis. The shortening of the working day is its fundamental premise. [Emphasis added.]

Marx, like Maimonides—and in contrast to Christian and to other Jewish teachings of salvation—does not postulate a final eschatological solution; the discrepancy between Man and nature remains, but the realm of necessity is brought under human control as much as possible: "But it always remains a realm of necessity." The goal is *that development of human power which is its own end, the true realm of freedom*" (emphasis added). Maimonides' view that "the preoccupation of the whole world will be to know the Lord" is to Marx the "development of human power . . . [as] its own end."

Having and being as two different forms of human existence are at the center of Marx's ideas for the emergence of new Man. With these modes Marx proceeds from economic to psychological and anthropological categories, which are, as we have seen in our discussion of the Old and New Testaments and Eckhart, at the same time fundamental "religious" categories. Marx wrote: "Private property has made us so stupid and partial that an object is only ours when we have it, when it exists for us as capital or when it is directly eaten, drunk, worn, inhabited, etc., in short, *utilized* in some way. . . . Thus *all* the physical and intellectual senses have been replaced by the simple alienation of *all* these senses; the sense of *having*. The human being had to be reduced to this absolute poverty in order to be able to give birth to all his inner wealth. (On the category of *having* see Hess in *Einundzwanzig Bogen*.)"*

Marx's concept of being and having is summarized in his sentence: "The less you *are* and the less you express your life —the more you *have* and the greater is your alienated life. . . . Everything the economist takes away from you in the way of life and humanity, he restores to you in the form of money and wealth."

The "sense of having" about which Marx speaks here is precisely the same as the "egoboundness" of which Eckhart speaks, the craving for things and for one's ego. Marx refers to the *having mode of existence*, not to possession as such, not

---

*This and the following passages are from Marx's *Economic and Philosophical Manuscripts*, translated in *Marx's Concept of Man*.

to unalienated private property as such. The goal is not luxury and wealth, nor is it poverty; in fact, *both* luxury and poverty are looked upon by Marx as vices. Absolute poverty is the condition for giving birth to one's inner wealth.

What is this act of giving birth? It is the active, unalienated expression of our faculty toward the corresponding objects. Marx continues: "All his [Man's] *human* relations to the world —seeing, hearing, smelling, tasting, touching, thinking, observing, feeling, desiring, acting, loving—in short all the organs of his individuality . . . are in their objective action [their *action in relation to the object*] the appropriation of this object, the appropriation of human reality." This is the form of appropriation in the mode of *being,* not in the mode of having. Marx expressed this form of nonalienated activity in the following passage:

> Let us assume *man* to be *man,* and his relation to the world to be a human one. Then love can only be exchanged for love, trust for trust, etc. If you wish to enjoy art, you must be an artistically cultivated person; if you wish to influence other people, you must be a person who really has a stimulating and encouraging effect upon others. Every one of your relations to man and to nature must be a *specific expression,* corresponding to the object of your will, of your *real individual* life. If you love without evoking love in return, i.e., if you are not able, by the *manifestation* of yourself as a loving person, to make yourself a *beloved person,* then your love is impotent and a misfortune.

But Marx's ideas were soon perverted, perhaps because he lived a hundred years too soon. Both he and Engels thought that capitalism had already reached the end of its possibilities and, hence, that the revolution was just around the corner. But they were thoroughly mistaken, as Engels was to state after Marx's death. They had pronounced their new teaching at the very height of capitalist development and did not foresee that it would take more than a hundred years for capitalism's decline and the final crisis to begin. It was a historical necessity that an anticapitalist idea, propagated at the very peak of capitalism, had to be utterly transformed into the capitalist spirit if it was to be successful. And this is what actually happened.

Western social democrats and their bitter opponents, communists within and without the Soviet Union, transformed socialism into a purely economic concept, the goal of which was maximum consumption, maximum use of machines. Khrushchev, with his concept of "goulash" communism, in his simple and folksy manner let the truth out of the bag: The aim of socialism was to give the whole population the same pleasure of consumption as capitalism gave only to a minority. Socialism and communism were built on the bourgeois concept of materialism. Some phrases of Marx's earlier writings (which, on the whole, were denigrated as "idealistic" errors of the "young" Marx) were recited as ritualistically as the words of the gospels are cited in the West.

That Marx lived at the height of capitalist development had another consequence: as a child of his time Marx could not help adopting attitudes and concepts current in bourgeois thought and practice. Thus, for instance, certain authoritarian inclinations in his personality as well as in his writings were molded by the patriarchal bourgeois spirit rather than by the spirit of socialism. He followed the pattern of the classical economists in his construction of "scientific" versus "utopian" socialism. Just as the economists claimed that economics was following its own laws quite independently of human will, Marx sensed the need to prove that socialism would *necessarily* develop according to the laws of economics. Consequently, he sometimes tended to develop formulations that could be misunderstood as deterministic, not giving a sufficient role to human will and imagination in the historical process. Such unintended concessions to the spirit of capitalism facilitated the process of perverting Marx's system into one that was not fundamentally different from capitalism.

If Marx had pronounced his ideas today, at the beginning
—and rapidly increasing—decline of capitalism, his *real* message would have had a chance to be influential or even victorious, provided one can make such a historical conjecture. As
it is, even the words "socialism" and "communism" are com-
promised. At any rate, every socialist or communist party that
could claim to represent Marxian thought would have to be
based on the conviction that the Soviet regimes are *not* socialist systems in any sense, that socialism is incompatible with a
bureaucratic, thing-centered, consumption-oriented social
system, that it is incompatible with the materialism and cere-
bralization that characterize the Soviet, like the capitalist, system.

The corruption of socialism explains the fact that genuine
radical humanist thoughts often come from groups and individuals who were not identified with the ideas of Marx or
who were even opposed to them, sometimes after having
been active members of the communist movement.

While it is impossible to mention here all the radical humanists of the post-Marxian period, some examples of their
thinking are given on the following pages. Though the con-
ceptualizations of these radical humanists differed widely, and
sometimes seem to contradict each other completely, they all
share the following ideas and attitudes:

- that production must serve the real needs of the people, not the
  demands of the economic system;
- that a new relation must be established between people and
  nature, one of cooperation not of exploitation;
- that mutual antagonism must be replaced by solidarity;
- that the aim of all social arrangements must be human well-
  being and the prevention of ill-being;
- that not maximum consumption but sane consumption that
  furthers well-being must be striven for;
- that the individual must be an active, not a passive, participant
  in social life.*

*The socialist humanists' views may be found in E. Fromm, ed., *Socialist Humanism.*

Albert Schweitzer starts from the radical premise of the imminent crisis of Western culture. "It is obvious to everybody," he states, "that we are in a process of cultural self-destruction. What is left is also not secure any more. It still stands because it was not exposed to the destructive pressure to which the rest has already succumbed. But it too is built on gravel [Geröll]. The next landslide [Bergrutsch] can take it along. . . . The cultural capacity of modern Man is diminished because the circumstances which surround him diminish him and damage him psychically."*

Characterizing the industrial being as "unfree . . . unconcentrated . . . incomplete . . . in danger of losing his humanity," he continues:

> Because society with its developed organization exercises a hitherto unknown power over Man, Man's dependency on it has grown to a degree that he almost has ceased to live a mental [geistig] existence of his own. . . . Thus we have entered a new Middle Ages. By a general act of will freedom of thought has been put out of function, because many give up thinking as free individuals, and are guided by the collective to which they belong. . . . With the sacrifice of independence of thought we have—and how could it be otherwise—lost faith in truth. Our intellectual-emotional life is disorganized. *The overorganization of our public affairs culminates in the organization of thoughtlessness* [emphasis added].

He sees industrial society characterized not only by lack of freedom but also by "overeffort" (*Überanstrengung*). "For two or three centuries many individuals have lived only as *working* beings and not as *human* beings." The human substance is stunted and in the upbringing of children by such stunted parents, an essential factor for their human development is

---

*This and the following Schweitzer passages are my translations of quotations from *Die Schuld der Philosophie an dem Niedergang der Kultur*, first published in 1923, but sketched from 1900 to 1917.

lacking. "Later on, himself subjected to overoccupation, the adult person succumbs more and more to the need for superficial distraction. . . . *Absolute passivity, diverting attention from and forgetting of oneself are a physical need for him*" (emphasis added). As a consequence Schweitzer pleads for reduction of work and against overconsumption and luxury.

Schweitzer, the Protestant theologian, insists, as does Eckhart, the Dominican monk, that Man's task is not to retire into an atmosphere of spiritual egotism, remote from the affairs of the world, but to lead an active life in which one tries to contribute to the spiritual perfection of society. "If among modern individuals there are so few whose human and ethical sentiments are intact, not the least reason is the fact that they sacrifice constantly their personal morality on the altar of the fatherland, *instead of being in constant living interchange with the collective and of giving it the power which drives the collective to its perfection*" (emphasis added).

He concludes that the present cultural and social structure drives toward a catastrophe, from which only a new Renaissance "much greater than the old one will arise"; that we must renew ourselves in a new belief and attitude, unless we want to perish. "Essential in this Renaissance will be the principle of activity, which rational thinking gives into our hands, the only rational and pragmatic principle of the historical development produced by Man. . . . I have confidence in my faith *that this revolution will occur if we decide to become thinking human beings*" (emphasis added).

It is probably because Schweitzer was a theologian and is best known, at least philosophically, for his concept of "reverence for life" as the basis of ethics that people have generally ignored that he was one of the most radical critics of industrial society, debunking its myth of progress and general happiness. He recognized the decay of human society and the world through the practice of industrialized life; at the beginning of this century he already saw the weakness and dependency of the people, the destructive effect of obsessional work, the need for less work and less consumption. He postulated the necessity for a Renaissance of collective life that would be organized by the spirit of solidarity and reverence for life.

This presentation of Schweitzer's thought should not be concluded without pointing to the fact that Schweitzer, in contrast to the metaphysical optimism of Christianity, was a metaphysical skeptic. This is one of the reasons he was strongly attracted by Buddhist thought, in which life has no meaning that is given and guaranteed by a supreme being. He came to this conclusion: "If one takes the world as it is, it is impossible to endow it with meaning in which the aims and goals of Man and of Mankind make sense." The only meaningful way of life is activity in the world; not activity in general but the activity of giving and caring for fellow creatures. Schweitzer gave this answer in his writing and by living it.

There is a remarkable kinship in the ideas of the Buddha, Eckhart, Marx, and Schweitzer: their radical demand for giving up the having orientation; their insistence on complete independence; their metaphysical skepticism; their godless religiosity,* and their demand for social activity in the spirit of care and human solidarity. However, these teachers are sometimes unconscious of these elements. For instance, Eckhart is usually unconscious of his nontheism; Marx, of his religiosity. The matter of interpretation, especially of Eckhart and Marx, is so complex that it is impossible to give an adequate presentation of the nontheistic religion of caring activism that makes these teachers the founders of a new religiosity fitting the necessities of new Man. In a sequel to this volume I shall analyze the ideas of these teachers.

Even authors whom one cannot call radical humanists, since they hardly transcend the transpersonal, mechanistic attitude of our age (such as the authors of the two reports commissioned by the Club of Rome), do not fail to see that

---

*In a letter to E. R. Jacobi, Schweitzer wrote that the "religion of love can exist without a world-ruling personality" (*Divine Light,* 2, No. 1 [1967]).

a radical inner human change is the only alternative to economic catastrophe. Mesarovic and Pestel demand a "new
world consciousness . . . a new ethic in the use of material
resources . . . a new attitude toward nature, based on harmony
rather than on conquest . . . a sense of identification with
future generations. . . . For the first time in Man's life on earth,
he is being asked to refrain from doing what he can do; he is
being asked to restrain his economic and technological advancement, or at least to direct it differently from before; he
is being asked by all the future generations of the earth to
share his good fortune with the unfortunate—not in a spirit
of charity but in a spirit of necessity. He is being asked to
concentrate now on the organic growth of the total world
system. Can he, in good conscience, say no?" They conclude
that without these fundamental human changes, *"Homo sapiens*
is as good as doomed."

The study has some shortcomings—to me the most outstanding one being that it does not consider the political,
social, and psychological factors that stand in the way of any
change. To indicate the trend of necessary changes in general
is useless until it is followed up by a serious attempt to consider the real obstacles that impede all their suggestions. (It
is to be hoped that the Club of Rome comes to grips with the
problem of those social and political changes that are the
preconditions for attaining the general goals.) Nevertheless
the fact remains that these authors have attempted for the first
time to show the economic needs and resources of the whole
world, and that, as I wrote in the Introduction, for the first
time a demand is made for an ethical change, not as a consequence of ethical beliefs but as the rational consequence of
economic analysis.

Within the past few years, a considerable number of books
in the United States and in Germany have raised the same
demand: to subordinate economy to the needs of the people,
first for our sheer survival, second for our well-being. (I have
read or examined about thirty-five such books, but the num-

ber available is at least twice that.) Most of these authors agree that material increase of consumption does not necessarily mean increase in well-being; that a characterological and spiritual change must go together with the necessary social changes; that unless we stop wasting our natural resources and destroying the ecological conditions for human survival, catastrophe within a hundred years is foreseeable. I mention here only a few of the outstanding representatives of this new humanistic economy.

The economist E. F. Schumacher shows in his book *Small Is Beautiful* that our failures are the result of our successes, and that our techniques must be subordinated to our real human needs. "Economy as a content of life is a deadly illness," he writes, "because infinite growth does not fit into a finite world. That economy *should not* be the content of life has been told to mankind by all its great teachers; that it *cannot* be is evident today. If one wants to describe the deadly illness in more detail, one can say that it is similar to an addiction, like alcoholism or drug addiction. It does not matter too much whether this addiction appears in a more egotistical or more altruistic form, whether it seeks its satisfaction only in a crude materialistic way or also in an artistically, culturally, or scientifically refined way. Poison is poison, even if wrapped in silver paper. . . . If spiritual culture, the culture of the inner Man, is neglected, then selfishness remains the dominating power in Man and a system of selfishness, like capitalism, fits this orientation better than a system of love for one's fellow beings."

Schumacher has translated his principles by devising minimachines that are adapted to the needs of nonindustrialized countries. It is especially noteworthy that his books are more popular every year—and not by a big advertising campaign but by the word-of-mouth propaganda of his readers.

Paul Ehrlich and Anne Ehrlich are two American authors whose thinking is similar to Schumacher's. In their *Population,*

Resources, Environment: Issues in Human Ecology they present the following conclusions about "the present world situation":

1. Considering present technology and patterns of behavior our planet is grossly overpopulated now.

2. The large absolute number of people and the rate of population growth are major hindrances to solving human problems.

3. The limits of human capability to produce food by conventional means have very nearly been reached. Problems of supply and distribution already have resulted in roughly half of humanity being undernourished or malnourished. Some 10–20 million people are starving to death annually now.

4. Attempts to increase food production further will tend to accelerate the deterioration of our environment, which in turn will eventually *reduce* the capacity of the earth to produce food. It is not clear whether environmental decay has now gone so far as to be essentially irreversible; it is possible that the capacity of the planet to support human life has been permanently impaired. Such technological "successes" as automobiles, pesticides, and inorganic nitrogen fertilizers are major causes of environmental deterioration.

5. There is reason to believe that population growth increases the probability of a lethal worldwide plague and of a thermonuclear war. Either could provide an undesirable "death rate solution" to the population problem; each is potentially capable of destroying civilization and even of driving *Homo sapiens* to extinction.

6. There is no technological panacea for the complex of problems composing the population-food-environment crisis, although technology properly applied in such areas as pollution abatement, communications, and fertility control can provide massive assistance. *The basic solutions involve dramatic and rapid changes in human*

attitudes, especially those relating to reproductive behavior, economic growth, technology, the environment, and conflict resolution. [Emphasis added.]

E. Eppler's *Ende oder Wende* (End or change) is another
recent work that bears mention. Eppler's ideas are similar to
Schumacher's, though less radical, and his position is perhaps
especially interesting because he is the leader of the Social
Democratic party in Baden-Württemberg and a convinced
Protestant. Two books I wrote are of the same orientation,
The Sane Society and *The Revolution of Hope.*

Even among the Soviet bloc writers, where the idea of the
restriction of production has always been tabu, voices are
beginning to suggest that consideration be given to an economy without growth. W. Harich, a dissident Marxist in the
German Democratic Republic, proposes a static, worldwide
economic balance, which alone can guarantee equality and
avert the danger of irreparable damage to the biosphere.
Also, in 1972 some of the most outstanding natural scientists,
economists, and geographers in the Soviet Union met to discuss "Man and His Environment." On their agenda were the
results of the Club of Rome studies, which they considered in
a sympathetic and respectful spirit, pointing to the considerable merits of the studies, even though not agreeing with them.
(See "Technologie und Politik" in the Bibliography, for a
report of this meeting.)

The most important contemporary anthropological and
historical expression of the humanism that is common to
these various attempts at humanist social reconstruction is to
be found in L. Mumford's *The Pentagon of Power* and in all his
previous books.

VIII

Conditions for Human Change and the Features of the New Man

Assuming the premise is right—that only a fundamental change in human character from a preponderance of the having mode to a predominantly being mode of existence can save us from a psychologic and economic catastrophe—the question arises: Is large-scale characterological change possible, and if so, how can it be brought about?

I suggest that human character *can* change if these conditions exist:

1. We are suffering and are aware that we are.
2. We recognize the origin of our ill-being.
3. We recognize that there is a way of overcoming our ill-being.
4. We accept that in order to overcome our ill-being we must follow certain norms for living and change our present practice of life.

These four points correspond to the Four Noble Truths that form the basis of the Buddha's teaching dealing with the general condition of human existence, though not with cases of human ill-being due to specific individual or social circumstances.

The same principle of change that characterizes the methods of the Buddha also underlies Marx's idea of salvation. In order to understand this it is necessary to be aware that for Marx, as he himself said, communism was not a final goal, but a step in the historical development that was to liberate human beings from those socioeconomic and political conditions that make people inhuman—prisoners of things, machines, and their own greed.

Marx's first step was to show the working class of his time, the most alienated and miserable class, *that* they suffered. He tried to destroy the illusions that tended to cover the workers' awareness of their misery. His second step was to show the *causes* of this suffering, which he points out are in the nature of capitalism and the character of greed and avarice and dependence that the capitalistic system produces. This analysis of the causes of the workers' suffering (but not *only* theirs) contributed the main thrust of Marx's work, the analysis of capitalistic economy.

His third step was to demonstrate that the suffering could be removed if the conditions for suffering were removed. In the fourth step he showed the new practice of life, the new social system that would be free of the suffering that the old system, of necessity, had to produce.

Freud's method of healing was essentially similar. Patients consulted Freud because they suffered and they were aware *that* they suffered. But they were usually not aware *what* they suffered *from*. The psychoanalyst's usual first task is to help patients give up their illusions about their suffering and learn what their ill-being really consists of. The diagnosis of the nature of individual or societal ill-being is a matter of interpretation, and various interpreters can differ. The patients' own picture of what they suffer from is usually the least reliable datum for a diagnosis. The essence of the psychoanalytic process is to help make patients aware of the *causes* of their ill-being.

As a consequence of such knowledge, patients can arrive at the next step: the insight that their ill-being can be cured, provided its causes are done away with. In Freud's view this meant to lift the repression of certain infantile events. Traditional psychoanalysis seems essentially not to agree on the need for the fourth point, however. Many psychoanalysts seem to think that, by itself, insight into the repressed has a curative effect. Indeed, this is often the case, especially when the patient suffers from circumscribed symptoms, such as hysterical or obsessional symptoms. But I do not believe anything lasting can be achieved by persons who suffer from a general ill-being and for whom a change in character is necessary, *unless they change their practice of life in accordance with the change in character they want to achieve.* For instance, one can analyze the dependency of individuals until doomsday, but all the insights gained will accomplish nothing while they stay in the same practical situations they were living in before arriving at these insights. To give a simple example: a woman whose suffering is rooted in her dependency on her father, even though she has insight into deeper causes of the dependency, will not really change unless she changes her practice of life, for instance separates from her father, does not accept his favors, takes the risk and pain that these practical steps toward independence imply. *Insight separated from practice remains ineffective.*

The New Man

The function of the new society is to encourage the emergence of a new Man, beings whose character structure will exhibit the following qualities:

• Willingness to give up all forms of having, in order to fully *be.*

• Security, sense of identity, and confidence based on faith in what one *is,* on one's need for relatedness, interest, love, solidarity with the world around one, instead of on one's desire to have, to possess, to control the world, and thus become the slave of one's possessions.

• Acceptance of the fact that nobody and nothing outside

oneself give meaning to life, but that this radical independence and no-thingness can become the condition for the
fullest activity devoted to caring and sharing.

• Being fully present where one is.

• Joy that comes from giving and sharing, not from hoarding and exploiting.

• Love and respect for life in all its manifestations, in the
knowledge that not things, power, all that is dead, but life and
everything that pertains to its growth are sacred.

• Trying to reduce greed, hate, and illusions as much as one
is capable.

• Living without worshiping idols and without illusions, because one has reached a state that does not require illusions.

• Developing one's capacity for love, together with one's
capacity for critical, unsentimental thought.

• Shedding one's narcissism and accepting the tragic limitations inherent in human existence.

• Making the full growth of oneself and of one's fellow
beings the supreme goal of living.

• Knowing that to reach this goal, discipline and respect for
reality are necessary.

• Knowing, also, that no growth is healthy that does not
occur in a structure, but knowing, too, the difference between
structure as an attribute of life and "order" as an attribute of
no-life, of the dead.

• Developing one's imagination, not as an escape from intolerable circumstances but as the anticipation of real possibilities, as a means to do away with intolerable circumstances.

• Not deceiving others, but also not being deceived by others; one may be called innocent, but not naive.

• Knowing oneself, not only the self one knows, but also the
self one does not know—even though one has a slumbering
knowledge of what one does not know.

• Sensing one's oneness with all life, hence giving up the

aim of conquering nature, subduing it, exploiting it, raping it, destroying it, but trying, rather, to understand and cooperate with nature.

• Freedom that is not arbitrariness but the possibility to be oneself, not as a bundle of greedy desires, but as a delicately balanced structure that at any moment is confronted with the alternative of growth or decay, life or death.

• Knowing that evil and destructiveness are necessary consequences of failure to grow.

• Knowing that only a few have reached perfection in all these qualities, but being without the ambition to "reach the goal," in the knowledge that such ambition is only another form of greed, of having.

• Happiness in the process of ever-growing aliveness, whatever the furthest point is that fate permits one to reach, for living as fully as one can is so satisfactory that the concern for what one might or might not attain has little chance to develop.

To suggest what people living in contemporary cybernetic, bureaucratic industrialism—whether in its "capitalist" or "socialist" version—could do to break through the having form of existence and to increase the being sector is not within the scope of this book. In fact, it would require a book by itself, one that might appropriately be titled "The Art of Being." But many books have been published in recent years about the road to well-being, some helpful, and many others made harmful by their fraudulence, exploiting the new market that caters to people's wish to escape their malaise. Some valuable books that might be helpful to anyone with a serious interest in the problem of achieving well-being are listed in the Bibliography.

IX

Features of the New Society

A New Science of Man

The first requirement in the possible creation of the new society is to be aware of the almost insurmountable difficulties that such an attempt must face. The dim awareness of this difficulty is probably óne of the main reasons that so little effort is made to make the necessary changes. Many think: "Why strive for the impossible? Let us rather act as if the course we are steering will lead us to the place of safety and happiness that our maps indicate." Those who unconsciously despair yet put on the mask of optimism are not necessarily wise. But those who have not given up hope can succeed only if they are hardheaded realists, shed all illusions, and fully appreciate the difficulties. This sobriety marks the distinction between *awake* and *dreaming* "utopians."

To mention only a few of the difficulties the construction of the new society has to solve:

• It would have to solve the problem of how to continue the industrial mode of production without total centralization, i.e., without ending up in fascism of the old-fashioned type or, more likely, technological "fascism with a smiling face."

• It would have to combine overall planning with a high degree of decentralization, giving up the "free-market economy," that has become largely a fiction.

• It would have to give up the goal of unlimited growth for

selective growth, without running the risk of economic disaster.

• It would have to create work conditions and a general spirit in which not material gain but other, psychic satisfactions are effective motivations.

• It would have to further scientific progress and, at the same time, prevent this progress from becoming a danger to the human race by its practical application.

• It would have to create conditions under which people experience well-being and joy, not the satisfaction of the maximum-pleasure drive.

• It would have to give basic security to individuals without making them dependent on a bureaucracy to feed them.

• It must restore possibilities for individual initiative in living, rather than in business (where it hardly exists any more anyway).

As in the development of technique some difficulties seemed insurmountable, so the difficulties listed above seem insurmountable now. But the difficulties of technique were not insurmountable because a new science had been established that proclaimed the principle of observation and knowledge of nature as conditions for controlling it (Francis Bacon: *Novum Organum,* 1620). This "new science" of the seventeenth century has attracted the most brilliant minds in the industrialized countries up to this day, and it led to the fulfillment of the technical Utopias the human mind had been dreaming of.

But today, roughly three centuries later, we need an entirely different new science. We need a Humanistic Science of Man as the basis for the Applied Science and Art of Social Reconstruction.

Technical Utopias—flying, for example—have been achieved by the new science of nature. The *human Utopia* of the Messianic Time—a united new humankind living in solidarity and peace, free from economic determination and from war and class struggle—can be achieved, provided we spend the same energy, intelligence, and enthusiasm on the realization of the human Utopia as we have spent on the realization of our technical Utopias. One cannot construct submarines by reading Jules Verne; one cannot construct a humanist society by reading the prophets.

Whether such a change from the supremacy of natural science to a new social science will take place, nobody can tell. If it does, we might still have a chance for survival, but whether it will depends on one factor: how many brilliant, learned, disciplined, and caring men and women are attracted by the new challenge to the human mind, and by the fact that this time *the goal is not control over nature but control over technique and over irrational social forces and institutions that threaten the survival of Western society, if not of the human race.*

It is my conviction that our future depends on whether, given awareness of the present crisis, the best minds will mobilize to devote themselves to the new humanistic science of Man. For nothing short of their concerted effort will help to solve the problems already mentioned here, and to achieve the goals discussed below.

Blueprints with such general aims as "socialization of the means of production" have turned out to be socialist and communist shibboleths mainly covering up the absence of socialism. "Dictatorship of the proletariat" or of an "intellectual elite" is no less nebulous and misleading than the concept of the "free market economy" or, for that matter, of the "free" nations. Earlier socialists and communists, from Marx to Lenin, had no concrete plans for a socialist or communist society; this was the great weakness of socialism.

New social forms that will be the basis of being will not arise without many designs, models, studies, and experiments that *begin to bridge the gap between what is necessary and what is possible.* This will eventually amount to large-scale, long-run planning and to short-term proposals for first steps. The problem is the will and the humanist spirit of those who work on them; besides, when people can see a vision and simultaneously recognize what can be done step by step in a concrete way to achieve it, they will begin to feel encouragement and enthusiasm instead of fright.

If the economic and political spheres of society are to be subordinated to human development, *the model of the new society must be determined by the requirements of the unalienated, being-oriented individual.* This means that human beings shall neither live in inhuman poverty—still the main problem of the majority of people—nor be forced—as are the affluent of the industrial world—to be a *Homo consumens* by the inherent laws of capitalist production, which demand continuous growth of production and, hence, enforce growing consumption. If human beings are ever to become free and to cease feeding industry by pathological consumption, a radical change in the economic system is necessary: *we must put an end to the present situation where a healthy economy is possible only at the price of unhealthy human beings.* The task is to construct a healthy economy for healthy people.

The first crucial step toward this goal is that production shall be directed for the sake of "sane consumption."

The traditional formula "Production for *use* instead of for *profit*" is insufficient because it does not qualify what kind of use is referred to: healthy or pathological. At this point a most difficult practical question arises: Who is to determine which needs are healthy and which are pathogenic? Of one thing we can be certain: to force citizens to consume what the state decides is best—even if it *is* the best—is out of the question. Bureaucratic control that would forcibly block consumption would only make people all the more consumption hungry. Sane consumption can take place only if an ever-increasing number of people *want* to change their consumption patterns and their lifestyles. And this is possible only if people are offered a type of consumption that is more attractive than the one they are used to. This cannot happen overnight or by decree, but will require a slow educational process, and in this the government must play an important role.

The function of the state is to establish norms for healthy

consumption, as against pathological and indifferent consumption. In principle, such norms can be established. The U.S. Food and Drug Administration offers a good example; it determines which foods and which drugs are harmful, basing its determination on the expert opinion of scientists in various fields, often after prolonged experimentation. In similar fashion, the value of other commodities and services can be determined by a panel of psychologists, anthropologists, sociologists, philosophers, theologians, and representatives of various social and consumer groups.

But the examination of what is life-furthering and what is life-damaging requires a depth of research that is incomparably greater than that necessary for resolving the problems of the FDA. Basic research on the nature of needs that has hardly been touched will have to be done by the new science of Man. We will need to determine which needs originate in our organism; which are the result of cultural progress; which are expressions of the individual's growth; which are synthetic, forced upon the individual by industry; which "activate" and which "passivate"; which are rooted in pathology and which in psychical health.

In contrast to the existing FDA, the decisions of the new humanist body of experts would not be implemented by force, but would serve only as guidelines, to be submitted to the citizens for discussion. We have already become very much aware of the problem of healthful and unhealthful food; the results of the experts' investigations will help to increase society's recognition of all other sane and pathological needs. People would see that most consumption engenders passivity; that the need for speed and newness, which can only be satisfied by consumerism, reflects restlessness, the inner flight from oneself; they would become aware that looking for the next thing to do or the newest gadget to use is only a means of protecting oneself from being close to oneself or to another person.

The government can greatly facilitate this educational process by subsidizing the production of desirable commodities and services, until these can be profitably produced. A large educational campaign in favor of sane consumption would have to accompany these efforts. It is to be expected that *a concerted effort to stimulate the appetite for sane consumption is likely to change the pattern of consumption.* Even, if the brainwashing advertising methods that industry now uses are avoided—and this is an essential condition—it does not seem unreasonable to expect this effort to have an effect that is not too far behind that of industrial propaganda.

A standard objection to the whole program of selective consumption (and production) according to the principle of "What furthers well-being?" is that in the free market economy the consumers get precisely what they want, and hence there is no need for "selective" production. This argument is based on the assumption that consumers want what is good for them, which is, of course, blatantly untrue (in the case of drugs, or perhaps even cigarettes, nobody would use this argument). The important fact that the argument plainly ignores is that the wishes of the consumer are manufactured by the producer. In spite of competing brands, the overall effect of advertising is to stimulate the craving for consumption. All firms help each other in this basic influence via their advertising; the buyer exercises only secondarily the doubtful privilege of choosing between several competing brands. One of the standard examples offered by those who argue that the consumers' wishes are all-powerful is the failure of the Ford company's "Edsel." But the Edsel's lack of success does not alter the fact that even the advertising propaganda for it was *propaganda to buy automobiles*—from which all brands profited, except the unfortunate Edsel. Furthermore, industry influences taste by *not* producing commodities that would be more healthful to human beings but less profitable to industry.

Sane consumption is possible only if we can drastically curb the right of the stockholders and management of big enterprises to determine their production solely on the basis of profit and expansion.

Such changes could be effected by law without altering the constitutions of Western democracies (we already have many laws that restrict property rights in the interest of the public welfare). What matters is the power to direct production, not ownership of capital. In the long run, the tastes of the consumers will decide what is to be produced, once the suggestive power of advertising is ended. Either the existing enterprises will have to convert their facilities in order to satisfy the new demands, or where that is not possible, the government must spend the capital necessary for the production of new products and services that are wanted.

All these changes can only be made gradually, and with the consent of the majority of the population. But they amount to a new form of economic system, one that is as different from present-day capitalism as it is from the Soviet centralized state capitalism and from the Swedish total welfare bureaucracy.

Obviously, from the very beginning the big corporations will use their tremendous power to try to fight such changes. Only the citizens' overwhelming desire for sane consumption could break the corporations' resistance.

One effective way that citizens can demonstrate the *power of the consumer* is to build a militant consumer movement that will use the threat of "consumer strikes" as a weapon. Assume, for instance, that 20 percent of the American car-consuming population were to decide not to buy private automobiles any more, because they believed that, in comparison with excellent public transportation, the private automobile is economically wasteful, ecologically poisonous, and psychologically damaging—a drug that creates an artificial feeling of power, increases envy, and helps one to run away from oneself. While only an economist could determine how great an economic threat it would be to the automobile industry—and, of course, to the oil companies—clearly if such a consumer strike were to happen, a national economy centered around automobile production would be in serious trouble. Of course, nobody wants the American economy to be in serious trouble, but such a threat, if it can be made credible (stop using cars for one month, for instance), would give consumers a powerful leverage to induce changes in the whole system of production.

The great advantages of consumer strikes are that they do not require government action, that they are difficult to combat (unless the government were to take the step of forcing citizens to buy what they do not want to buy), and that there would be no need to wait for the accord of 51 percent of the citizens to bring enforcement by government measures. For, indeed, a 20 percent minority could be extremely effective in inducing change. Consumer strikes could cut through political lines and slogans; conservative as well as liberal and "left" humanists could participate, since one motivation would unite them all: the desire for sane and humane consumption. As the first step to calling off a consumer strike, the radical humanist consumer movement leaders would negotiate with big industry (and with the government) for the demanded changes. Their method would be basically the same as that used in negotiations to avert or end a workers' strike.

The problem in all this lies in making the consumers aware of (1) their partly unconscious protest against consumerism and (2) their potential power, once the humanist-minded consumers are organized. Such a consumers' movement would be a manifestation of genuine democracy: the individuals would express themselves directly and try to change the course of social development in an active and nonalienated fashion. And all this would be based on personal experience, not on political slogans.

But even an effective consumers' movement will not suffice as long as the power of the big corporations remains as great as it is now. For even the remnant of democracy that still exists is doomed to yield to technocratic fascism, to a society of well-fed, unthinking robots—the very type of society that was so much feared under the name of "communism"—unless the giant corporations' big hold on the government (which becomes stronger daily) and on the population (via thought control through brainwashing) is broken. The United States has a tradition of curbing the power of giant enterprises, expressed in its antitrust laws. A powerful public sentiment could move that the spirit of these laws be applied to the existing corporate superpowers, so that those superpowers would be broken up into smaller units.

To achieve a society based on being, all people must actively participate in their economic function and as citizens. Hence, our liberation from the having mode of existence is possible only through the full realization of industrial and political participatory democracy.

This demand is shared by most radical humanists.

Industrial democracy implies that each member of a large industrial or other organization plays an active role in the life of the organization; that each is fully informed and participates in decision-making, starting at the level of the individual's own work process, health and safety measures (this has already been successfully tried by a few Swedish and American enterprises) and eventually participating in decision-making at higher, general policy levels of the enterprise. It is essential that the employees themselves, and not representatives of trade unions, represent the workers in the respective bodies of codetermination. Industrial democracy means also that the enterprise is not only an economic and technical institution, but a social institution in whose life and manner of functioning every member becomes active and, therefore, interested.

The same principles apply to the implementation of *political democracy*. Democracy can resist the authoritarian threat if it is transformed from a passive "spectator democracy" into an active "participatory democracy"—in which the affairs of the community are as close and as important to the individual citizens as their private affairs or, better, in which the well-being of the community becomes each citizen's private concern. By participating in the community, people find life becomes more interesting and stimulating. Indeed, a true political democracy can be defined as one in which life is just that, *interesting*. By its very nature such participatory democracy—in contrast to the "people's democracies" or "centralistic democracy"—is unbureaucratic and creates a climate that virtually excludes the emergence of demagogues.

Devising the methods for participatory democracy is probably far more difficult than was the elaboration of a democratic constitution in the eighteenth century. Many competent people will be required to make a gargantuan effort to devise the new principles and the implementing methods for building the participatory democracy. As just one of many possible suggestions for achieving this end, I should like to restate one I made more than twenty years ago in *The Sane Society:* that hundreds of thousands of face-to-face groups (of about five hundred members each) be created, to constitute themselves permanent bodies of deliberation and decision-making with regard to basic problems in the fields of economics, foreign policy, health, education, and the means to well-being. These groups would be given all pertinent information (the nature of this information is described later), would discuss this information (without the presence of outside influences), and would vote on the issue (and, given our current technological methods, all their votes could be collected within a day). The totality of these groups would form a "Lower House," whose decisions, along with those of other political organs, would have crucial influence on legislation.

"Why make these elaborate plans," it will be asked, "when opinion polls can perform the task of eliciting the whole population's opinion in an equally short time?" This objection touches upon one of the most problematical aspects of the expression of opinion. What is the "opinion" on which the polls are based but the views a person has without the benefit of adequate information, critical reflection, and discussion? Furthermore, the people polled know that their "opinions" do not count and, thus, have no effect. Such opinions only constitute people's conscious ideas at a given moment; they tell us nothing about the underlying trends that might lead to the opposite opinions if circumstances were to change. Similarly, the voters in a political election know that once they have voted for a candidate, they have no further real influence on the course of events. In some respects, voting in a political election is even worse than the opinion polls because of the dulling of thinking by semihypnotic techniques. Elections become an exciting soap opera, with the hopes and aspirations of the candidates—not political issues—at stake. The voters can even participate in the drama by giving their votes to the candidate with whom they side. Even though a large part of the population refuses to make this gesture, most people are fascinated by these modern Roman spectacles in which politicians, rather than gladiators, fight in the arena.

At least two requirements are involved in the formation of a genuine conviction: *adequate information and the knowledge that one's decision has an effect.* Opinions formed by the powerless onlooker do not express his or her conviction, but are a game, analogous to expressing a preference for one brand of cigarette over another. For these reasons the opinions expressed in polls and in elections constitute the worst, rather than the best, level of human judgment. This fact is confirmed by just two examples of people's best judgments, i.e., *people's decisions are far superior to the level of their political decisions (a)* in their private affairs (especially in business, as Joseph Schumpeter has so clearly shown) and *(b)* when they are members of juries. Juries are comprised of average citizens, who have to make decisions in cases that are often very intricate and difficult to understand. But the panel members get all pertinent information, have the chance for extended discussion, and know that their judgment decides the life and happiness of the persons they are mandated to judge. The result is that, by and large, their decisions show a great deal of insight and objectivity. In contrast, uninformed, half-hypnotized, and powerless people cannot express serious convictions. Without information, deliberation, and the power to make one's decision effective, democratically expressed opinion is hardly more than the applause at a sports event.

Active participation in political life requires maximum decentralization throughout industry and politics.

Because of the immanent logic of existing capitalism, enterprises and government grow ever larger and eventually become giants that are administered centrally from the top through a bureaucratic machine. One of the requisites of a humanistic society is that this process of centralization should stop and large-scale decentralization take place. There are several reasons for this. If a society is transformed into what Mumford has called a "megamachine" (that is, if the whole of a society, including its people, is like a large, centrally directed machine), fascism is almost unavoidable in the long run because *(a)* people become sheep, lose their faculty for critical thinking, feel powerless, are passive, and necessarily long for a leader who "knows" what to do—and everything else *they* do not know, and *(b)* the "megamachine" can be put in operation by anybody with access to it, simply by pushing the proper buttons. The megamachine, like an automobile, essentially runs itself: i.e., the person behind the wheel of the car has only to push the right buttons, manage the steering and the braking, and pay some attention to a few other similarly simple details; what in a car or other machine are its many wheels, in the megamachine are the many levels of bureaucratic administration. Even a person of mediocre intelligence and ability can easily run a state once he or she is in the seat of power.

Government functions must not be delegated to states—which are themselves huge conglomerates—but to relatively small districts where people can still know and judge each other and, hence, can actively participate in the administration of their own community affairs. Decentralization in industry must give more power to small sections within a given enterprise and break up the giant corporations into small entities.

Active and responsible participation further requires that humanistic management replace bureaucratic management.

Most people still believe that every kind of large-scale administration must necessarily be "bureaucratic," i.e., an alienated form of administration. And most people are unaware of how deadening the bureaucratic spirit is and how it pervades all spheres of life, even where it seems not to be obvious, as in physician-patient and husband-wife relationships. The bureaucratic method can be defined as one that *(a)* administers human beings as if they were things and *(b)* administers things in quantitative rather than qualitative terms, in order to make quantification and control easier and cheaper. The bureaucratic method is governed by statistical data: the bureaucrats base their decisions on fixed rules arrived at from statistical data, rather than on *response to the living beings who stand before them;* they decide issues according to what is statistically most likely to be the case, at the risk of hurting the 5 or 10 percent of those who do not fit into that pattern. Bureaucrats fear personal responsibility and seek refuge behind their rules; their security and pride lie in their loyalty to rules, not in their loyalty to the laws of the human heart.

Eichmann was an extreme example of a bureaucrat. Eichmann did not send the hundreds of thousands of Jews to their deaths because he hated them; he neither hated nor loved anyone. Eichmann "did his duty": he was dutiful when he sent the Jews to their deaths; he was just as dutiful when he was charged simply with expediting their emigration from Germany. All that mattered to him was to obey the rules; he felt guilty only when he had disobeyed them. He stated (damaging his own case by this) that he felt guilty on only two counts: for having played truant as a child, and for having disobeyed orders to take shelter during an air raid. This does

not imply that there was not an element of sadism in Eichmann and in many other bureaucrats, i.e., the satisfaction of
controlling other living beings. But this sadistic streak is only
secondary to the primary elements in bureaucrats: their lack
of human response and their worship of rules.

I am not saying that all bureaucrats are Eichmanns. In the
first place, many human beings in bureaucratic positions are
not bureaucrats in a characterological sense. In the second
place, in many cases the bureaucratic attitude has not taken
over the whole person and killed his or her human side. Yet
there are many Eichmanns among the bureaucrats, and the
only difference is that they have not had to destroy thousands
of people. But when the bureaucrat in a hospital refuses to
admit a critically sick person because the rules require that the
patient be sent by a physician, that bureaucrat acts no differently than Eichmann did. Neither do the social workers who
decide to let a client starve, rather than violate a certain rule
in their bureaucratic code. This bureaucratic attitude exists
not only among administrators; it lives among physicians,
nurses, schoolteachers, professors—as well as in many hus-
bands in relation to their wives and in many parents in relation to their children.

Once the living human being is reduced to a number, the
true bureaucrats can commit acts of utter cruelty, not because
they are driven by cruelty of a magnitude commensurate to
their deeds, but because they feel no human bond to their
subjects. While less vile than the sadists, the bureaucrats are
more dangerous, because in them there is not even a conflict
between conscience and duty: their conscience *is* doing their
duty; human beings as objects of empathy and compassion do
not exist for them.

The old-fashioned bureaucrat, who was prone to be unfriendly, still exists in some old-established enterprises or in
such large organizations as welfare departments, hospitals,
and prisons, in which a single bureaucrat has considerable
power over poor or otherwise powerless people. The bureau-

crats in modern industry are not unfriendly and probably have little of the sadistic streak, even though they may get some pleasure from having power over people. But again, we find in them that bureaucratic allegiance to a thing—in their case, the *system:* they believe in *it.* The corporation is their home, and its rules are sacred because the rules are "rational."

But neither the old nor the new bureaucrats can coexist in a system of participatory democracy, for the bureaucratic spirit is incompatible with the spirit of active participation by the individual. The new social scientists must devise plans for new forms of nonbureaucratic large-scale administration that is directed by response (that reflects "responsibility") to people and situations rather than by the mere application of rules. Nonbureaucratic administration *is* possible provided we take into account the potential spontaneity of response in the administrator and do not make a fetish of economizing.

Success in establishing a society of being depends on many other measures. In offering the following suggestions, I make no claim to originality; on the contrary, I am encouraged by the fact that almost all of these suggestions have been made in one form or another by humanist writers.*

• *All brainwashing methods in industrial and political advertising must be prohibited.*

These brainwashing methods are dangerous not only because they impel us to buy things that we neither need nor want, but because they lead us to choose political representatives we would neither need nor want *if* we were in full control of our minds. But we are *not* in full control of our minds because hypnoid methods are used to propagandize us. To combat this ever-increasing danger, *we must prohibit the use of all hypnoid forms of propaganda, for commodities as well as for politicians.*

*In order not to overburden this book I refrain from quoting the large literature that contains similar proposals. Many titles may be found in the Bibliography.

The hypnoid methods used in advertising and political propaganda are a serious danger to mental health, specifically to clear and critical thinking and emotional independence. I have no doubt that thorough studies will show that the damage caused by drug addiction is only a fraction of the damage done by our methods of brainwashing, from subliminal suggestions to such semihypnotic devices as constant repetition or the deflection of rational thought by the appeal to sexual lust ("I'm Linda, fly me!"). The bombardment with purely suggestive methods in advertising, and most of all in television commercials, is stultifying. This assault on reason and the sense of reality pursues the individual everywhere and daily at any time: during many hours of watching television, or when driving on a highway, or in the political propaganda of candidates, and so on. The particular effect of these suggestive methods is that they create an atmosphere of being half-awake, of believing and not believing, of losing one's sense of reality.

Stopping the poison of mass suggestion will have a withdrawal effect on consumers that will be little different from the withdrawal symptoms drug addicts experience when they stop taking drugs.

• *The gap between the rich and the poor nations must be closed.*

There is little doubt that the continuation and further deepening of that gap will lead to catastrophe. The poor nations have ceased to accept the economic exploitation by the industrial world as a God-given fact. Even though the Soviet Union is still exploiting its own satellite states in the same colonialist manner, it uses and reinforces the protest of the colonial peoples as a political weapon against the West. The increase in oil prices was the beginning—and a symbol—of the colonial peoples' demand to end the system that requires them to sell raw materials cheap and buy industrial products dear. In the same way, the Vietnam war was a symbol of the beginning of the end of the colonial peoples' political and military domination by the West.

What will happen if nothing crucial is done to close the gap? Either epidemics will spread into the fortress of the white society or famines will drive the population of the poor nations into such despair that they, perhaps with the help of sympathizers from the industrial world, will commit acts of destruction, even use small nuclear or biological weapons, that will bring chaos within the white fortress.

This catastrophic possibility can be averted only if the conditions of hunger, starvation, and sickness are brought under control—and to do that, the help of the industrial nations is vitally necessary. The methods for such help must be free from all interests in profits and political advantages on the side of the rich countries; this means also that they must be free from the idea that the economic and political principles of capitalism are to be transferred to Africa and Asia. Obviously, *the* most efficient way for economic help to be given (especially, for instance, in terms of services) is a matter for economic experts to determine.

But only those who can qualify as true experts can serve this cause, individuals who have not only brilliant brains but humane hearts that impel them to seek the optimal solution. In order for these experts to be called in, and their recommendations to be followed, the having orientation must greatly weaken, and a sense of solidarity, of caring (not of pity) must emerge. Caring means caring not only for our fellow beings on this earth but also for our descendants. Indeed, nothing is more telling about our selfishness than that we go on plundering the raw materials of the earth, poisoning the earth, and preparing nuclear war. We hesitate not at all at leaving our own descendants this plundered earth as their heritage.

Will this inner transformation take place? No one knows. But one thing the world should know is that without it the clash between poor and rich nations will become unmanageable.

• *Many of the evils of present-day capitalist and communist societies would disappear with the introduction of a guaranteed yearly income.* *

The core of this idea is that all persons, regardless of whether they work or not, shall have the unconditional right not to starve and not to be without shelter. They shall receive not more than is basically required to sustain themselves— but neither shall they receive less. This right expresses a new concept for today, though a very old norm, demanded by Christianity and practiced in many "primitive" tribes, that human beings have an *unconditional right to live, regardless of whether they do their "duty to society."* It is a right we guarantee to our pets, but not to our fellow beings.

The realm of personal freedom would be tremendously enlarged by such a law; no person who is economically dependent on another (e.g., on a parent, husband, boss) could any longer be forced to submit to the blackmail of starvation; gifted persons wanting to prepare for a different life could do so provided they were willing to make the sacrifice of living in a degree of poverty for a time. Modern welfare states have accepted this principle—almost . . . which actually means "not really." A bureaucracy still "administers" the people, still controls and humiliates them. But a guaranteed income would require no "proof" of need for any person to get a simple room and a minimum of food. Thus no bureaucracy would be needed to administer a welfare program with its inherent waste and its violations of human dignity.

The guaranteed yearly income would ensure real freedom and independence. For that reason, it is unacceptable to any system based on exploitation and control, particularly the various forms of dictatorship. It is characteristic of the Soviet system that even suggestions for the simplest forms of free goods (for example, free public transportation or free milk) have been consistently rejected. Free medical service is the exception, but only apparently so, since here the free service

*I proposed this in 1955 in *The Sane Society;* the same proposal was made in a mid-1960s symposium (edited by A. Theobald; see Bibliography).

is in response to a clear condition: one must be sick to receive it.

Considering the present-day cost of running a large welfare bureaucracy, the cost of treating physical, especially psychosomatic, illnesses, criminality, and drug addiction (all of which are largely forms of protest against coercion and boredom), it seems likely that the cost of providing any person who wanted it with a guaranteed annual income would be less than that of our present system of social welfare. The idea will appear unfeasible or dangerous to those who believe that "people are basically lazy by nature." This cliché has no basis in fact, however; it is simply a slogan that serves as a rationalization for the resistance against surrendering the sense of power over those who are helpless.

• *Women must be liberated from patriarchal domination.*

The freedom of women from patriarchal domination is a fundamental factor in the humanization of society. The domination of women by men began only about six thousand years ago in various parts of the world when surplus in agriculture permitted the hiring and exploitation of workers, the organization of armies, and the building of powerful city-states.* Since then, not only Middle Eastern and European societies but most of the world's cultures have been conquered by the "associated males" who subdued the women. This victory of the male over the female of the human species was based on the men's economic power and the military machine they built.

The war between the sexes is as old as the war between the classes, but its forms are more complicated, since men have needed women not only as working beasts but also as mothers, lovers, solace-givers. The forms of the war between the sexes are often overt and brutal, more often hidden. Women yielded to superior force, but fought back with their own weapons, their chief one being ridicule of the men.

---

*I have discussed the early "matriarchate" and the literature related to it in *The Anatomy of Human Destructiveness.*

The subjugation of one half of the human race by the other has done, and still does, immense harm to both sexes: the men assume the characteristics of the victor, the women those of the victim. No relation between a man and a woman, even today, and even among those who consciously protest against male supremacy, is free from the curse either, among men, of feeling superior or, among women, of feeling inferior. (Freud, the unquestioning believer in male superiority, unfortunately assumed that women's sense of powerlessness was due to their alleged regret that they have no penis, and that men were insecure because of their alleged universal "fear of castration." What we are dealing with in this phenomenon are symptoms of the war between the sexes, not biological and anatomical differences as such.)

Many data show how much men's control over women resembles one group's control over other powerless populations. As an example, consider the similarity between the picture of the blacks in the American South a hundred years ago and that of women at that time, and even up to today. Blacks and women were compared to children; they were supposed to be emotional, naive, without a sense of reality, so that they were not to be trusted with making decisions; they were supposed to be irresponsible, but charming. (Freud added to the catalogue that women had a less developed conscience [superego] than men and were more narcissistic.)

The exercise of power over those who are weaker is the essence of existing patriarchy, as it is the essence of the domination of nonindustrialized nations and of children and adolescents. The growing movement for women's liberation is of enormous significance because it is a threat to the principle of power on which contemporary society (capitalist and communist alike) lives—that is, if the women clearly mean by liberation that they do not want to share the men's power over other groups, such as the power over the colonial peoples. If the movement for the liberation of women can identify its own role and function as representative of "antipower," women will have a decisive influence in the battle for a new society.

Basic liberating changes have already been made. Perhaps a later historian will report that the most revolutionary event in the twentieth century was the beginning of women's liberation and the downfall of men's supremacy. But the fight for the liberation of women has only just begun, and men's resistance cannot be overestimated. Their whole relation to women (including their sexual relation) has been based on their alleged superiority, and they have already begun to feel quite uncomfortable and anxious vis-à-vis those women who refuse to accept the myth of male superiority.

Closely related to the women's liberation movement is the antiauthoritarian turn of the younger generations. This antiauthoritarianism had its peak in the late sixties; now, through a number of changes, many of the rebels against the "establishment" have essentially become "good" again. But the starch has nonetheless been washed out of the old worship of parental and other authorities, and it seems certain that the old "awe" of authority will not return.

Paralleling this emancipation from authority is the liberation from guilt about sex: sex certainly seems to have ceased being unspeakable and sinful. However people may differ in their opinions regarding the relative merits of the many facets of the sexual revolution, one thing is sure: sex no longer frightens people; it can no longer be used to develop a sense of guilt, and thereby to force submission.

• *A Supreme Cultural Council, charged with the task of advising the government, the politicians, and the citizens in all matters in which knowledge is necessary, should be established.*

The cultural council members would be representative of the intellectual and artistic elite of the country, men and women whose integrity was beyond doubt. They would determine the composition of the new, expanded form of the FDA and would select the people to be responsible for disseminating information.

There is a substantial consensus on who the outstanding representatives of various branches of culture are, and I believe it would be possible to find the right members for such a council. It is of decisive importance, of course, that this council should also represent those who are opposed to established views: for instance, the "radicals" and "revisionists" in economics, history, and sociology. The difficulty is not in *finding* the council members but in *choosing* them, for they cannot be elected by popular vote, nor should they be appointed by the government. Yet other ways of selecting them may be found. For instance, start with a nucleus of three or four persons and gradually enlarge the group to its full size of, say, fifty to a hundred persons. This cultural council should be amply financed so that it would be able to commission special studies of various problems.

• *A system of effective dissemination of effective information must also be established.*

Information is a crucial element in the formation of an effective democracy. Withholding information or falsifying it in the alleged interests of "national security" must be ended. But even without such illegitimate withholding of information, the problem remains that at present the amount of real and necessary information given to the average citizen is almost zero. And this holds true not only for the average citizen. As has been shown abundantly, most elected representatives, members of government, the defense forces, and business leaders are badly informed and to a large extent misinformed by the falsehoods that various government agencies spread, and the news media repeat. Unfortunately, most of these same people, in turn, have at best a purely manipulative intelligence. They have little capacity to understand the forces operating beneath the surface and, hence, to make sound judgments about future developments, not to speak of their selfishness and dishonesty, of which we have heard enough. But even to be an honest and intelligent bureaucrat is not enough to solve the problems of a world facing catastrophe.

With the exception of a few "great" newspapers, even the factual information on political, economic, and social data is extremely limited. The so-called great newspapers inform better, but they also misinform better: by not publishing all the news impartially; by slanting headlines, in addition to writing headlines that often do not conform with their accompanying text; by being partisan in their editorials, written under the cover of seemingly reasonable and moralizing language. In fact, the newspapers, the magazines, television, and radio produce a commodity: *news,* from the raw material of events. Only news is salable, and the news media determine which events are news, which are not. At the very best, information is ready-made, concerns only the surface of events, and barely gives the citizens an opportunity to penetrate through the surface and recognize the deeper causes of the events. As long as the sale of news is a business, newspapers and magazines can hardly be prevented from printing what sells (in various degrees of unscrupulousness) their publications and does not antagonize the advertisers.

The information problem must be solved in a different way if informed opinion and decision are to be possible. As an example of such a way I mention only one: that one of the first and most important functions of the Supreme Cultural Council would be to gather and disseminate all the information that would serve the needs of the whole population and, particularly, would serve as the basis for discussion among the face-to-face groups in our participatory democracy. This information should contain basic facts and basic alternatives in all areas in which political decisions take place. It is of special importance that in case of disagreement the minority opinion *and* the majority opinion would be published, and that this information would be made available to every citizen and particularly to the face-to-face groups. The Supreme Cultural Council would be responsible for supervising the work of this new body of news reporters, and, of course, radio and television would have an important role in disseminating this kind of information.

• *Scientific research must be separated from application in industry and defense.*

While it would be hobbling of human development if one set any limits to the demand for knowledge, it would be extremely dangerous if practical use were made of all the results of scientific thinking. As has been emphasized by many observers, certain discoveries in genetics, in brain surgery, in psychodrugs, and in many other areas can and will be misused to the great damage of Man. This is unavoidable as long as industrial and military interests are free to make use of all new theoretical discoveries as they see fit. Profit and military expediency must cease to determine the application of scientific research. This will require a control board, whose permission would be necessary for the practical application of any new theoretical discovery. Needless to say, such a control board must be—legally and psychologically—completely independent of industry, the government, and the military. The Supreme Cultural Council would have the authority to appoint and supervise this control board.

• While all the suggestions made in the foregoing pages will be difficult enough to realize, our difficulties become almost insurmountable with the addition of another necessary condition of a new society: *atomic disarmament.*

One of the sick elements in our economy is that it needs a large armament industry. Even today, the United States, the richest country in the world, must curtail its expenses for health, welfare, and education in order to carry the load of its defense budget. The cost of social experimentation cannot possibly be borne by a state that is making itself poor by the production of hardware that is useful only as a means of suicide. Furthermore, the spirit of individualism and activity cannot live in an atmosphere where the military bureaucracy, gaining in power every day, continues to further fear and subordination.

The New Society: Is There a Reasonable Chance?

Considering the power of the corporations, the apathy and powerlessness of the large mass of the population, the inadequacy of political leaders in almost all countries, the threat of nuclear war, the ecological dangers, not to speak of such phenomena as weather changes that alone could produce famines in large parts of the world, *is there a reasonable chance for salvation?* From the standpoint of a business deal, there is no such chance; no reasonable human beings would bet their fortunes when the odds represent only a 2 percent chance of winning, or make a large investment of capital in a business venture with the same poor chance of gain. But when it is a matter of life and death, "reasonable chance" must be translated into "real possibility," however small it may be.

Life is neither a game of chance nor a business deal, and we must seek elsewhere for an appreciation of the real possibilities for salvation: in the healing art of medicine, for example. If a sick person has even the barest chance for survival, no responsible physician will say, "Let's give up the effort," or will use only palliatives. On the contrary, everything conceivable is done to save the sick person's life. Certainly, a sick society cannot expect anything less.

Judging present-day society's chances for salvation from the standpoint of betting or business rather than from the standpoint of life is characteristic of the spirit of a business society. There is little wisdom in the currently fashionable technocratic view that there is nothing seriously wrong in keeping ourselves busy with work or fun, in not feeling, and that even *if* there is, perhaps technocratic fascism may not be so bad, after all. But this is wishful thinking. Technocratic fascism must necessarily lead to catastrophe. Dehumanized Man will become so mad that he will not be able to sustain a viable society in the long run, and in the short run will not be able to refrain from the suicidal use of nuclear or biological weapons.

Yet there are a few factors that can give us some encouragement. The first is that a growing number of people now recognize the truth that Mesarovic and Pestel, Ehrlich and Ehrlich, and others have stated: that *on purely economic grounds* a new ethic, a new attitude toward nature, human solidarity, and cooperation are necessary if the Western world is not to be wiped out. This appeal to reason, even aside from any emotional and ethical considerations, may mobilize the minds of not a few people. It should not be taken lightly, even though, historically, nations have again and again acted against their vital interests and even against the drive for survival. They could do so because the people were persuaded by their leaders, and they persuaded themselves, that the choice between "to be or not to be" did not confront them. Had they recognized the truth, however, the normal neurophysiological reaction would have taken place: their awareness of vital threats would have mobilized appropriate defense action.

Another hopeful sign is the increasing display of dissatisfaction with our present social system. A growing number of people feel *la malaise du siècle:* they sense their depression; they are conscious of it, in spite of all kinds of efforts to repress it. They feel the unhappiness of their isolation and the emptiness of their "togetherness"; they feel their impotence, the meaninglessness of their lives. Many feel all this very clearly and consciously; others feel it less clearly, but are fully aware of it when someone else puts it into words.

So far in world history a life of empty pleasure was possible for only a small elite, and they remained essentially sane because they knew they had power and that they had to think and to act in order not to lose their power. Today, the empty life of consumption is that of the whole middle class, which economically and politically has no power and little personal responsibility. The major part of the Western world knows the benefits of the consumer type of happiness, and growing numbers of those who benefit from it are finding it wanting. They are beginning to discover that having much does not create well-being: traditional ethical teaching has been put to the test—and is being confirmed by experience.

Only in those who live without the benefits of middle-class luxury does the old illusion remain untouched: in the lower middle classes in the West and among the vast majority in the "socialist" countries. Indeed, the bourgeois hope for "happiness through consumption" is nowhere more alive than in the countries that have not yet fulfilled the bourgeois dream.

One of the gravest objections to the possibilities of overcoming greed and envy, namely that their strength is inherent in human nature, loses a good deal of its weight upon further examination. Greed and envy are so strong not because of their *inherent intensity* but because of the difficulty in resisting the public pressure to be a wolf with the wolves. Change the social climate, the values that are either approved or disapproved, and the change from selfishness to altruism will lose most of its difficulty.

Thus we arrive again at the premise that the being orientation is a strong potential in human nature. Only a minority is completely governed by the having mode, while another small minority is completely governed by the being mode. Either can become dominant, and which one does depends on the social structure. In a society oriented mainly toward being, the having tendencies are starved and the being mode is fed. In a society like ours, whose main orientation is toward having, the reverse occurs. But the new mode of existence is always already present—though repressed. No Saul becomes a Paul if he was not already a Paul before his conversion. The change from having to being is actually a tipping of the scales, when in connection with social change the new is encouraged and the old discouraged. Besides, this is not a question of new Man as different from the old as the sky is from the earth; it is a question of a change of direction. One step in the new direction will be followed by the next, and taken in the right direction, these steps mean everything.

Yet another encouraging aspect to consider is one that,

paradoxically, concerns the degree of alienation that characterizes the majority of the population, including its leaders.
As pointed out in the earlier discussion of the "marketing
character," the greed to have and to hoard has been modified
by the tendency to merely function well, to exchange oneself
as a commodity who is—nothing. It is easier for the alienated,
marketing character to change than it is for the hoarding
character, which is frantically holding onto possessions, and
particularly its ego.

A hundred years ago, when the major part of the population consisted of "independents," the greatest obstacle to
change was the fear of and resistance to loss of property and
economic independence. Marx lived at a time when the working class was the only large dependent class and, as Marx
thought, the most alienated one. Today, the vast majority of
the population is *dependent;* virtually all people who work are
employed (according to the 1970 U.S. Census report, only 7.82
percent of the total working population over age sixteen is
self-employed, i.e., "independent"); and—at least in the
United States—it is the blue-collar workers who still maintain
the traditional middle-class hoarding character, and who,
consequently, are less open to change than is today's more
alienated middle class.

All this has a most important political consequence: while
socialism was striving for the liberation of all classes—i.e.,
striving for a classless society—its immediate appeal was to
the "working class," i.e., the manual workers; today the working class is (in relative terms) even more of a minority than
it was a hundred years ago. In order to gain power, the social
democratic parties need to win the votes of many members of
the middle class, and in order to achieve this goal, the socialist
parties have had to cut back their program from one with a
socialist vision to one offering liberal reforms. On the other
hand, by identifying the working class as the lever of humanistic change, socialism necessarily antagonized the members of
all other classes, who felt that their properties and privileges
were going to be taken away by the workers.

Today, the appeal of the new society goes to all who suffer from alienation, who are employed, and whose property is not threatened. In other words, it concerns the majority of the population, not merely a minority. It does not threaten to take anybody's property, and as far as income is concerned, it would raise the standard of living of those who are poor. High salaries for top executives would not have to be lowered, but if the system worked, they would not want to be symbols of times past.

Furthermore, the ideals of the new society cross all party lines: many conservatives have not lost their ethical and religious ideals (Eppler calls them "value conservatives"), and the same holds true of many liberals and leftists. Each political party exploits the voters by persuading them that it represents the true values of humanism. Yet behind all political parties are only two camps: *those who care and those who don't care.* If all those in the camp that cares could rid themselves of party clichés and realize that they have the same goals, the possibility of change would seem to be considerably greater; especially so since most citizens have become less and less interested in party loyalty and party slogans. People today are yearning for human beings who have wisdom and convictions and the courage to act according to their convictions.

Given even these hopeful factors, however, the chances for necessary human and social changes remain slim. Our only hope lies in the energizing attraction of a new vision. To propose this or that reform that does not change the system is useless in the long run because it does not carry with it the impelling force of a strong motivation. The "utopian" goal is more realistic than the "realism" of today's leaders. The realization of the new society and new Man is possible only if the old motivations of profit, power, and intellect are replaced by new ones: being, sharing, understanding; if the marketing character is replaced by the productive, loving character; if cybernetic religion is replaced by a new radical-humanistic spirit.

Indeed, for those who are not authentically rooted in theistic religion the crucial question is that of conversion to a humanistic "religiosity" without religion, without dogmas and institutions, a "religiosity" long prepared by the movement of nontheistic religiosity, from the Buddha to Marx. We are not confronted with the choice between selfish materialism and the acceptance of the Christian concept of God. Social life itself—in all its aspects in work, in leisure, in personal relations—will be the expression of the "religious" spirit, and no separate religion will be necessary. This demand for a new, nontheistic, noninstitutionalized "religiosity" is not an attack on the existing religions. It does mean, however, that the Roman Catholic Church, beginning with the Roman bureaucracy, must convert *itself* to the spirit of the gospel. It does not mean that the "socialist countries" must be "desocialized," but that their fake socialism shall be replaced by genuine humanistic socialism.

Later Medieval culture flourished because people followed the vision of the *City of God.* Modern society flourished because people were energized by the vision of the growth of the *Earthly City of Progress.* In our century, however, this vision deteriorated to that of the *Tower of Babel,* which is now beginning to collapse and will ultimately bury everybody in its ruins. If the City of God and the Earthly City were *thesis* and *antithesis,* a new *synthesis* is the only alternative to chaos: the synthesis between the spiritual core of the Late Medieval world and the development of rational thought and science since the Renaissance. This synthesis is *The City of Being.*

Bibliography

Included in the Bibliography are all books cited in the text, although not all sources used in the preparation of this work. Books especially recommended for collateral reading are marked with a single asterisk; a second asterisk denotes books for readers with limited time.

Aquinas, Thomas. 1953. *Summa Theologica*. Edited by P. H. M. Christmann. OP. Heidelberg: Gemeinschaftsverlage, F. H. Kerle; Graz: A. Pustet.

Arieti, Silvano, ed. 1959. *American Handbook of Psychiatry*, vol. 2. New York: Basic Books.

Aristotle. *Nicomachean Ethics*. Cambridge: Harvard University Press, Loeb Classical Library.

*Artz, Frederick B. 1959. *The Mind of the Middle Ages: An Historical Survey: A.D. 200–1500*. 3rd rev. ed. New York: Alfred A. Knopf.

Auer, Alfons. "Die Autonomie des Sittlichen nach Thomas von Aquin" [The anatomy of ethics according to Thomas Aquinas]. Unpublished paper.

———. 1975. "Ist die Sünde eine Beleidigung Gottes?" [Is sin an insult to God?]. In *Theol. Quartalsschrift*. Munich, Freiberg: Erich Wewel Verlag.

*———. 1976. *Utopie, Technologie, Lebensqualität* [Utopia, technology, quality of life]. Zurich: Benziger Verlag.

*Bachofen, J. J. 1967. *Myth, Religion and the Mother Right: Selected Writings of Johann Jakob Bachofen*. Edited by J. Campbell; translated by R. Manheim. Princeton: Princeton University Press. (Original ed. *Das Mutterrecht*, 1861.)

Bacon, Francis. 1620. *Novum Organum*.

Bauer, E. *Allgemeine Literatur Zeitung 1843/4.* Quoted by K. Marx and F. Engels; q.v.

*Becker, Carl L. 1932. *The Heavenly City of the Eighteenth Century Philosophers.* New Haven: Yale University Press.

Benveniste, Emile. 1966. *Problèmes de Linguistique Général.* Paris: Ed. Gallimard.

Benz, E. See Eckhart, Meister.

Blakney, Raymond B. See Eckhart, Meister.

Bloch, Ernst. 1970. *Philosophy of the Future.* New York: Seabury Press.

———. 1971. *On Karl Marx.* New York: Seabury Press.

*———. 1972. *Atheism in Christianity.* New York: Seabury Press.

Cloud of Unknowing, The. See Underhill, Evelyn.

Darwin, Charles. 1969. *The Autobiography of Charles Darwin 1809–1882.* Edited by Nora Barlow. New York: W. W. Norton. Quoted by E. F. Schumacher; q.v.

Delgado, J. M. R. 1967. "Aggression and Defense Under Cerebral Radio Control." In *Aggression and Defense: Neural Mechanisms and Social Patterns. Brain Function,* vol. 5. Edited by C. D. Clemente and D. B. Lindsley. Berkeley: University of California Press.

De Lubac, Henri. 1943. *Katholizismus als Gemeinschaft.* Translated by Hans-Urs von Balthasar. Einsiedeln/Cologne: Verlag Benziger & Co.

De Mause, Lloyd, ed. 1974. *The History of Childhood.* New York: The Psychohistory Press, Atcom Inc.

Diogenes Laertius. 1966. In *Lives of Eminent Philosophers.* Translated by R. D. Hicks. Cambridge: Harvard University Press.

Du Marais. 1769. *Les Véritables Principes de la Grammaire.*

Dumoulin, Heinrich. 1966. *Östliche Meditation und Christliche Mystik.* Freiburg/Munich: Verlag Karl Alber.

**Eckhart, Meister. 1941. *Meister Eckhart: A Modern Translation.* Translated by Raymond B. Blakney. New York: Harper & Row, Torchbooks.

———. 1950. Edited by Franz Pfeifer; translated by C. de B. Evans. London: John M. Watkins.

———. 1969. *Meister Eckhart, Deutsche Predigten und Traktate.* Edited and translated by Joseph L. Quint. Munich: Carl Hanser Verlag.

———. *Meister Eckhart, Die Deutschen Werke.* Edited and translated by Joseph L. Quint. In *Gesamtausgabe der deutschen und lateinischen Werke.* Stuttgart: Kohlhammer Verlag.

———. *Meister Eckhart, Die lateinischen Werke, Expositio Exodi 16.* Edited by E. Benz et al. In *Gesamtausgabe der deutschen und lateinischen Werke.* Stuttgart: Kohlhammer Verlag. Quoted by Otto Schilling; q.v.

*Ehrlich, Paul R., and Ehrlich, Anne H. 1970. *Population, Resources, Environment: Essays in Human Ecology.* San Francisco: W. H. Freeman.

Engels, F. See Marx, K., jt. auth.

Eppler, E. 1975. *Ende oder Wende* [End or change]. Stuttgart: W. Kohlhammer Verlag.

Farner, Konrad. 1947. "Christentum und Eigentum bis Thomas von Aquin." In *Mensch und Gesellschaft,* vol. 12. Edited by K. Farner. Bern: Francke Verlag. Quoted by Otto Schilling; q.v.

Finkelstein, Louis. 1946. *The Pharisees: The Sociological Background of Their Faith,* vols. 1, 2. Philadelphia: The Jewish Publication Society of America.

Fromm, E. 1932. "Die psychoanalytische Charakterologie und ihre Bedeutung für die Sozialforschung." *Ztsch. f. Sozialforschung.* 1: 253–277. "Psychoanalytic Characterology and Its Relevance for Social Psychology." In E. Fromm, *The Crisis of Psychoanalysis;* q.v.

———. 1941. *Escape from Freedom.* New York: Holt, Rinehart and Winston.

———. 1942. "Faith as a Character Trait." In *Psychiatry 5.* Reprinted with slight changes in E. Fromm, *Man for Himself;* q.v.

———. 1943. "Sex and Character." In *Psychiatry 6:* 21–31. Reprinted in E. Fromm, *The Dogma of Christ and Other Essays on Religion, Psychology, and Culture;* q.v.

*———. 1947. *Man for Himself: An Inquiry into the Psychology of Ethics.* New York: Holt, Rinehart and Winston.

———. 1950. *Psychoanalysis and Religion.* New Haven: Yale University Press.

———. 1951. *The Forgotten Language: An Introduction to the Understanding of Dreams, Fairy Tales, and Myths.* New York: Holt, Rinehart and Winston.

*———. 1955. *The Sane Society.* New York: Holt, Rinehart and Winston.

———. 1956. *The Art of Loving.* New York: Harper & Row.

———. 1959. "On the Limitations and Dangers of Psychology." In

W. Leibrecht, ed. *Religion and Culture: Essays in Honor of Paul Tillich;* q.v.

**——. 1961. *Marx's Concept of Man.* New York: Frederick Ungar.

——. 1963. *The Dogma of Christ and Other Essays on Religion, Psychology, and Culture.* New York: Holt, Rinehart and Winston.

——. 1964. *The Heart of Man.* New York: Harper & Row.

——, ed. 1965. *Socialist Humanism.* Garden City, N.Y.: Doubleday & Co.

——. 1966. "The Concept of Sin and Repentance." In E. Fromm, *You Shall Be as Gods;* q.v.

——. 1966. *You Shall Be as Gods.* New York: Holt, Rinehart and Winston.

*——. 1968. *The Revolution of Hope.* New York: Harper & Row.

——. 1970. *The Crisis of Psychoanalysis: Essays on Freud, Marx, and Social Psychology.* New York: Holt, Rinehart and Winston.

**——. 1973. *The Anatomy of Human Destructiveness.* New York: Holt, Rinehart and Winston.

——, and Maccoby, M. 1970. *Social Character in a Mexican Village.* Englewood Cliffs, N.J.: Prentice-Hall.

——, Suzuki, D. T., and de Martino, R. 1960. *Zen Buddhism and Psychoanalysis.* New York: Harper & Row.

*Galbraith, John Kenneth. 1969. *The Affluent Society.* 2nd ed. Boston: Houghton Mifflin.

*——. 1971. *The New Industrial Society.* 2nd rev. ed. Boston: Houghton Mifflin.

*——. 1974. *Economics and the Public Purpose.* Boston: Houghton Mifflin.

*Habermas, Jürgen. 1971. *Toward a Rational Society.* Translated by J. Schapiro. Boston: Beacon Press.

——. 1973. *Theory and Practice.* Edited by J. Viertel. Boston: Beacon Press.

Harich, W. 1975. *Kommunismus ohne Wachstum.* Hamburg: Rowohlt Verlag.

Hebb, D. O. "Drives and the CNS [Conceptual Nervous System]." *Psych. Rev.* 62, 4: 244.

Hess, Moses. 1843. "Philosophie der Tat" [The philosophy of action]. In *Einundzwanzig Bogen aus der Schweiz.* Edited by G. Herwegh. Zurich: Literarischer Comptoir. Reprinted in Moses Hess,

Ökonomische Schriften. Edited by D. Horster. Darmstadt: Melzer Verlag, 1972.

*Illich, Ivan. 1970. *Deschooling Society*. World Perspectives, vol. 44. New York: Harper & Row.

————. 1976. *Medical Nemesis: The Expropriation of Health*. New York: Pantheon.

*Kropotkin, P. A. 1902. *Mutual Aid: A Factor of Evolution*. London.

Lange, Winfried. 1969. *Glückseligkeitsstreben und uneigennützige Lebensgestaltung bei Thomas von Aquin*. Diss. Freiburg im Breisgau.

Leibrecht, W., ed. 1959. *Religion and Culture: Essays in Honor of Paul Tillich*. New York: Harper & Row.

Lobkowicz, Nicholas. 1967. *Theory and Practice: The History of a Concept from Aristotle to Marx*. International Studies Series. Notre Dame, Ind.: University of Notre Dame Press.

*Maccoby, Michael. Forthcoming, fall 1976. *The Gamesmen: The New Corporate Leaders*. New York: Simon and Schuster.

Maimonides, Moses. 1963. *The Code of Maimonides*. Translated by A. M. Hershman. New Haven: Yale University Press.

*Marcel, Gabriel. 1965. *Being and Having: An Existentialist Diary*. New York: Harper & Row, Torchbooks.

Marx, K. 1844. *Economic and Philosophical Manuscripts*. In *Gesamtausgabe (MEGA)* [Complete works of Marx and Engels]. Moscow. Translated by E. Fromm in E. Fromm, *Marx's Concept of Man;* q.v.

————. 1909. *Capital*. Chicago: Charles H. Kerr & Co.

————. *Grundrisse der Kritik der politischen Ökonomie*. [Outline of the critique of political economy]. Frankfurt: Europaische Verlagsanstalt, n.d. McClellan, David, ed. and trans. 1971. *The Grundrisse*, Excerpts. New York: Harper & Row, Torchbooks.

————, and Engels, F. 1844/5. *The Holy Family, or a Critique of Critical Critique*. London: Lawrence & Wishart, 1957. *Die Heilige Familie, der Kritik der kritischen Kritik*. Berlin: Dietz Verlag, 1971.

Mayo, Elton. 1933. *The Human Problems of an Industrial Civilization*. New York: Macmillan.

Meadows, D. H., et al. 1972. *The Limits to Growth*. New York: Universe Books.

*Mesarovic, Mihajlo D., and Pestel, Eduard. 1974. *Mankind at the Turning Point*. New York: E. P. Dutton.

Mieth, Dietmar. 1969. *Die Einheit von Vita Activa und Vita Contemplativa*. Regensburg: Verlag Friedrich Pustet.

―――. 1971. *Christus—Das Soziale im Menschen*. Düsseldorf: Topos Taschenbücher, Patmos Verlag.

Mill, J. S. 1965. *Principles of Political Economy*. 7th ed., reprint of 1871 ed. Toronto: University of Toronto/Routledge and Kegan Paul.

Millan, Ignacio. Forthcoming. *The Character of Mexican Executives*.

Morgan, L. H. 1870. *Systems of Sanguinity and Affinity of the Human Family*. Publication 218, Washington, D.C.: Smithsonian Institution.

**Mumford, L. 1970. *The Pentagon of Power*. New York: Harcourt Brace Jovanovich.

**Nyanaponika Mahatera. 1962; 1970. *The Heart of Buddhist Meditation*. London: Rider & Co.; New York: Samuel Weiser.

*―――, ed. 1971; 1972. *Pathways of Buddhist Thought: Essays from the Wheel*. London: George Allen & Unwin; New York: Barnes & Noble, Harper & Row.

Phelps, Edmund S., ed. 1975. *Altruism, Morality and Economic Theory*. New York: Russell Sage Foundation.

Piaget, Jean. 1932. *The Moral Judgment of the Child*. New York: The Free Press, Macmillan.

Quint, Joseph L. See Eckhart, Meister.

*Rumi. 1950. Selected, translated and with Introduction and Notes by R. A. Nicholson. London: George Allen & Unwin.

Schecter, David E. 1959. "Infant Development." In Silvano Arieti, ed. *American Handbook of Psychiatry*, vol. 2; q.v.

Schilling, Otto. 1908. *Reichtum und Eigentum in der Altkirchlichen Literatur*. Freiburg im Breisgau: Herderische Verlagsbuchhandlung.

Schulz, Siegried. 1972. *Q, Die Spruchquelle der Evangelisten*. Zurich: Theologischer Verlag.

**Schumacher, E. F. 1973. *Small Is Beautiful: Economics as if People Mattered*. New York: Harper & Row, Torchbooks.

*Schumpeter, Joseph A. 1962. *Capitalism, Socialism, and Democracy*. New York: Harper & Row, Torchbooks.

Schweitzer, Albert. 1923. *Die Schuld der Philosophie an dem Niedergang der Kultur* [The responsibility of philosophy for the decay of culture]. Gesammelte Werke, vol. 2. Zurich: Buchclub Ex Libris.

————. 1923. *Verfall und Wiederaufbau der Kultur* [Decay and restoration of civilization]. *Gesammelte Werke,* vol. 2. Zurich: Buchclub Ex Libris.

*————. 1973. *Civilization and Ethics.* Rev. ed. Reprint of 1923 ed. New York: Seabury Press.

Simmel, Georg. 1950. *Hauptprobleme der Philosophie.* Berlin: Walter de Gruyter.

Sommerlad, T. 1903. *Das Wirtschaftsprogramm der Kirche des Mittelalters.* Leipzig. Quoted by Otto Schilling; q.v.

Spinoza, Benedictus de. 1927. *Ethics.* New York: Oxford University Press.

Staehelin, Balthasar. 1969. *Haben und Sein.* [Having and being]. Zurich: Editio Academica.

Stirner, Max. 1973. *The Ego and His Own: The Case of the Individual Against Authority.* Edited by James J. Martin; translated by Steven T. Byington. New York: Dover. (Original ed. *Der Einzige und Sein Eigentum.*)

Suzuki, D. T. 1960. "Lectures on Zen Buddhism." In E. Fromm et al. *Zen Buddhism and Psychoanalysis;* q.v.

Swoboda, Helmut. 1973. *Die Qualität des Lebens.* Stuttgart: Deutsche Verlagsanstalt.

*Tawney, R. H. 1920. *The Acquisitive Society.* New York: Harcourt Brace.

"Technologie und Politik." *Attuell Magazin,* July 1975. Rheinbeck bei Hamburg: Rowohlt Taschenbuch Verlag.

Theobald, Robert, ed. 1966. *The Guaranteed Income: Next Step in Economic Evolution.* New York: Doubleday.

Thomas Aquinas. See Aquinas, Thomas.

Titmuss, Richard. 1971. *The Gift Relationship: From Human Blood to Social Policy.* London: George Allen & Unwin.

*Underhill, Evelyn, ed. 1956. *A Book of Contemplation the Which Is Called The Cloud of Unknowing.* 6th ed. London: John M. Watkins.

Utz, A. F. OP. 1953. "Recht und Gerechtigkeit." In Thomas Aquinas, *Summa Theologica,* vol. 18; q.v.

Yerkes, R. M., and Yerkes, A. V. 1929. *The Great Apes: A Study of Anthropoid Life.* New Haven: Yale University Press.

Index

Aaron, 52
Abraham, 48, 109
activity, 5, 25, 47, 73, 88–97, 100–02, 135, 162, 163, 181
advertising and propaganda, 127, 178, 179, 187–88; *see also* communications, media
alienation, 5, 19, 21–22, 32, 33, 38–39, 90–91, 92, 105, 110, 112–13, 122–25, 149, 150–51, 157, 169, 200; *see also* passivity
antagonism, 111–16; class war, 6, 114, 174
Aquinas, St. Thomas, 7, 59, 93, 121–22, 122*n.*, 124
Aristippus, 3–4
Aristotle, 4, 92–93, 94
Artz, Frederick B., 140–41
Auer, Alfons, 121–22, 122*n.*, 124
Augustine, St., 124, 141
authority, exercise of, 36–39, 78, 81, 83, 120, 121–22, 124, 125, 147, 158, 191, 192, 193; and children, 11, 36, 38, 70, 76, 80, 121, 186, 192; sexual prohibitions, 78–80; *see also* bureaucracy; patriarchal society; property; rebellion and revolution
automobile, importance of, 5, 27, 72–73, 178, 179–80

Baader, Franz von, 154
Bachofen, J. J., 145
Bacon, Francis: *Novum Organum*, 174
Basho, 16, 17, 18
Basilius, 58
Bauer, Edgar, 20–21
Becker, Carl, 144

behaviorism, 64, 97
being (mode of existence), 20, 23, 24, 87–107, 170–72; and authority, 36, 37–38, 124–25; biblical concept, 48–59 *passim* (*see also* New Testament; Old Testament); in daily experience, 28–47, 87, 127–29; exists in the here and now, 127–28; and faith, 41, 42–44, 128; freedom and growth, 1, 25–26, 76, 78–81, 110, 172, 191–93; happiness and pleasure, 100–01, 115–20 *passim*, 172; and having, difference between, 15–27, 87, 100, 105–06; and having, existential, 85; interest, 30, 31, 34, 101, 170; knowledge, 39–41; knowledge of reality, 23, 24, 25–26, 31, 39, 40, 61–63, 97–100, 168; in language and speech, 23–24, 34; and learning, 29–30, 101; life, affirmation of, 16, 20, 24, 104, 105, 110, 125–27, 171–72; philosophical concepts of, 25–26; and reading, 35, 36; and remembering, 30–32, 33, 128; security, 108–09, 110, 170, 174, 190–91; and sex, 45, 46–47, 115, 117; solidarity and union, 20, 24, 104, 105, 111–16, 170, 189; well-being and joy, 4, 6, 18–19, 93, 111, 116–20, 128, 171, 198–99; *see also* activity; Buddha; Eckhart, Master; Jesus; love/loving; Marx, Karl
Benveniste, Emile, 23–24
Benz, E., 65
Bible, 4, 140; *see also* New Testament; Old Testament
Blakney, Raymond B., 40, 59–63 *passim*, 119

About the Author

Erich Fromm is a practicing psychoanalyst and the author of such influential books as *The Art of Loving, Escape from Freedom, Beyond the Chains of Illusion, The Revolution of Hope, The Heart of Man,* and *Man for Himself.* Born in Frankfurt, Germany, in 1900, he studied at the universities of Heidelberg and Munich, and at the Psychoanalytic Institute in Berlin. He has taught in Germany and in Mexico, where he was Professor of Psychoanalysis at the National University, in Mexico, and in the United States at Bennington College, Yale, Michigan State, and New York universities.

About the Editor of This Series

Ruth Nanda Anshen, philosopher and editor, plans and edits *World Perspectives, Religious Perspectives, Credo Perspectives, Perspectives in Humanism,* and *The Science of Culture Series.* She also writes and lectures on the relationship of knowledge to the nature and meaning of man and his existence. Her book, *The Reality of the Devil: Evil in Man,* a study in the phenomenology of evil, is published by Harper & Row.